Cognitive Science, Religion,
and Theology

TEMPLETON SCIENCE AND RELIGION SERIES

In our fast-paced and high-tech era, when visual information seems so dominant, the need for short and compelling books has increased. This conciseness and convenience is the goal of the Templeton Science and Religion Series. We have commissioned scientists in a range of fields to distill their experience and knowledge into a brief tour of their specialties. They are writing for a general audience, readers with interests in the sciences or the humanities, which includes religion and theology. The relationship between science and religion has been likened to four types of doorways. The first two enter a realm of "conflict" or "separation" between these two views of life and the world. The next two doorways, however, open to a world of "interaction" or "harmony" between science and religion. We have asked our authors to enter these latter doorways to judge the possibilities. They begin with their sciences and, in aiming to address religion, return with a wide variety of critical viewpoints. We hope these short books open intellectual doors of every kind to readers of all backgrounds.

Series Editors: J. Wentzel van Huyssteen & Khalil Chamcham
Project Editor: Larry Witham

Cognitive Science, Religion, *and* Theology

FROM HUMAN MINDS TO DIVINE MINDS

Justin L. Barrett

TEMPLETON PRESS

Templeton Press
300 Conshohocken State Road, Suite 550
West Conshohocken, PA 19428
www.templetonpress.org

Designed and typeset by Gopa and Ted2, Inc.

Library of Congress Cataloging-in-Publication Data

Barrett, Justin L., 1971–
  Cognitive science, religion, and theology : from human minds
to divine minds / Justin L. Barrett.
      p. cm. — (Templeton science and religion series)
   Includes bibliographical references and index.
   ISBN 978-1-59947-381-9 (pbk.)
   1. Psychology, Religious. 2. Cognitive science. I. Title.
   BL53.B332 2011
   200.1'9—dc23

                                        2011021825

Printed in the United States of America

11   12   13   14   15   16   10   9   8   7   6   5   4   3   2   1

 Contents

 Preface

AT SOCIAL EVENTS when I need to make small talk or meet new people, the question I dread is, "So, what's your field?" My dread isn't because I don't value what I do or don't like to talk about my work—like most academics, I have a probably unjustifiably high opinion of my field. My fear is that my answer will only lead to more confusion:

"I do cognitive science."

"What is that?" comes the inevitable next question.

"The science of the mind and how we think." Such a curt answer for such a vast and important field only invites confusion and more questions. My aim for this book is to give a more complete answer to the question, "What is cognitive science?" But my task is also to highlight the potential for this scientific area to have exciting and challenging things to say about religion and theology.

The engagement between "science" and "religion" is often presented as a dialogue between two individuals. Science and Theology talk to each other. Science tells Theology what its latest and greatest accomplishments are and then Theology scurries to figure out how to accommodate those findings. Theology points out the dependence of Science on certain prescientific assumptions and commitments that are often supplied by Theology, and insists that without Theology to inform discussions concerning values (what we ought and should think or do), the findings of Science are just as likely to be harmful as beneficial. In this dialogue, Science tells Theology what it knows, and Theology tells Science what it knows.

As interesting and important as this dialogue can be, it isn't the only dimension in which a science-religion engagement can happen. Some sciences (particularly the psychological and social sciences) can apply the tools of science to the study of religion. This second dimension of the science-and-religion dialogue also has two types of activity. Perhaps the most common scientific study of religion is the investigation of the consequences of religious commitments, thoughts, practices, and organizations. The political scientist might wonder how being religious or not changes voting practices. The demographer might wonder whether religious identification changes fertility rates. The psychologist might explore whether some religious practices encourage or discourage mental health. These types of studies treat some dimension of religion as a cause, predictor variable, or *explanas* of some effect, outcome variable, or *explanadum*. But we might want to try to explain various dimensions of religion as well. Why do people tend to be religious? Why do religious practices take the forms they do? Why are some beliefs more common than others? These too are topics for scientific exploration at the hands of the human sciences.

Cognitive science can be a fruitful dialogue partner with religion on both dimensions and in all four ways. (1) Findings from cognitive science can potentially support or challenge theological claims. (2) Theological positions can inform how and why one does cognitive science, and what we should do with what we find. (3) The outcomes of religion can be studied through cognitive science. (4) Cognitive science can uncover causes for features of religion, including why people tend to have certain theological commitments. Few sciences have this potential breadth of engagement with religion and theology. My chief aim for this book is to convince readers of the tremendous positive possibilities for such engagement—that findings from cognitive science merit our attention whether we are scholars, religious leaders, or generally educated citizens. I hope to also encourage some readers to get involved with teaching or researching in this area that is blossoming with potential.

In recent years conflict between "science" and "religion" has generated considerable heat, but far less light. My secondary aim for this book, then, is to demonstrate that in this particularly exciting area of science, we can move beyond a simple conflict thesis and see that cognitive science is not simply a friend or foe for religious or nonreligious people. It is a useful tool for learning. Sometimes we learn things that make us change or abandon our beliefs and behaviors, and at other times we learn new things that build upon or further our existing beliefs and behaviors. Cognitive science should and will do likewise. Those committed to discovering truth, and confident that their worldview is true, should see a rigorous and robust cognitive science as a valuable companion.

The view I present of cognitive science is much more an invitation to explore than a summary of completed journeys. After introducing cognitive science as a field of study (chapter 1), I sketch a general working model of the mind and how we form beliefs of any kind (chapters 2 and 3). In the next section (chapters 4 through 6), I begin filling in this model by considering how humans naturally make sense of the basic furniture of the world, how we make sense of other humans, and how such ordinary thought makes us prone to religious thought. The final section of the book (chapters 7 through 9) turns more directly to applications of cognitive science for religion and theology, including questions concerning religious experience, practice, revelation, and education.

To try to make this book broadly accessible, I shared early drafts of the manuscript with an interdisciplinary group of Oxford University scholars at different career levels. We met periodically to discuss the text and harvest feedback. I have done my best to incorporate their comments and criticisms into the final version, but in doing so was forced to make some difficult decisions about word choices and just how much time to spend on particular topics. A topic that bored the linguist excited the astrophysicist. A term that meant one thing to the economist meant something entirely different to the philosopher.

I share this background as a warning, particularly to philosophers and theologians. Though I raise some philosophical and theological issues—and offer some suggestions pertaining to the relationship among cognitive science, religion, and theology—this is not a book of philosophy for philosophers or of theology for theologians, and I will thank both camps for their patience (and mercy). Usually when I take up such issues here, my motivation is only to discourage those (usually scientists) who regard the implications of cognitive science for religious and theological beliefs as simple and straightforward. I am not trying to solve any philosophical or theological problems here but only indicate the sorts of problems to which findings from cognitive science might fruitfully contribute. I leave proper treatments to the proper experts.

Cognitive Science, Religion, *and* Theology

CHAPTER 1
What Is Cognitive Science?

THE POINT IS ALMOST so obvious that it hardly needs stating: humans are distinctive because of their ability to think, reason, imagine, and learn—their cognitive abilities. When Hamlet trumpets the greatness of humans, it is the human mind that takes center stage:

> What a piece of work is a man! how noble in reason! how infinite in faculty! in form and moving how express and admirable! in action, how like an angel! in apprehension, how like a god! the beauty of the world, the paragon of animals; and yet to me, what is this quintessence of dust? (*Hamlet*, act 2, scene 2)

The words *reason, faculty, action,* and *apprehension* point to humans' ability to think and direct their actions apart from mere instincts. Shakespeare recognizes as well a tension between the marvels of the human mind and the less lofty biological ("paragon of animals") and physical ("quintessence of dust") nature. The great thinkers throughout the ages and the world's religious traditions have sought to embrace this tension in their treatments of human nature. In the Genesis creation story, humanity is presented as derived from the dust of the earth and yet above all animals, and ultimately separated from God by succumbing to the temptation of knowledge:

> And the serpent said to the woman, "You will not surely
> die. For God knows that in the day you eat of it your eyes
> will be opened, and you will be like God, knowing good
> and evil." So when the woman saw the tree was good for
> food, that it was pleasant to the eyes, and a tree desir-
> able to make one wise, she took of its fruit and ate. (Gen.
> 3:4–6, NKJV)

It is the gifts of the mind that separate humans from the other animals, and on the basis of mental prowess humans vie to "be like God." In Buddhism too we see ambivalence about thought: it distracts and enslaves us to worldly concerns, and yet it is through disciplining our thought (such as meditative practice, *vipassanā*) that genuine wisdom or insight (*paññā*) can be achieved. Understanding how humans think, then, may be critical in understanding distinctive features of human nature, how we may relate to the transcendent, and the key to human thriving.

In a direct hand-to-hand combat with a wolf, leopard, bear, Tasmanian devil, or ape, an average human would fare poorly. Without natural weapons such as claws or powerful teeth and jaws, and lacking impressive quickness and power, humans are not terribly formidable foes. Human babies, in particular, are relatively helpless. A two-year-old human is known as a "toddler" because of its clumsiness, but the same aged chimpanzee can swing from tree to tree, and the two-year-old wildcat or canine is already an adult, able to catch an antelope on the run and tear it to bits. Lacking impressive physical attributes, human survival and thriving are critically dependent upon the power of our minds.

The obvious importance and distinctiveness of human thought do not mean its scientific study—cognitive science—is so obvious. In fact, very well educated people do not even realize that cognitive science exists. In this chapter I give a brief explanation of what cognitive science is and what it is cognitive scientists do, laying the groundwork for an exploration of cognitive science as it relates to religious expression and theological issues. After all, how the human mind handles religious information may provide insights into the nature of revelation, how people understand scripture, and how they "read" the natural world for messages from the divine.[1] Understanding the prerequisite kind of mind for being religious could also amplify accounts of the origins of religion for humanity and in individual lives. For religious ideas and practices to spread and persist, they must ride on cognitive equipment. It may be, then, that just how cognition supports religious thought and action might have practical implications for religious communities—for instance, how to successfully teach children, what impact changing a ritual might have on participants, and identifying which points of doctrine might be most subject to distortion. On the other hand, perhaps religious thought and practices are not just informed and shaped by human cognition, but can also change our thought-producing equipment in important ways: religious practice might impact human cognition beyond merely filling in content. Before turning to these big questions, an introduction to cognitive science is required.

Surveying the Terrain of Cognitive Science

Cognitive science is the interdisciplinary area of scholarship that considers what the human mind is and how it functions; how people think. Thinking includes everything from perceiving what is in the world around us to reflectively and abstractly reasoning about hypothetical worlds that are not around us. I am not including all human behavior as the object of cognitive science. A psychologist or a physiologist may study sneezing, yawning, or sleeping, but that isn't cognitive science. Cognitive science concerns imagining, recalling, watching, wondering, pondering, and deciding. Without denying or affirming animal thought (another fascinating matter), my focus here is on human thought. That said, in some cases the study of nonhuman animals provides special insights into the character of the human mind.

Recently my family and I had a Sunday supper with friends and afterward played a wonderful game that required each of us in turn to try to provide clues for everyone else to guess what was depicted on a card. The card could present a famous person, an occupation, a location, an object, an event, or any number of different things. A roll of a die determined the restricted range of clues that the player could provide. They could be a drawing, a wordless performance (think charades with sound effects), words all beginning with the same letter, or a comparison with two other things (for instance, one successful clue was "smaller than a swimming pool, bigger than a mattress" for the answer "waterbed"). This group effort was a race against time. Not only was the game a lot of fun, it was fascinating watching various types of human thought at work. The clue givers had to figure out what critical information would trigger the right association in the minds of at least one member of the audience within the constraints of the rule-types. The guessers had to try to infer a concept from the very strange and indirect clues—almost mind reading. One seemingly amazing instance was when my wife gave a two-second hula dance and then mimed opening a can with a pull-tab. The whole act lasted less than three seconds and in a heartbeat my daughter (correctly) answered, "Spam!" How? Cognitive scientists are interested in every step of interactions like these. How does a person (my daughter) perceive another person's body (my wife's)? Understand the movement of that person as an example of a known dance (hula)? Regard that dance as indicating a particular culture or place (Hawaii)? Recognize a cupped hand, first, as a hand and, next, as indicating holding something that isn't actually there? Recognize a movement as representing opening a familiar container type (a tin with a pull-tab) that isn't actually present? Put the concepts HAWAII and TIN-WITH-PULL-TAB together to trigger a memory that Hawaiians are inordinately fond of Spam and get the correct answer "Spam"? How did my daughter do all of this in a fraction of a second? And how did my wife suspect that someone would be able to rapidly piece all of this together and choose this performance strategy? And why did we all feel surprise and amusement at this exchange?

Cognitive Science Is Not Neuroscience

These questions are the sorts that animate cognitive scientists, questions about how human minds work, how we think. Notice, however, that few of us would be satisfied if we answered these questions by simple appeals to brains or biological structures. Consider: Question, "How did my daughter get from hula and can-opening motions to Spam?" Answer, "Her brain did it." Not terribly satisfying, right? Even if we narrow the scope a little, "This part of the brain and that part of the brain did it," we're still left with the wrong kind of answer. Though the brain sciences can and do make important contributions to cognitive science, cognitive science is not first and foremost about where things "happen" in the brain. It isn't really about brains at all. It is about minds.

If someone asks you how the United States federal government works, you wouldn't answer by saying that it is located in Washington, or even specifying that the White House is at 1600 Pennsylvania Avenue and the Capitol is about one-and-a-half miles ESE of there and the Supreme Court building is a bit over a quarter mile to the east of there. How the U.S. government works isn't (usually) answered by appeal to the physical structures involved. To use the familiar comparison with our office computers: cognitive science isn't about the "hardware" of human minds—silicon chips, circuit boards, and the like. Cognitive science is about the "software" of human minds: How does this word processor work? Why do I get an error message when I try to open this file? What can I do to import information from my spreadsheet to my presentation file? If my IT officer answered any of these sorts of questions by explaining how semiconductors work in my computer's micro-circuits, I'd show him the door. It isn't that computer hardware isn't interesting; it just isn't the right level of explanation for the sorts of questions being asked. Similarly, I think brain science is fascinating, but that doesn't mean it is the right level of explanation for the questions that cognitive scientists are (usually) trying to answer.

You may have noticed that I keep putting "usually" in parentheses here and there. The reason is that in some small proportion of cases, the physical structures of the brain do play a role in illuminating why we think the way we do. The area of cognitive neuroscience considers these cases, and I will say more about it below. I am belaboring the brain-mind distinction here because so many people—academics and nonacademics alike—confuse cognitive science with brain sciences. Snazzy pictures of brain scans make for good television and print media, but that can lead to the *mis*perception that brain science is the direction that *all* science of the mind and behavior is headed.

Brain sciences, neuroscience, and related areas pertaining to the anatomy and physiology of our nervous system contribute greatly to our understanding of human behavior and provide tools for medical solutions when things go wrong. My very first publication was a coauthored paper arguing that the failure of a subcellular structure in certain neurons could account for bipolar disorder and features of its treatment with lithium.[2] A feature of neuron function arguably has an impact on the wide range of manic and depressive behaviors that characterize bipolar disorder. Understanding the biology of the brain and the rest of the nervous system matters, sometimes in surprising ways. But not all of neuroscience is cognitive science. The kind of neuroscience I dabbled in at the beginning of my academic career was not cognitive science. The identification of a subcellular neural structure failure might have helped explain episodes of mania, but it didn't explain anything about language use, analogical reasoning, or learning during manic episodes. Other areas of neuroscience are even further afield, concerned with the nuts-and-bolts of how neurons communicate with each other or how brain structures develop without meaningful reference to thoughts and feelings at all.

TOPICS OF STUDY

The cognitive science umbrella covers a wide range of topics—as broad as the innumerable domains of human thought. In just one issue of *Trends in Cognitive Sciences* (December 2004), a leading professional journal in the area, you can find essays on:

: How value and probability are represented by brain structures such that they can be used to make decisions
: Immediate, "working" memory in sign language versus spoken language
: Children's developing understanding of other's mental states
: Understanding the unspoken implications of conversation
: Why certain muscular actions become rhythmical when they are learned
: What it would mean for a robot to have emotions

In just this sample of topics we can see a range from very general thought activities such as decision-making to very specific problems such as keeping sign language in memory as one uses it.

Grouping the various topics that cognitive scientists consider can be done in many different ways. Commonly, however, problems are grouped by the general cognitive process or activity that seems most critical. These processes include:

: Perception—how do we use our senses to identify patterns and objects in the environment? How do we recognize the furniture of the world? How much is perception influenced by situation, personal history, and cultural context?
: Attention—how do we focus on some ideas or incoming information as opposed to others? What are the limits on human attention? How much can it be divided among tasks? Can attention be expanded through practice?
: Memory—how is memory structured? Do we have different

types of memory? How can we put ideas, images, events, or action-sequences into memory? How do we retrieve information from memory? Why do we forget? Are there techniques that can be used to improve memory?

: Conceptualization—where do our concepts come from? How do we categorize ideas? How do collections of ideas or experiences of events become knowledge structures? How do we form stereotypes and think with them?

: Communication—how do we communicate with others? How do we use language, gestures, facial expressions, and other actions to convey ideas or feelings? How do we understand the messages others try to send? How do we acquire language, including grammar and vocabulary? What role does language play in thought?

: Reasoning—reasoning overlaps with decision-making and conceptualization, but places an emphasis on conscious, careful reflection on ideas, on what we know and don't know, and on how to solve problems. How do we come up with answers to questions? When are we able to reason using the rules of logic or probability?

: Learning—we reason *from* something we know *to* something else (inference). We make decisions regarding ideas we have acquired somehow. Before cognitive science was born, the scientific study of learning principally concerned how animals (including human animals) acquire behaviors that are not simply instinctual. The cognitive science of learning emphasizes how new information, ideas, concepts, and words are acquired.

: Decision-making—how do we form judgments? What thought strategies do we use automatically to decide whether something is or isn't the case? How do we decide to do one thing as opposed to another? How do we string many decisions together to make complex plans?

: Imagination—just as we can form *percepts* (impressions from perceptual systems) through all of our senses, perhaps we can form all of these kinds of images "in our heads," from images of what a cat's fur feels like to what baking bread smells like to what a sunrise looks like. How accurate are these mental representations? How do we use them in thought? How does this sort of image-based imagination compare to language-based imagination? How are we able to think about things that are not necessarily so?

These processes are not discretely partitioned from each other but interact in most real-world thought and action. Cognitive scientists also consider how these various processes interact. For instance, how does attention impact memory? Does language modify perception and concept formation? Can forming visual images improve memory or problem-solving? How do concepts impact communication or imagination?

Another category of cognition deserves mention here even though it does not really constitute a different process parallel to the categories above. Our feelings or *emotions* can be considered in any of these general processes. For this reason, I consider emotions a dimension of cognition rather than a separate process or activity. A cognitive scientist might be interested in why certain types of thought might get infused with certain emotional qualities and how different physiological states can acquire meaningful content that lead to the rich diversity of feelings people report experiencing. Do particulars of language change our feelings? How does intensity of emotion impact memory, attention, or perception? What role does emotion play in reasoning or decision-making?

Similarly, across all of these categories we might consider how consciously accessible dynamics differ from nonconscious dynamics. Is there more going on in our thoughts than we can introspectively become aware of? If so, how do these nonconscious cognitive processes impact conscious ones?

PROBLEMS THAT ANIMATE COGNITIVE SCIENCE

At universities today, you will rarely find something called the Department of Cognitive Science. Many of the scholars who engage in cognitive science do not even identify themselves as "cognitive scientists." They are tucked away in various university departments. Cognitive science is not an academic discipline as much as an inter-disciplinary field that falls at the intersection of several other disciplines: psychology, computer science, linguistics, neuroscience, philosophy, and anthropology (including archaeology). Each of these disciplines has subareas or specialties that contribute to cognitive science (see Table 1).

We must tread softly when we use the term *scientist* as we delve into the broad field of cognitive science. Some investigators might be natural scientists (neuroscientists and some psychologists), others are applied scientists (many computer scientists and some psychologists), social scientists (many psychologists, linguists, and anthropologists), or not scientists at all (philosophers and some linguists and anthropologists). Not all cognitive scientists are *scientists* in the sense that their research constitutes the collection of empirical data through scientific methods, and quantitative analysis of those data to test models and hypotheses.

What earns them all the title *cognitive scientists*—even the philosophers—is that they bring scientific evidence to bear on claims and predictions about how humans think and the character of the human mind, and attempt to discover naturalistic explanations for the phenomena the data reveal.[3] What they have in common, in other words, is a common set of problems. Everyone in cognitive science is looking at a few major threads of concern. Many of these threads are theoretical "pure" science issues, but others are applied problems. We can divide these into theoretical problems and applied problems.

TABLE 1. Constituent Disciplines of Cognitive Science

Cognitive science is an interdisciplinary field that falls at the intersection of several other disciplines. Each of these disciplines has subareas or specialties that contribute to cognitive science.

PSYCHOLOGY

Psychology, the study of thought and behavior, overlaps considerably with cognitive science. Those areas of psychology closest to cognitive science are cognitive psychology (the psychological study of thought), cognitive development (how cognitive systems develop and change across the lifespan), social cognition, and psycholinguistics (the psychology of language), an area shared with linguistics.

COMPUTER SCIENCE

An important branch of computer science tries to develop artificial intelligent systems with computers and robots in order to model or mimic human intelligence. These Artificial Intelligence (or AI) projects can serve to generate solutions to computational problems that serve as analogs for how human minds might solve comparable problems. Conversely, discoveries in the broader cognitive sciences can give computer scientists fresh ideas for solving Artificial Intelligence problems. Computer science has also created computer-based artificial "neural networks" that help model different ways in which cognitive systems might be structured and work. They can suggest how a human mind "could" work. Computer scientists are constantly creating new research instruments and methods applicable across the various sciences, including cognitive science.

LINGUISTICS

Some aspects of linguistics—the study of the diversity, history, and use of language—make valuable contributions to cognitive science. It asks, for instance, could we use any symbolic communication system equally well (binary code? semaphore flags?), or do we have natural predilections that make some languages easier? How is language acquired during early childhood, and how does this compare to second language learning later in life? What is the relationship between thought and language? Do the particulars of a language (say, German or Hindi) impact the way the speaker thinks, feels, and learns? Does human cognition shape the way languages evolve over time? Because language is so intimately tied to many areas of reflective higher-order thought, cognitive science is inseparable from linguistics.

Continued

Neuroscience

Neuroscience, at its core, is about how neurons function individually or in concert, but increasingly it contributes evidence relevant to deciding how human thought works, an area called *cognitive neuroscience*. For instance, some cognitive scientists are concerned with how people use mental images, the kinds of images you experience if I ask you to imagine the face of your mother, or picture in your mind walking from your house to the nearest grocery store. Do we really think with images, or is this just an illusion? Among the different types of evidence we might use to answer this question, neuroscientific evidence can be especially telling. If we really do use visual images, we might expect the same circuits of the brain to be active when we conjure up a visual image and inspect it "in our heads" as when we inspect a visual image in the external world. Likewise, we might expect that if someone has a particular disability when it comes to making sense of scenes or objects, that person might have a comparable disability imagining scenes or objects. On both counts, affirmative evidence that we really think with images has been found through the application of neuroscience.*

Philosophy

The study of the mind had once been the sole domain of philosophy. It has long addressed topics of introspection and reflection, reasoned discussions about how we know and how we should know, and debates about consciousness and the relationship between the mind and body. This continues to be a contribution to cognitive science, especially regarding the study of consciousness, the relationship between minds and brains, and evaluating competing models of how the human mind works. Philosophy helps us see how different levels of explanation and different types of evidence from the various constituent disciplines can be successfully integrated.

Anthropology and Archaeology

Although most of anthropology and archaeology concerns human behavior and organization, cultural expression, human evolution, human remains and artifacts, it assists cognitive science with the investigation of how culture interacts with human cognition. For instance, can the recurring expression of human activities such as sports, music, and religion be anchored in the human mental processes? This is an important question for religion and the cognitive science of religion (CSR), which draws extensively on anthropology. The same importance can be applied to the study of ancient tools as evidence of how human cognition worked in the past.

---

*For a review of evidence, see Stephen M. Kosslyn, Giorgio Ganis, and William L. Thompson, "Neural Foundations of Imagery," *National Review of Neuroscience* 2, no. 9 (2001): 635–42.

Theoretical Problems

Numerous theoretical questions energize cognitive scientists, but one or more of three broad questions seem to lurk in the background of nearly every discussion in cognitive science: what is innate and what isn't, how to best characterize the mind, and how minds and bodies are related.

What is "innate"?

We seem to hear a lot these days about different behaviors, personality dispositions, or ways of thinking being *innate* or *hardwired into the brain* or *in your genes*. Behind all of these figures of speech is the idea that some aspects of our minds might be a fixed part of our biology. Just as humans have brains, hearts, and livers, we also have (barring developmental disorder) the ability to see, the desire for touch, and the drive to eat. Perhaps much more subtle and interesting features of human thought are also "innate." On the other hand, surely some aspects of our thought are not fixed. Whether someone is a Red Sox fan or a Yankees fan or does not care about baseball is not innate (regardless of what a colleague of mine insists).[4] Clearly the *particular* language we speak, foods we prefer, music we enjoy, and a host of other preferences and aspects of who we are are not endowed to us by our genes but are acquired through our social environment. Perhaps, however, some aspects of even these seemingly arbitrary aspects of our thinking are not so independent of our biology after all. These questions—sometimes expressed as the nature-nurture debate—have been animating cognitive science since its birth. In the next chapter and again later in this book I return to these issues.

How do we best characterize the mind?

It is helpful to think about the mind as a computer, similar to the silicon-based machines that we use for doing accounting, word processing, surfing the Internet, and a host of other tasks. Minds, like personal computers, have some basic hardware (our bodies, including brains and nervous system) that limits what we can and can't do and how well we do things. Additionally, human minds have "programming" that has come from elsewhere that shapes how we operate. For computers, human programmers have provided this information. For human minds, this sort of information comes from our natural and cultural environment. When functioning ("thinking"), computers receive inputs from the human users (or other computers) and then process the information to produce outputs. Similarly, human minds receive information from the immediate situation around them (including from other humans) and then process the information to produce outputs (facial expressions, speech, actions, etc.). This metaphor of the mind as computer has been enormously productive in cognitive science.

Perhaps the "mind as computer" characterization has been so useful in part because it isn't wholly metaphorical. When I add 2 + 3 or when I cut a cake into approximately equal slices, my mind is doing computations. We know too that brains, like other biological systems, can be accurately characterized as doing computations. If minds reflect this computational aspect of the biological substrate that gives them shape, then we shouldn't be surprised if minds too are computational. We might say that minds *are* computers if by "computers" we mean things that do computations.

Nevertheless, it could be that not all mental activities are usefully characterized as computational, and even those that are might be importantly different in the type of computation they do. Cognitive scientists have used different characterizations of human minds depending upon the type of function that they are studying. Philosopher Paul Thagard notes that cognitive scientists have regarded the mind as working in at least six different ways depending upon the problem under consideration: by using logic, rules, concepts, analogies, images, or connected networks of units.[5] These approaches are not mutually exclusive. When deciding whether to buy an article of clothing for my wife, I might imagine what it would look like on her, I could use rules (e.g., "orange doesn't go with red hair"), or I could think conceptually ("this is my wife's kind of thing"). Cognitive scientists try to determine how people normally tend to think in various situations. In solving certain types of problems, for instance, do people predominantly use logic or analogy? By and large, cognitive scientists do not try to use one approach to address all questions in cognitive science, but are happy to take a piecemeal approach.

In addition to deciding which cognitive activities can be fruitfully regarded as computation and which cannot, characterizing the mind carries the heavy burden of linking mental activities to various types of conscious experiences. Even well before the cognitive revolution, psychologists such as Freud and Jung recognized the need to model human minds as having both conscious features and activities and nonconscious or unconscious ones. The problem of linking these two types of mental activity remains with us. I will discuss an instance of this problem concerning the formation of beliefs in chapter 3, leaving aside the even thornier issue of how both conscious and nonconscious activities might map onto brains.

How do we connect minds and mental states to brains and bodies?
As I suggested above, brains and minds are not the same thing. Explaining something on the level of brain activity is not the same as explaining it on the cognitive or psychological level. If you hang upside down, you might be right to say that "Blood is rushing to my brain," but you wouldn't say that "Blood is rushing to my mind." If someone "changes their mind," we don't suppose they have swapped brains. Beliefs can be true or false, right or wrong, good or bad; but can any of these evaluations be applied to electrical and chemical processes of the brain? When I say a scene is "breathtaking," I refer to my subjective experience of the scene, not the particular activation of my visual cortex. Brains and minds are not equivalent, but they aren't wholly independent either. If part of my brain is damaged (or stimulated), I may lose the ability to speak,

or the ability to recognize people, or I may feel someone touching my body when no one is doing so.[6] A blow to the head can disrupt memory not because the mind has been jarred, but because the body (brain) has. Just how the mind and brain are related is an active area of concern in cognitive science, particularly among philosophers and neuroscientists.

I will say more about these matters in the next chapter, but at no point will I attempt to "solve" the mind-body problem or commit to a definitive position on the status of minds in contrast with bodies. Rather, I adopt a pragmatic position in which we recognize that explanations in terms of minds and those in terms of bodies (including brains) are not the same level of explanation. For the purposes of seeking understanding, minds are not the same as brains, but they are not wholly unrelated either.[7]

A related problem concerns whether our biology deterministically causes our thought. If minds are just functional properties of bodies, and bodies operate by deterministic biological and physical laws, then might minds too be causally determined? This philosophical problem has potentially important consequences for everyone, but it may have especially pointed conflict with many traditional, religious views of human nature. I return to this issue later in this book.

Applied Problems

Perhaps because of the intimate involvement of computer scientists, cognitive science has always had a strong applied face concerning Artificial Intelligence systems, from building intelligent machines to human-computer interactions. Cognitive science applications have also readily extended to education, law enforcement (e.g., the dangers of memory distortion in eyewitness testimony), product design (e.g., arranging a machine's controls to capitalize on conceptual predilections), and advertising (how can attitudes be shaped and preferences formed?), to name just a few. At the heart of these varied applications are at least three core applied questions: how can we build thinking machines, how can we get people to think (and learn) better, and how can we make tools or systems best fit with what we know about human cognition so that people can use them most effectively?

TOWARD A COGNITIVE SCIENCE RELEVANT TO RELIGION AND THEOLOGY

When I ran cross-country in high school, my coach taught us that when you run a long uphill, don't watch the top of the hill. Doing so can encourage bad running form, lead to missteps, and be demoralizing too. Rather, keep your gaze fixed on the bit of course just ahead, only occasionally glancing up. This strikes me as good advice for cognitive science as well. Cognitive science has some huge problems looming large ahead—such as the mind-body problem, and determining whether anything general can be said about how the mind works—but fixating on those will only discourage strong progress on the more manageable problems at hand. In this book, I'll mostly pay attention to the problems that cognitive scientists do seem to be solving, and I'll try to draw implications for understanding religion and theology rather than spending too much time speculating on what the more mountainous problems might mean. Many of the implications I discuss will come from an area of research called *cognitive science of religion* (CSR).

You will notice too that unlike introductions to many science disciplines, I do not (and will not) tick through lots of facts of the field. The reason is simple: cognitive science is a very young science with a lot to discover. Unlike the old big three sciences (physics, chemistry, and biology), cognitive science is only a little over fifty years old. The birth year of the *cognitive revolution* is often set at 1956, the year Elvis Presley hit number one with "Blue Suede Shoes" and "Hound Dog" and helped boost rock and roll into the music mainstream. Cognitive science is about the same age as rock and roll. We might (perhaps somewhat arbitrarily) say that modern physics was "born" with Newton's *Principia* in 1687. That was when Giovanni Battista degli Antoni was hot on the Baroque music scene with his music for cello. A very different age indeed! Telling you all of the "facts" uncovered by cognitive science would be a bit like a textbook laying out the "facts" discovered by physics in say, 1740. Some ideas would be fine, but others would be importantly missing the mark. Physics has changed, and so will cognitive science. There is no way to avoid being embarrassed by history, so I beg readers to realize that all of the findings and theories presented here are bound to be elaborated, expanded, modified, or even rejected, but I will do the best that I can with the state-of-the-art as I see it and stick to relatively solid facts and theories.

I opened this chapter with the observation that the human mind gives people a special place in the natural world—an observation not lost on secular and religious thinkers. To appreciate what it is that is so special about the human mind requires a robust science of the mind, precisely what cognitive science aims to offer.

CHAPTER 2
Features of Human Thought

IN THE 1996 FILM *Phenomenon*, John Travolta plays George, an ordinary man who experiences a strange flash of light that changes his life. Suddenly he begins demonstrating astounding cognitive abilities such as being able to read full-length books in a matter of minutes, learning new languages by just flipping through language textbooks, and even moving objects with his mind (telekinesis). Later doctors discover that George is dying from a brain tumor, and we are led to believe that his amazing cognitive abilities are the result of this tumor stimulating more and greater brain functions than is normally the case. The captivating part of this story is the tantalizing possibility that the limitations we experience in thinking, learning, and remembering might be overcome. The plausibility of the tale derives in part from real-life individuals with remarkable abilities.

Psychology textbooks are littered with stories of savants who can memorize telephone directories or perform instantaneous multiplication of five-digit numbers or play (and win) a dozen chess games simultaneously without viewing the chessboards. People with a trait called *synesthesia* experience the world differently than the rest of us, actually seeing color in numbers or tasting words or otherwise having sensations normally associated with one domain in a completely different domain.[1] Less exotically, a former Oxford colleague famous for his prolific writing allegedly enjoys not only a photographic memory but also the ability to type upward of 100 words per minute: he could practically "think onto the page." These cases, real or fictitious, may prompt us to enviously speculate about how people could fully realize more of their cognitive potential, but should also remind us that limitations are there. Even in Travolta's character, it is a change in the biology of the brain that changes George's abilities. He is still a prisoner of his brain (if it is even sensible to talk that way).

In this chapter I offer some examples of ways in which the human mind exhibits general tendencies that inform and constrain the way we think. The picture they help paint is that the human mind is no blank slate waiting for any and all "writing" at the hand of the cultural environment or a passive sponge that simply absorbs whatever is around it equally well. Rather, minds have *natural* limitations, tendencies, and biases that make some ways of thinking more fluent than others. I will also introduce what I mean by *natural* in contrast to *innate* and then argue that some of our natural propensities turn out to be very important for the acquisition of religious and theological ideas, something that other animals do not seem to have.

Perhaps behind visions of unbridled memory, learning, or thinking abilities is the idea that our bodies (brains included) only exert trivial influence on how and what we think. The real action, we might suppose, is in our environment. Surrounded by enough educational opportunities, showered with encouragement, and maybe practicing special mind-development techniques, our minds can do amazing things that we can't even dream of. This is a *tabula rasa* or *blank slate* view of the mind.[2] The mind is a passive receptor just waiting to be written upon. Early psychologist J. B. Watson famously wrote:

> Give me a dozen healthy infants, well-formed, and my own specified world to bring them up in and I'll guarantee to take any one at random and train him to become any type of specialist I might select—doctor, lawyer, artist, merchant-chief and, yes, even beggar-man and thief,

regardless of his talents, penchants, tendencies, abilities, vocations, and race of his ancestors. I am going beyond my facts and I admit it, but so have the advocates of the contrary and they have been doing it for many thousands of years.[3]

Putting aside the chilling image of giving any psychologist a dozen infants to manipulate, the spirit behind such boasts has been taken by many to be refreshingly optimistic. The suggestion is that we're all the same under the skin and have enough potential for nearly any endeavor. Just discovering the right educational technologies and organizing society to implement them would eliminate inequalities in achievement and life satisfaction. Unfortunately (or fortunately), we can now be confident that the mind is not as pliable as Watson thought.

Underlying the view that only the environment (importantly) limits or promotes our cognitive capacities is an assumption that bodies (including brains) are trivial when it comes to human thought. We return, then, momentarily to the mind-body problem.

MINDS CONSTRAINED BY BODIES

Attributes of the mind and its activities such as thoughts and feelings are different than the attributes that can be sensibly applied to the brain or body. Conceptually, then, the two are separable. This observation does not entail that human minds are actually separable from bodies. Some philosophers and scientists say that they are, others say they aren't. This dispute is at the heart of the mind-body problem. Those who say that minds and bodies are separable are called *dualists,* and those who say that they are not separable but different aspects of the same thing are *monists.*[4] Both positions (and the various shades in between) have numerous subproblems to solve. For dualists, if the mind is separable from the body, then how does it interact with the body as in when I will my hand to move and it then does? How does a mind come to be *in* a body? Why does it look like the body impinges on properties of the mind? For monists, the tricky questions are different. For instance, how do we get subjective experience and consciousness from purely physical substances and reactions (the body)? What kind of bodies produce minds and how? If minds are nothing but the product of bodies acting in accordance with physical laws, why should I trust my thoughts to give me true beliefs (including the belief that my mind is nothing but the product of a body acting in accordance with physical laws)?

For my purposes here it is enough to insist that even if minds are separable from and not identical to bodies, it seems clear enough that our minds are, in fact, embodied. That is, it may be that my mind could leave my body (say, at death) and perhaps even be placed in another body, but the fact remains that at the very least my mind is part of or joined to my body for the time being. The fact that when I am tired or hungry or have had too much coffee my mind acts differently than when I am well-rested or sated or haven't had coffee indicates that there is at least a working relationship between my body and mind—let alone cases of brain injury that change someone's personality, destroy their ability to form new autobiographical memories, change their ability to organize thoughts, or eliminate their ability to recognize familiar people or objects. What happens to my body can affect my mind. Further, if I will part of my body to move, it usually does. I can learn to slow my heartbeat through concentration. If I engage in years of meditation or learning, my brain's structure will change.[5] In short, what happens to my mind can affect my body.

If some relationship between the mind and body is granted, then clearly the possibility exists for particulars of bodies to exert important limitations and influences on the properties of minds. Why would we expect our mental activities to float free of bodily constraints when our other activities are firmly grounded by our bodies? Consider sports and let's rework Watson's claim in the following way:

> Give me a dozen healthy infants, well-formed, and my own specified world to bring them up in and I'll guarantee to take any one at random and train him to become any type of world-class athlete I might select—sprinter, marathoner, weight lifter, high jumper, rugby star, swimmer, and yes, even footballer.

Ridiculous, right? I was reasonably healthy and "well-formed" as an infant, but there is simply no way I could have ever become an offensive lineman for the Pittsburgh Steelers, a 100 meter dash specialist for the Jamaican national team, or a center for the Los Angeles Lakers. I simply have physical limitations (height, bone structure, musculature) that would have made such feats impossible for me. Even elite athletes have physical limitations that direct them to one sport over another—or merely keep them from leaping tall buildings in a single bound. If our bodies shape and limit our athletic capacities, why wouldn't they shape and limit our intellectual capacities?

We would find Watson's boast absurd if applied to a dozen healthy chimpanzees, dogs, dolphins, elephants, or gray parrots—and these are all clever animals. We recognize that other animals have instincts and predilections that are part of their nature. Would we expect that humans are the only animals whose thought and behavior are not importantly informed and limited by their nature?

THE PROBLEM WITH NATURE-NURTURE AND INNATE

A major theme in cognitive science, as well as psychology and a number of other human sciences, is the nature-nurture debate. Which aspects of human thought, behavior, and character are part of our *nature* and which are part of our *nurture*? Nature, in this context, is usually taken to mean our fixed biology whereas nurture refers primarily to our distinctive social or cultural environments, including things that people deliberately teach us. For some (cognitive) reason, catchy little alliterative clichés can take on a life of their own to dominate and direct discussion, sometimes in not-so-helpful ways. I am afraid that *nature-nurture* is one such cliché.

The trouble with thinking in terms of nature *versus* nurture is that it invites an unrealistic, idealized view of how cognition and biology work. No aspect of our biological development, let alone our cognitive development occurs without important contributions from both our biological endowment and our environment. Cells don't divide and multiply without a steady stream of chemical nourishment from their environment, prenatal development is dependent upon hormones and nutrients from the mother, and babies simply cannot survive, let alone develop properly, without massive environmental inputs. When it comes to human thought and behavior, we see more of the same. If eyes do not receive stimulation from the environment, our ability to see properly is compromised, but without eyes and the visual cortex, we won't see properly either. Learning a language requires exposure to that language but also requires the right biological substrate. You cannot teach a rabbit German because it does not have the right biological substrate. For any cognitive capacity or any behavior you come up with, the answer to "Is it nature or nurture?" is always "Both," and deciding if it is more one than the other may prove impossible because "nature" and "nurture" are so vague. If seeing requires exposure to retinal stimulation (environment), does that make seeing *more* nurture than nature? How do we quantify the amount of contribution of each?

Similarly, I do not much care for another popular way of trying to characterize certain cognitive capacities: "Is it *innate*?" The term *innate* invites confusion. What would it mean for something to be innate? It cannot mean determined by our biology because nothing, strictly, is determined by our biology absent important environmental qualifications. Does it mean present at birth? But what makes birth special—especially now that we regularly schedule and induce birth? Consider the ability to hold one's head up. It isn't in place at birth, but what makes it less "innate" than opening eyes? In some species the babies cannot open eyes at birth but can hold their heads up and even walk. Is walking, then, innate but eye-opening not in those animals? What about predictable but late-arriving traits such as speech, teeth, and armpit hair?

In recent years we have begun to hear cognitive traits referred to as *hard-wired*. This problematic metaphor comes from electrical systems. If you have a hard-wired appliance, it is part of the electrical system of (for instance) your house and you cannot simply unplug it. Overhead light fixtures are hard-wired, but floor lamps that you plug into the wall are not. Smoke alarms may be hard-wired into the electrical system of the house, but battery-operated smoke alarms are not. Applied to cognitive systems, "hard-wired" is sometimes used to mean invariable or fixed in some way by the circuitry of the brain. For those of us who think that we think through our brain (or more strongly, that our brain thinks), it is a little odd to say that some cognition is part of our brain circuitry whereas other cognition is not: it is *all* part of our electrical system. So the emphasis added by hard-wired just means degree of rigidity, automaticity, or invariance. But this is an issue of degree whereas to be hard-wired (in electrical systems) is a discrete concept—either hard-wired or not.

I find terms like *innate* and *hard-wired* problematic and the nature-nurture distinction misleading, but surely they are all pointing toward an important consideration regarding human cognition: just how much is a given trait or capacity *variable* from one person to another because of environmental factors, and *variable* across situations in a given individual based on context or volition? To capture these questions, I will use a distinction proposed by philosopher of cognitive science Robert McCauley, but with slight modification.

COGNITIVE NATURALNESS

McCauley uses *naturalness* to refer to thought processes or behaviors that are characterized by ease, automaticity, and fluency. Those abilities that require little conscious attention or effort are *natural* in McCauley's sense. Speaking a native language, adding 2 + 2, and walking are natural for most of us in this respect. McCauley goes on to observe that this kind of naturalness can come about in two basic ways. *Practiced naturalness* arises through lots and lots of practice, training, tuition, and cultural support (including relevant artifacts) as in gaining chess mastery or becoming a concert pianist. In contrast, *maturational naturalness* seems to just appear as a matter of developmental course—as in learning to walk or talk or add small numbers.[6] Of course, many forms of cultural expression that we find "natural" bear some marks of both practiced and maturational naturalness. Literacy, which requires practice, training, tuition, and writing tools, for instance, can get so automatic and fluent that we find it hard to turn off. The Stroop Test famously demonstrates the naturalness of literacy in adults.[7]

In the Stroop Test an experimenter presents a fully literate adult with a list of words written in colored ink and the task for the participant is to simply say the color of the ink. The words, however, are color names that sometimes match and sometimes mismatch with the ink. When the ink is blue, for instance, and the word is "RED," people name the color more slowly than when the ink is red. Why? The meaning of the word interferes with the demand to name a different color. The naturalness of reading the words cannot be simply turned off or overridden to solve the task. Naming the ink color requires extra cognitive effort and, hence, extra time (even if only fractions of seconds).[8]

Literacy, then, can become cognitively natural, but it rides on the back of both practiced and maturational naturalness. Language use is maturationally natural, but writing and reading language requires instruction, practice, and special cultural conditions that include writing systems and writing implements.

Though many (if not all) forms of expression we would call cultural show signs of both practiced and maturational naturalness, not all cognitive systems that underlie these forms of expression have this dual character. Some cognitive capacities are decidedly maturationally natural. I wish to focus on these maturationally natural capacities because they bear the important feature of being present in essentially all normally developing humans of any cultural group. Indeed, a good rule of thumb McCauley suggests for identifying such maturationally natural cognition is whether its absence in your child would make you worry that an abnormality is present. If your five-year-old child just can't develop chess mastery even after many lessons and lots of practice, you would probably just shrug, but if your five-year-old still is not speaking, you would be concerned. Maturationally natural cognitive capacities typically arise early in development (in the first five years of life) as a matter of course.[9] It follows that they are broadly present across cultures in largely similar forms. These capacities are the foundations upon which cultural learning and expertise are built.

Note that this view of maturationally natural cognition does not entail that the capacities are present at birth, biologically determined, hard-wired, or innate. Some of these capacities could be largely fixed before birth or impervious to environmental inputs (outside of normal biological needs). Other maturationally natural capacities might be largely a product being tuned up by environmental regularities that occur in any cultural context: rocks are solid everywhere, plants require sunlight, babies have mothers, and so on. We often overlook just how regular many aspects of the world (including the social world) are. Identifying something as maturationally natural doesn't commit one to a hard stance on any of these issues.

The regularity and early development of maturationally natural capacities make me think these capacities map on to what we normally think of as part of human nature or as natural cognition. For this reason, and for linguistic economy, I will use *natural* to mean maturationally natural. In contrast, I will refer to practiced naturalness as *expertise*.

Natural General Cognition[10]

The most obvious and least controversial features of natural cognition are *general* limitations such as limits on perception, attention, and memory. Though it may not be obvious at first, the general limitations we have on perception, attention, and memory have important consequences for knowledge acquisition and cultural learning because they force use of another type of cognition, *content-specific* cognition, as explained below.

We know full well from our own experiences that we cannot remember everything we might want to remember. Cognitive scientists have usefully decomposed memory into specific types of memory such as semantic memory, episodic memory, and procedural memory. Semantic memory is a type of long-term memory pertaining to the information we know. As anyone who has tried to learn massive amounts of information can attest, semantic memory seems to have some practical limitations. Episodic memory is memory for particular episodes or events in one's life. Do you remember all of the events of last Thursday? No? Then you have fallible episodic memory. Procedural memory is memory for how to do things, how to execute a series of actions. If you've ever forgotten how to do something, you have experienced the limitations we have in procedural memory. Most of us take these kinds of memory limitations for granted—we can't remember everything—but we can readily integrate this kind of naturalness into the old *blank slate* or *sponge* view of the human mind. The slate is blank but it is only so big; the sponge soaks up anything equally well but gets saturated and can't soak up more. These sorts of limitations are not directly relevant to the *content* or type of information we acquire but only how much.

Semantic, episodic, and procedural memory are types of long-term memory—memory that can slip out of conscious attention and be brought back again, maybe even after delays of many years. A type of short-term memory, working memory, featured importantly in the early days of cognitive science. Working memory refers to the amount of information that can be consciously attended to, *held in mind*, at the same time. Working memory is also not infinite. We can only attend to so many units of information at one time. In fact, one of the first sallies in the "cognitive revolution" that began cognitive science was research by George Miller investigating working memory.[11] His experiments led to the claim that working memory is limited to approximately seven-plus-or-minus-two chunks of information—a claim that has undergone some modification but still is in the right ballpark: we can (usually) only keep up to around seven chunks of information in attention at once, and sometimes less than that. *Chunks* might sound crude, but it means roughly the largest conceptually meaningful unit a person recognizes. So the digits [0], [7], [0], [4], [1], [7], [7], [6] may be represented as eight chunks (one for each digit) or recognized as the date July 4, 1776, and be represented as either three chunks, if that is just an arbitrary date with no particular significance, one chunk for [July], one for [4], and one for [1776]; or as just one chunk, [American Independence Day]. Knowledge, then, impacts chunk sizes, but big or small, it is still unusual to be able to keep more than seven or so chunks of information in working memory.

This observation about working memory being limited might seem as trivial as the limitations on long-term memory, but it has important consequences for perception, thought, and communication. Applied to perception, a limit on working memory suggests restrictions on how rich a representation of the world around us we can maintain. Simply too much information comes pouring in at one time for us to focus on it all. Sights, sounds, smells, tastes, and feelings of various sorts bombard us constantly. We cannot attend to it all—certainly not consciously. In a series of experiments, psychologists Daniel Simons and Daniel Levin demonstrated just how impoverished our real-world perception is.[12] For instance, they asked adults to look at series of photographs, each one followed by a blank screen and then another photo. Their task was to answer whether the second photo of each pair was the same as the first. Easy, right? Depending upon the variation, adults were no better than guessing, mistakenly saying the photo was the same even when large changes (in terms of the proportion of the photo) were made such as completely changing the color of a building or removing prominent trees, changing a car into a dumpster, and the like. Similarly, they found that when viewers watched a film of a dialogue between two people sitting at a table with plates and food in front of them, that the clothing of the actors, the food location, the color of the plates, and numerous other changes could be made from one cut to the next without viewers noticing. They refer to this phenomenon as *change blindness*, and it illustrates that we have much thinner perceptual representations of the world around us than we suppose, in part because we cannot consciously attend to it all.[13] We have the *illusion* of a complete representation of the world around us, particularly in familiar environments, because we know what should be there. That is, our knowledge automatically, nonconsciously fills in the blanks. We only have to attend to enough details about the environment to trigger the right conceptual information or the right course of actions. Sometimes amusingly, if there is something in the environment that does not belong— that our understanding of the situation does not "fill in" for us, we may fail to notice it all together. Daniel Simons has famously demonstrated this with his studies in which viewers are asked to watch two teams of three players each pass around a basketball, but only count the passes of the team wearing white, not the one wearing black. As the viewers count the passes, a person in a gorilla costume walks into the middle of the players, turns to the camera and pounds his chest, and then walks off. In this task only about half of viewers notice the gorilla at all! Keeping track of passes consumes too much attentional capacity for us to have much left over for a surprising event.[14]

Our working memory limitations also mean that when we have to rapidly solve problems, draw inferences, or make predictions, there is only so much information we can consciously attend to and so we often take reasoning shortcuts that simplify things. We use heuristics—rules of thumb that work reasonably well and reasonably quickly—instead of doing the difficult (or impossible) work of carefully reasoning things out. I will describe one particularly important heuristic, the *accessibility heuristic,* in the next chapter: we tend to treat as correct those ideas that are easy to consciously access.

To get around our working memory limitations in thinking, we also make heavy use of what might be termed *intuitive* or *tacit* knowledge. This is knowledge we typically don't even know we have, but once it is pointed out it just seems right—it is intuitive. To illustrate, we tacitly know that animals have babies like themselves. Dogs, for instance, have baby dogs. Cats have baby cats. This fact is so banal that it is rarely stated, nor does it even need to be stated. If I tell you that a manoby in the local zoo had babies, I don't need to tell you that it had baby manobies instead of baby wallabies—that information is there automatically, tacitly, intuitively. In fact, you also tacitly know that the manoby moves to obtain nutrition, has parts inside of it that make it go, is made of organic matter, is a bounded physical object that cannot pass directly through other objects, and a host of other pieces of information—even though you have never heard of a manoby before (because I made it up). This intuitive knowledge is built into the chunk *manoby* and so doesn't take up precious working memory space.

Because this extra conceptual information gets smuggled in

"free of charge" to working memory, it serves as an important prop for communication. Real-time face-to-face verbal communication makes working memory demands that could easily outstrip seven-plus-or-minus-two chunks if not for conceptual information that can be assumed. Again, if I tell you that the local zoo has a manoby that gave birth, I don't have to tell you that it grows, requires food, and the rest. The consequence is efficient communication. I only need to communicate enough information to trigger this conceptual background information and trust your mind to fill in the rest.[15] Note, however, that if I am trying to tell you about something for which you don't naturally possess background conceptual information that can flesh out the skeleton of verbal communication, I have the increased burden of detailing all of this information and you have the burden of keeping enough of it in working memory at a time that it can be comprehended enough to be encoded into long-term memory for later use. It follows that ideas that are largely composed of the conceptual building materials we already have are more easily and readily communicated. Ideas that deviate from our intuitive knowledge require more effort, attention, and repetition (or other devices) for successful communication.

I have spent this time discussing the general limitations we have on long-term and working memory systems that might seem trivial and boring at first glance because they end up having huge implications for all of our knowledge acquisition and cultural learning, including religious learning. Working memory and attendant attentional limitations cause us to be dependent upon intuitive knowledge for rapid reasoning, communicating, and learning. As ideas that make good use of existing intuitive knowledge will be easiest to acquire, use, and communicate, then knowing something about what kind of intuitive knowledge people are likely to have is critically important in knowing what they can readily acquire, use, and communicate. And it may come as no surprise that the intuitive knowledge that most people will share has its origins in (maturationally) natural cognition.[16]

Natural Content-Specific Cognition

Above I discussed some natural cognition that imposes general limitations on how we process information. Whether the information is about rocks or cows, people or chairs, or comes in through words or through scenes, certain basic restrictions apply when it comes to memory and attention. Perception too seems to have some basic limitations regardless of the type of objects you are trying to perceive. In contrast to this natural *general* cognition, we also have limitations and tendencies when it comes to specific domains of cognitive content. Not all information about all topics is treated the same. In my experience, this claim is more surprising and more controversial, and so even though I will spend more time in subsequent chapters detailing such natural *content-specific* biases, I want to provide a few examples now.

A view of the mind as a blank slate just waiting for culture to write on it or a sponge ready to absorb any and all information equally well or a pitcher open to being filled can readily accommodate the general limitations discussed above. One might think, "Sure, the mind cannot limitlessly attend, perceive, or remember, but it still attends, perceives, or remembers all information in pretty much the same way. The slate is blank, but it isn't infinitely large. The sponge isn't particular about what it soaks up, but it does get saturated and unable to take in more. The pitcher can get full."

I suspect something like these models represent the way most people think about minds: limited in capacity but not having interesting limits in terms of the particular content. The pitcher can only hold a gallon, but it is just as happy with a gallon of lemonade as of water. Certainly the way intelligence is traditionally treated—as a general capacity that is greater or less from one person (or species) to another—is consistent with this view. We talk about dogs being smarter than cats or one person being smarter than another. What we probably mean in most of these cases is that one person has more general capacity to learn or think than another.

Challenging such a picture of the mind is evidence that we seem to naturally take in some kinds of information better than others, and have characteristic ways of treating some information that does not apply to others. Here are a few examples to make the point.

Humans (and monkeys) have a natural disposition to become afraid of snakes. It is very easy for a person to become afraid of snakes compared to flowers or butterflies. People have been shown to rapidly detect snakelike objects, and to be readily conditioned to fear snakes—even when they are not consciously aware of having seen the snake. Infants readily associate snakes with fearful stimuli: when presented with a photo of a snake and another animal (e.g., a hippo) and they hear a voice speaking in a frightened tone, they preferentially look at the snake, but not when the voice uses a happy tone. If you suspect that this rapid fear association with snakes is due to cultural peculiarities, consider this: monkeys raised without exposure to snakes (in captivity) can acquire a long-lasting fear of snakes merely by watching another monkey react in fear to a snake. Not so with watching a monkey react in fear to a bunny. Monkeys and humans alike have a *preparedness* to become afraid of snakes. Why might this be? As snakes might prove dangerous and are rarely a dominant source of food or other survival aid, a good survival strategy is to simply avoid snakes. Having a natural bias to become afraid of snakes would be adaptive for monkeys, humans, and other animals.[17]

Newborn babies differentially detect faces and imitate their expressions. From immediately following birth (within hours), human babies already attend more to human faces in their environment as compared with other sorts of things out there. The baby in the delivery-room bassinet would rather look at its mother's face than a pile of rags, the colorful wallpaper, or the nearby sphygmomanometer. Even more surprising is that within a few hours after birth, babies can imitate some facial expressions such as sticking out the tongue.[18] Think what is involved in this feat: among the blurry mass of novel stimuli, a baby detects something in her environment (the face) and maps the thing's appearance and movement onto her own facial musculature to create a comparable expression. And the baby doesn't even know she has a face yet! (Or does she?) Again, as impressive as this is for a newborn with very poor visual acuity, the finding makes sense. Spotting and recognizing other humans is terribly important for human social success. Having some natural biases that give an advantage in processing faces (as compared with, say, trees, potatoes, or the faces of cows or chickens) would be helpful. This content-specific facility with human faces persists into adulthood: most adults are remarkably facile with identifying and remembering thousands of faces when compared with comparably complex and varied visual stimuli.

Humans partition the rainbow in similar ways. Ask the average educated adult how many colors there are in a rainbow and they will most likely answer either six or seven. The odd person will know that the truth is that a rainbow displays a whole spectrum of colors and there aren't just six or seven bands of color. The illusion of seeing color bands instead of a nice gradual swoosh of color is an instance of a recurrent perceptual bias called *categorical perception*: we impose boundaries on visual or auditory information where none really exist and see instances within those boundaries as more similar than they really are (e.g., all shades of blue being more similar to each other than to any neighboring shades of green). Some cases of categorical perception are clearly influenced by cultural particularities as in vowel and consonant sounds: if you do not have a distinction in your language (e.g., between "r" as in "raw" and "l" as in "law" or between the "er" sound at the end of "rather" and the "a" sound at the end of "idea"), you may *lose* the ability to hear certain differences. In contrast, seeing bands of color in a rainbow appears to be a natural instance of categorical perception. Studies with infants show that they see color boundaries in the same place as most adults. This categorical perception has been demonstrated now with a variety of tasks. One early and representative task was an experiment in which four-month-olds were shown either two colors from the same color band (e.g., that adults would say were both blue) or two colors that straddle a color band (e.g., one that adults would say is blue and one that adults would say is green), but the two pairs of colored panels were the same difference from each other in terms of actual wavelength of light that they reflected—that is, the colors straddling a boundary were just as far apart in the color spectrum as the two within the same color band. Babies were slower to stop looking at the two colors that straddled the boundary, indicating they registered the two types of displays as different. If these four-month-olds saw the world without color boundaries, they should have looked at the different displays for the same length of time.[19]

These three areas of content-specific natural cognitive bias—fearing snakes, detecting faces, and categorical color perception—are just the tip of the iceberg, but I hope they are sufficient to illustrate a key point: the mind as a whole is not helpfully compared to a blank slate. Rather, our minds preferentially attend to and differentially process some types of information over others, handling different domains of information in different ways. This does not mean that there are not general principles or some ways in which these differing classes of information are brought together on more equal footing, but it does mean that a blank slate view is too simplistic.

In the movie *Phenomenon*, John Travolta's character embodies the idea that if we could just get more of our brain involved or interconnected, then we could have supercognitive abilities. It does not take too much imagination to see parallels between these possibilities depicted in *Phenomenon* and ideas in another film that Travolta made in the same year (1996): *Orientation: A Scientology Information Film*. Many Scientologists, like practitioners of some forms of Buddhism, see the typical human's mind as shackled and restricted, but capable of so much more impressive cognitive abilities than are actualized. They could be right. Certainly the occasional super-genius gives us a glimpse of what we all might be. Cognitive science does not directly contradict such a view, but it does reduce optimism in the possibility that we could all be like George in *Phenomenon*.

If human minds are embodied (whether they must be or not), our bodies restrict our general cognitive capacities. Our natural cognition limits our perceptual and attentional abilities as well as long-term and working memory. Further, we naturally process some kinds of information more readily than others (such as human faces) and process some kinds of information differently than others (such as associating snakes with fear). Unless our minds fully escape our bodies, such limitations and predilections may never be completely avoided. But maybe being devoid of all such natural cognitive limitations or biases would mean no longer having a human mind. Suppose we did have better long-term memory or we could keep a few more chunks in working memory, or we no longer selectively processed some kinds of information as opposed to others. Such "enhancements" would radically change our human character. Perhaps we would no longer be human without the particular natural propensities of our minds.

If this speculation has merit, then examining more closely the character of natural cognition, particularly the content-specific variety, will help illuminate human distinctiveness—that something special that makes humans different from other animals.

CHAPTER 3
The Cognitive Origins of Beliefs

MANY THEOLOGIES, including some forms of Buddhism, Hinduism, and Judaism, downplay the importance of beliefs, instead favoring community identification or engagement in particular practices being regarded as the core features of religious expression. The term *belief* often carries connotations of commitment and devotion to a set of propositions that less intellectualist religious traditions find uncomfortable. But surely even these traditions affirm characteristic ideas that motivate or justify their community identifications and distinctive practices. To capture these affirmed ideas as well as confessional, propositional commitments, and because of its fit with human cognition, I adopt a particular meaning of *belief*. By *belief* I mean an instance of *mentally representing something as being the case in the generation of further thought and action*. The *something* could be information, associations, evaluations, and the like. These "beliefs," as I explain below, need not be held or represented in propositional form or even consciously or explicitly at all.[1] To believe something in this sense is similar to thinking that something is the case. I might hear that it is raining right now without being conscious of the fact but, nevertheless, form the belief that it is raining. On a nonconscious level I think (or represent) it as raining, and so I *believe* it is raining.

This narrower definition of beliefs skirts the problem of historical or cultural particularities surrounding "belief" and enables the recognition that beliefs, in the sense meant here, underlie every action—religious or otherwise—and all religious actions regardless of tradition, including ritual, prayer, and meditation. The construction and proclamation of every religious doctrine, likewise, hinge on the formation of beliefs. From this perspective, why people hold *religious* beliefs (beliefs that motivate *religious* action), and why religious beliefs tend to take the forms that they do across time and place are central questions to the study of any religion.

How one arrives at one's conscious beliefs and whether arriving at them was done reputably has occupied a prominent place in philosophy since the Enlightenment. How do we arrive at beliefs then? Does cognitive science have anything to contribute?

Our working memory limitations require us to use conceptual information to complete our percepts, communication, and general thinking. Because we cannot hold everything in consciousness, we need nonconscious information to be available as needed to fill in the blanks. Fortunate for us, we have enormous long-term stores of information, of which we need not be consciously aware, that can serve this function. Some of this information has been acquired through cultural expertise, but much of it is acquired as a natural part of being human. In this chapter I present how nonconscious information contributes to the formation of beliefs, an area of broad application and particularly relevant to religion and theology.

Testimony

Perhaps the factors relevant to belief formation that have received the most attention by psychologists concern the role of testimony.[2] Common sense tells us that much of what we believe was imparted to us by other people. The importance of testimony bears upon every domain of knowing, even in the sciences: we believe things because trusted others tell us that they are true. Arguably, we would know very little in life if we did not give testimony the benefit of the doubt—sometimes called the *credulity principle*. We trust others unless we have good reason not to do so.

One key to the power of testimony is the social context of the testimony: who is talking? If the sources are known and trusted individuals, we will tend to value their testimony all the more. Further, people have been shown to be subject to a number of *context biases* regarding to whom they listen: conformity bias, prestige bias, and similarity bias. These biases depend upon the social context rather than the content of the ideas or practices.[3]

Conformity Bias

"You just think that because everybody else does!" If we look at how contested beliefs are distributed, what is immediately obvious is that they are not uniformly scattered but tend to cluster. People who believe that Manchester United is the best football club in England are more common in Manchester than in Liverpool or Portsmouth. People who believe that Brad Paisley is a better guitarist than The Edge will be in higher proportions in Tennessee than Ireland. In part this is because beliefs can motivate social affiliation, but mostly because people tend to conform to the dominant views of people around them. When in doubt, the consensus opinion serves as one's default belief and is accepted as true.

Prestige Bias

The *conformity bias* is joined by a *prestige bias* in shaping those we choose to imitate in terms of behaviors or beliefs. When a strong consensus is lacking, who do we trust to have the truth or to imitate? Those who are highly regarded, have social power, or high status. Again, advertisers have known this for a long time and used celebrities and other high-status individuals to endorse their wares. Such prestigious affirmation of products ranges from sensible to absurd. Sensible endorsements are when we might expect that the high-status individual actually has relevant expertise, as when Michael Jordan endorses basketball shoes, something he uses more frequently and at a higher level than most people. Being a high-performing basketball player qualifies him to have an opinion worth considering when it comes to basketball shoes. But why should I care what hot dog he chooses? Or why should an actor's— even a very fine actor's—opinion on a political issue or candidate move me in the least? Rationally, it should not as a general principle, but humans seem to have a natural tendency to treat prestigious individuals as good targets for imitation regardless of how the prestige was achieved.

Similarity Bias

Politicians spend a lot of time trying to get the electorate to identify with them, to show that they are somehow similar to everyone else. In April 1993 President Bill Clinton appeared on MTV and famously informed the world that he wore briefs not boxers. Some political observers of the time decried the gross condescension of the presidency, but others praised Clinton's political acumen: at the time the vast majority of American men wore briefs and this was a great way to show he was a regular guy. But why, if he was a prestigious individual, did he need to communicate that he was a regular guy? When in doubt, we first trust those who are similar to us. This *similarity bias* is a fairly sensible strategy from a long-term perspective. Historically, people "like us" would have been most likely to possess reliable information relevant for people "like us." If you were a local angler and wanted to know where to catch fish in the local lake, you would ask another local angler, not a foreign angler, or a local sheepherder. The lesson extends to all kinds of cultural knowledge such as how I should behave in social settings, what is safe to eat, how to best build a house, and so on. Of course, we can use similarity bias together with prestige bias to produce the principle that one should learn from the most prestigious individual of the group of people with which one identifies.

I have only given a cursory treatment of these social biases that impact testimony because as important as these factors are in transmitting ideas and beliefs, these factors say little about cross-culturally recurrent patterns in the content of beliefs. Suppose we want to know why people in many parts of the world believe that ghosts (or similar entities) exist and act in the world. Answering, "Why do people believe in the existence of ghosts?" with "Because they were told about them," or "Because a prestigious individual told them," or "Because a majority of people around them believe in them" only pushes the question back a step: "But why did those who testified to the existence of ghosts believe in ghosts?" To answer this sort of question, we need a different sort of answer.[4] The rest of this chapter will look for such an answer.

Two-System Model of Reasoning

Advertisers have long known that a key to getting people to want your product—to believe that it will meet their needs—is repetition. Make the claim over and over again. Associate your product with joy, happiness, success, and satisfaction *repeatedly*. The same basic principle applies to political campaigns, education, and proselytizing. Such repetition changes attitudes, judgments, and beliefs, and these, in turn, change behaviors. Why is repetition often sufficient to win hearts and minds?

An important clue for how minds form beliefs comes from Nobel laureate Daniel Kahneman's research on judgments and choice. Together with Amos Tversky, Kahneman made huge contributions to an area Herbert Simon called *bounded rationality*.[5] These psychologists challenged the model of the mind once dominant in economics that people can be regarded as careful, rational decision-makers—rational in the sense that they consciously think through the evidence and reasons available and arrive at the optimal justifiable decision that is usually right. Instead, Kahneman's work has shown that people tend to form judgments and choose among options using processes that are not always rational.

Consider the following judgment problem. List the highest crime-rate cities in the United States. What cities come to mind? Los Angeles? New York? Miami? Las Vegas? Or alternatively, rank the following U.S. cities (given here alphabetically) in terms of serious crime rates from highest to lowest:

: Atlanta, Georgia
: Cincinnati, Ohio
: Flint, Michigan
: Las Vegas, Nevada
: Los Angeles, California
: New York, New York
: St. Louis, Missouri
: Washington, DC

When I have given this example in the past, generally educated people volunteer Los Angeles, New York, Las Vegas, and Miami near the tops of their lists. I have found, informally, that the amount of convergence in these rankings is moderately high, and very inaccurate. For instance, City-Data.com published the following 2008 crime data for these cities on a scale with 321 as the U.S. national average, and higher scores indicating higher crime rates:

: New York, 245
: Los Angeles, 349
: Las Vegas, 505
: Miami, 632
: Washington, 676
: Cincinnati, 734
: Atlanta, 787
: Flint, 932
: St. Louis, 1081

Los Angeles is actually near the national per capita average and New York is below average in serious crime. Why then, when people think of crime in America, do Los Angeles and New York spring to mind as top offenders, but St. Louis, Atlanta, and Cincinnati rarely come to mind? This association between crime and America's largest cities has been built up over repeated exposure to the pairing. Because they are large cities in terms of numbers of people, and they are media centers, more published reports about crime in those cities reach us. Further, television and film producers often choose cities like New York and Los Angeles for crime shows (*CSI: New York, Law & Order,* and *NCIS: Los Angeles*; but also *CSI,* set in Las Vegas, *Miami Vice,* and *CSI: Miami*).

These repeated associations between some cities and crime become part of our nonconscious cognition available to solve the judgment problem in the absence of other information, and rates are hard to judge. That is, we have the intuition that these are high crime-rate cities. Atlanta and Cincinnati just don't *seem* like high crime cities. This example illustrates a heuristic Kahneman calls *accessibility*. If an idea or association comes to mind rapidly, we are more likely to regard it as correct. Kahneman comments aptly: "People are not accustomed to thinking hard and are often content to trust a plausible judgment that quickly comes to mind."[6] In a sense, Kahneman is suggesting that we apply the credulity principle to the "testimony" of our own minds. What our minds tell us, we are inclined to believe.

Kahneman presents the impact of accessibility on judgment through a dual-processing or two-system view of cognition. Increasingly, cognitive scientists discuss human thought as reflecting two different general subsystems. One that might be labeled the "intuitive" system can be characterized as fast, automatic, effortless, and emotional; whereas the "reasoning" system is slow, controlled, effortful, flexible, and less emotional. The intuitive system generates impressions that are not voluntary or verbally explicit. The reasoning system creates explicit, verbally expressible judgments. Kahneman's argument is that these two systems are not independent, but when the intuitive system generates thoughts that come to mind seemingly spontaneously and effortlessly—thoughts that have high accessibility—they serve as basic material for the reasoning system to form an explicit judgment. A key question, then, is what makes an idea accessible? His answer: "The accessibility of a thought is determined jointly by the characteristics of the cognitive mechanisms that produce it and by the characteristics of the stimuli and events that evoke it."[7]

Concerning beliefs generated by perception or memory, the lesson from Kahneman is simple and timeworn. Our percepts and memories automatically and immediately deliver beliefs without intervening reflection. I believe there is a teacup in front of me because my visual perception system registers stimuli for which TEACUP is the most accessible matching object. I do not reason my way to this belief. Similarly, if you were to ask me how the teacup came to be sitting in front of me, my memory system immediately produces a memory of me filling the cup and placing it on the table in front of me. In the absence of overriding reasons to mistrust this memory, I believe it. In fact, most of the time when we rely on our percepts or memories, we do not even consciously consider whether the beliefs they deliver are true or false. Their high degree of accessibility makes them indubitable. We can think of these automatic, intuitive beliefs as the starting point or default assumption for further reflection or to just take at face value. Similar lessons apply to other beliefs that are not directly formed through perception or memory. I discuss these below.

Two Kinds of Belief

In a similar vein to Kahneman, and following anthropologist Dan Sperber, I find it helpful to talk about two kinds of "beliefs": *reflective* or *explicit beliefs*, and *nonreflective* or *intuitive beliefs*.

Reflective Beliefs

Reflective beliefs are those beliefs we consciously hold and explicitly endorse. Barring deception, simple verbal responses are the most direct measure of reflective beliefs. For instance, the answer "Yes" to the question "Do you think that dogs are better pets than cats?" indicates a belief in the superiority of dogs to cats as pets. Reflective belief, then, approximates common use of the term *belief*. In terms of the two-system model above, reflective beliefs are a product of the reasoning system. Reflective beliefs are typically represented as propositions. "The chair is ugly," "England won the last World Cup," "Bob is angry at Emma because Nick told Tom about Bob's secret," "Maple leaves have five points," and "Harvey is seven feet tall" are all examples of reflective beliefs. Note that reflective beliefs are not necessarily *inferential* in the sense of reflectively drawing inferences from consciously accessible evidence or reasons or inferring them from other beliefs, a point I return to below. Reflective beliefs may be true, false, or indeterminate, concerning fact or opinion.

One's reflective beliefs may appear to defy any attempt at a general explanation because they seem so idiosyncratic and dependent upon personal history, experiences, and cultural context.[8] In the case of a given individual's reflective beliefs, this resistance to explanation may be largely true. When considering why it is that people generally tend to hold the sorts of reflective beliefs that they do, including religious beliefs, however, cognitive science provides us with some explanatory traction. This traction derives in large part from considering intuitive, nonreflective beliefs and their relationship to reflective beliefs.

Nonreflective Beliefs

Nonreflective beliefs map closely onto what might be called tacit or intuitive knowledge. They are products of the intuitive system, and are likewise cognitively natural in McCauley's sense of having a high degree of automaticity and requiring little conscious effort to produce. These nonreflective beliefs are representations that we have whether or not we know we have them. They are nonreflective in that they do not require conscious, deliberate, reflective resources to form them. We might never be aware of many of our nonreflective beliefs even though they guide our information processing, speech, and other actions. Though unlikely to be represented as verbal propositions, for the sake of clarity I will present examples as propositions.

Nonreflective beliefs include such ideas as "Snakes are scary," "Rainbows have bands of color," "People have minds," "I am," "A definite article does not precede a proper name," "Unsupported solid objects fall," "The sun moves relative to the earth," and "Dogs have puppies." When cognitive scientists talk about what infants or chimpanzees think or know, they generally are referring to nonreflective beliefs—refusing to commit to whether these nonverbal animals are explicitly, reflectively aware of these beliefs. Note that whether a belief is true or false is independent of whether it is reflective or nonreflective. Likewise, nonreflective beliefs may be part of natural cognition or expertise.

Relating Reflective and Nonreflective Beliefs

Reflective beliefs are typically obtained through nonreflective beliefs by several means. First, nonreflective beliefs anchor and inform the range of likely reflective beliefs by serving as default positions. It is hard work to think, and so we are inclined to just accept nonreflective beliefs for our reflective ones. For instance, when confronted with a question that they have never consciously considered such as, "Do you believe snakes are dangerous?" people may have no explicit, reflective belief one way or the other, but must come to a decision. Unless relevant information, such as from previous education in zoology, comes to mind, the most likely reflective belief will be that option consistent with relevant nonreflective beliefs. If thinking about snakes triggers an association with fear and danger, as is often the case, then the nonreflective belief "Snakes are scary" seems right and serves as the starting point or default for the reflective belief "Snakes are scary and dangerous."

Consider the question of whether other people have conscious thoughts. Maybe it has never occurred to me to think explicitly about whether other people have conscious thoughts and I have not been exposed to related philosophical ruminations. So how do I form a reflective belief on the subject? I tap my intuitions and discover the nonreflective belief "People have conscious minds." Finding no reason to reject or override such an intuition, I accept it (at least initially) as my reflective belief. In the absence of salient, relevant, consciously accessible reasons not to do so, reflective beliefs are simply read off of nonreflective beliefs.[9]

Similarly, a second way in which nonreflective beliefs inform reflective beliefs is by lending credibility to reflective propositions. Consider, "Is it morally permissible to use a hedgehog as a polo ball?" One view of moral reasoning is that we rationally, reflectively arrive at moral norms and then apply them to a particular case. More typically, however, a particular moral question generates emotion-laden intuitions (of which we may become consciously aware) that we then reflectively justify.[10] Contemporary research on beliefs and decision-making in various domains often points to the important role of intuition or emotions.[11] When presented with a choice, decision, or judgment, we often have a *reflex*ive, emotional reaction and then we *reflect*ively generate reasons to justify the gut reaction. We report our reasons as why we believe what we do, but we might have settled on other rationalizations: the beliefs are driven most forcefully by intuitions and emotions. These intuitions are products of the intuitive system and, when they have meaningful content (e.g., "that action is repulsive"), are nonreflective beliefs. Explicit propositions will be more likely to feel right when they converge with implicitly held nonreflective beliefs.

This principle can be extended to cases in which multiple nonreflective beliefs bear upon an explicit proposition. Suppose someone tells you that somewhere on Tasmania there has been discovered an animal called a manoby that has babies of an entirely different species with metal organs inside of them. Manobies become invisible when people look at them, the exception being Thursdays, when they stay entirely visible. The proposition to consider is "Manobies exist." In this case, reflecting upon the possible existence of manobies, you probably have several different nonreflective beliefs that you draw upon to arrive at a reflective belief. You likely have the intuition (nonreflective belief) that animals do not have babies of a different species. Further, you know (via nonreflective belief) that animals do not have metal parts inside as part of their nature. You likely have the strong intuitions that animals cannot become invisible, and that visibility cannot be dependent upon whether something else is looking at it or the day of the week. Physical laws concerning visibility are constants, as you nonreflectively know. On the other hand, you have the sense that strange things live in Tasmania. All of these nonreflective beliefs weigh in on whether you believe in the existence of manobies. The more nonreflective beliefs that are consistent with manobies existing (versus nonreflective beliefs that are problematic for such a belief), the more likely one is to believe, and believe with confidence. Plausibility increases with the cumulative support of nonreflective beliefs. I have spelled out this evaluative process as if it were wholly consciously reasoned, but we may instead simply have the intuition that manobies could not exist and only generate reasons after already deciding.

These nonreflective beliefs that serve as defaults for reflective beliefs or lend plausibility to them may be products of (maturationally) natural cognition or expertise. As natural cognition is more broadly shared within and across populations, natural cognition will play the greatest role in anchoring and informing explicit, reflective beliefs that are recurrent within and across human populations.

Above I have described how reflective beliefs arise through nonreflective beliefs, but nonreflective beliefs can be reflectively created as well. Reflective beliefs may become nonreflective through rehearsal. Heavy repetition can train the "intuitive system," resulting in what might be called *expertise,* or what McCauley calls practiced naturalness.[12] For instance, I was once taught that one must mount a horse from the horse's left side. Previously I had no reflective or nonreflective beliefs about the way to mount a horse. I would approach the horse from either side. With practice, however, I have come to just feel like approaching the horse on its right is wrong and mounting from the left is right.[13] Because of rehearsal, I now have a nonreflective belief about the "right" way to mount a horse, but it began as a reflective belief delivered via authoritative testimony.

The nonreflective beliefs that reflective beliefs encourage via rehearsal will be instances of expertise, as in mounting the horse from the left or learning how a chess knight moves. Explicitly being taught that other people have consciousness or that dogs give birth to little dogs (and not little cats) may be possible, but it is redundant with the deliverances of natural cognition.[14]

So far I have been focusing on fairly direct impacts of reflective and nonreflective beliefs on each other. Indirectly, they may interact as well. As the nonreflective beliefs derived from natural cognition are essentially universal and early developing, they broadly ballast the rise of cultural systems and the kind of expertise one is likely to acquire. For instance, because quantum mechanics is so poorly supported by natural cognition, quantum beliefs are poorly distributed and unlikely to be encountered. Special *cultural scaffolding* such as educational systems, institutions, written record systems, artifacts, and the like may be required to transmit widely ideas that deviate too far from natural cognition. Modern science is an excellent case in point as the enormous scaffolding provided by specialized symbolic and mathematical systems, special observation tools, rules and procedures, schools and academies, academic journals, and other forms of cultural support enable scientists to generate and maintain bodies of knowledge that deviate dramatically from natural cognition.[15]

Reflective beliefs may similarly impact nonreflective beliefs via the cultural environment. To illustrate, the owner of the shop next to the grocery store might have a belief about aesthetics that leads her to place pink flamingos outside her shop. Eventually, the townsfolk know nonreflectively that pink flamingos are next to the gro-cery store. In this example, a reflective belief was instrumental in changing the environment such that it increased the likelihood of acquiring some specifiable nonreflective belief.

To summarize, natural cognition supplies nonreflective beliefs that constrain and inform reflective belief formation directly and indirectly. Reflective beliefs can importantly impact nonreflective beliefs that are part of expertise, either directly or indirectly. These new nonreflective beliefs can, in turn, constrain and inform other reflective belief formation.

The relatively invariable components of this belief formation process are the deliverances of natural cognition. We all have them. They tether what we are likely to learn, and they constrain cultural expression, which further influences what we are likely to learn. It follows that when trying to understand beliefs acquired as part of expertise or as part of natural cognition, we need to know what our content-specific natural cognition supplies to us.

COMBINING CONTENT AND CONTEXT BIASES

After noting that several context biases impact whom we are likely to imitate or regard as providers of trustworthy testimony (con-formity, prestige, and similarity), I have been focusing on dynam-ics that hinge on content-rich natural cognition. This distinction has sometimes been called *content biases* versus *context biases*. Of course, both are at play in belief formation. If a prestigious indi-vidual tells me something that deviates from my content-specific natural cognition, I may be more receptive to it than if a nonpres-tigious individual tells me the same thing. Such a dynamic hap-pens in higher education all the time: we are inclined to believe the (sometimes) outrageous things professors teach because they are esteemed experts. Ideas that too greatly violate the nonreflective beliefs from natural cognition, however, are unlikely to be believed by prestigious individuals in the first place.

What all of these observations converge upon is that our two-system way of thinking entails that our reflective beliefs are influenced by our nonreflective beliefs. In fact, typically, reflective beliefs are obtained through or derived from nonreflective beliefs, albeit through processes of which we might not be consciously aware.[16]

WHAT DOES THE BELIEF-FORMATION PROCESS SAY ABOUT WHETHER OUR BELIEFS ARE TRUE?

When worldviews collide—religious or nonreligious—beliefs become a big deal. It isn't uncommon during heated disagreement about the existence of a god to hear a skeptic challenge the religious person to "prove" that his or her beliefs are true, and regard it as a humiliating and decisive defeat for the believer when he or she fails to do so.

Kahneman's work on reasoning heuristics and biases are often presented in the context of showing how our ordinary judgment-making procedures frequently yield irrational, illogical, and false conclusions. It may be tempting, therefore, to conclude that these automatic, nonconscious cognitive dynamics that influence belief-formation cast a shadow of doubt over *all* beliefs thus formed. If automatic cognitive processes noninferentially deliver beliefs to us, then such beliefs cannot be trusted on the grounds that they have not been reasoned to. They have been foisted upon us by our cognitive machinery, right?

A full treatment of such epistemological issues falls beyond the scope of this book, but many of us cannot help but wonder whether explaining where reflective beliefs come from amounts to "explaining away" the beliefs themselves—particularly when it comes to religious beliefs. Allow me a few brief comments for now.

Surely identifying the causal mechanisms of reflective belief (e.g., that reflective beliefs come from nonreflective beliefs) does not, in itself, say anything about the truth of the beliefs. If we accept that our minds are embodied in some sense, it would be surprising if *any* beliefs did not have some causal explanations in terms of cognitive systems. All of our beliefs are at least partially caused by natural mechanisms whether they are true or false, good or bad, a point made elegantly by philosopher and early psychologist William James.[17] So identifying the causal chain behind a given belief does not imply that the belief is wrong.

That a causal story for reflective beliefs exists does not cast aspersions on the belief in question, but perhaps this *particular* account of where reflective beliefs come from is unsettling. Shouldn't beliefs be reflectively reasoned to from evidence, logic, and mathematics? Reflective beliefs arrived at via nonreflective beliefs appear to violate philosopher W. K. Clifford's dictum that "It is wrong, always and everywhere for anyone to believe anything on insufficient evidence."[18]

Clifford's assertion resonates with those of us brought up in the age of science and skepticism. We don't just accept what is told us or what seems right, but demand evidence, no? No. Certainly in *some* cases it is wrong to believe something without sufficient evidence, such as believing someone guilty of a crime, or believing that on a yet-to-be-discovered planet live green monkeys that enjoy backgammon. Nevertheless, it certainly cannot be wrong "always and everywhere" to believe things in the absence of sufficient evidence—that is, unless by "evidence" we include the automatic deliverances of our cognitive systems, our intuitions. All of our beliefs, at one point or another, rely at least in part upon unproven, undersupported intuitions—the sorts of intuitions described in the upcoming chapters. If we dismissed all beliefs that rely on intuitions for support, we would be left with no (or at least very few) beliefs at all. Surely Clifford has set the bar too high.

The point is, we can never fully escape the influence of nonreflective beliefs on the formation of our reflective beliefs. Accepting a position like Clifford's—rejecting all beliefs caused importantly by nonreflective beliefs—would leave us intellectually paralyzed, unable to believe anything, including believing that we can't believe anything and believing Clifford's position. Self-defeating positions are never good ones.

Rather than be trapped in a skeptical quagmire, unable to know anything (including that I can't know anything), I regard it as more prudent to adopt a position of initial trust toward my cognitive faculties and their ability to deliver to me, via nonreflective beliefs, true beliefs and genuine knowledge about the world. Undoubtedly we make mistakes in forming true and good reflective beliefs, but rather than being concerned that natural causes for our beliefs mean we should doubt their veracity until they are vindicated through evidence and reason independent of these natural causes (if that were possible), we are justified in holding them *until* evidence and reason suggest that they are problematic (including evidence from science when applicable).[19] In short, identifying the cognitive pedigree of a reflective belief does not automatically "explain away" the belief.

Our understanding of particular causes of belief formation, such as those identified by Kahneman, might give us reason to suspect that some of the causes for our beliefs lead us to predictable types of errors. But note that discovering the errors presumes that we have some reliable ways to form beliefs about which beliefs are in error and which are correct. We have to have general trust in our belief-forming equipment or we would not be able to tell when and where it goes wrong—nor could we even do science. Science is built on a qualified trust of our cognitive faculties: we can approach truth but require judicious use of reason and systematic observation to guard against error.

In the next three chapters I offer more details about the natural cognition that gives rise to these structuring nonreflective beliefs. Chapter 4 focuses on how we naturally think about the world around us. Chapter 5 concerns how we naturally understand other humans. These observations are combined in chapter 6 to build a case for the naturalness of belief in gods generally, and a super-knowing, perceiving, powerful, immortal creator God in particular. In none of these belief domains does specifying the cognitive, causal background automatically entail that the beliefs are wrong or unjustified.

CHAPTER 4

How We Conceive of the World

WE COME INTO the world eager to make meaning out of our surroundings. What is out there, why is it how it is, and how does it work are questions that drive our explorations of the environment in the early years. The result is an impressive body of nonreflective, natural beliefs in place by the time children are five years old—much of it developing in the first year of life. In addition to learning to control their bodies for movement and speech, one of the early tasks for babies is forming a conception of the world.

My doctoral alma mater, Cornell University, is located on a hillside overlooking Cayuga Lake, one of upstate New York's Finger Lakes, so named because they resemble the fingers of two hands. Indeed, indigenous people of the region regarded these lakes as the impressions of the creator's hands. From an adult perspective, we might suppose that conceptualizing the world is wildly variable. Consider the vast range of cultural accounts of the world. Some Native Americans picture the world as riding on the back of a great turtle. Some Hindus emphasize that the world is part of the divine being, whereas others take greater inspiration from the god Shiva dancing the world into existence. Christianity, Islam, and Judaism share the view that God spoke the world into existence. In some worldviews the world has always existed with plants, animals, and humans arriving at a later point; in others it had a definite start. In some, the world is radically different from the creator; in others it is part of a creator.

What this apparent diversity might mask is that questions of why and how concerning the world occupy us all. Even if it has not seemed important to all peoples to wonder where the universe came from, we do wonder where people originated, why a familiar landscape is the way it is, what accounts for rainbows, or the origins of fire. We come up with different answers, but we ask similar questions.

As we see in essentially all domains of thought, however, adult diversity of opinions does not entail childhood openness to any and all possibilities equally. Cognitive scientists have begun demonstrating that children think about the world in fairly regular ways. As explained in the previous chapter, this content-specific natural cognition concerning the world and what is in it structures our thought for the rest of our lives.

In this chapter I sketch how humans characteristically carve the world up into objects and then categorize these objects into what have been called *intuitive ontologies*—nonreflective categories of being. Depending upon category membership, different causal reasoning strategies are applicable. A standard strategy leads to very predictable ways for people—from before school age—to generate inferences about bounded physical objects (including natural and artificial ones), living things, and intentional agents. Evidence exists that people are also prone to see the world as purposeful and intentionally ordered, perhaps contributing to the resilience of creationist ideas and arguments for the existence of a creator god.

THE WHERE: SPATIAL LAYOUT

Our first move in making sense of the world appears to be to code the spatial layout that we are in: where are the barriers, where are the objects, and where is the space in which we can move? The geometry of the space might be particularly important and automatically processed to aid action and navigation. Experiments by psychologist Linda Hermer and colleagues showed that two-year-olds searching for an object, which they had previously seen hidden in the corner of a rectangular room, searched at comparable rates in the geometrically similar corners (e.g., the two corners with the long wall on the left), ignoring the single brightly colored wall that specified a unique location for the object. When performing a difficult *verbal-shadowing* task, adults performed similarly to toddlers. Such tasks increase cognitive load (and reduce available working memory stores), thereby eliminating the use of all but the most automatically processed information.[1] In this case, the geometry of the space seems to be more readily registered in a useful way than the color of walls. Similarly, Daniel Simons, in early change-detection research, found that changes in the spatial arrangement of objects were more readily detected than changes of the objects themselves (e.g., from a mug to a typewriter).[2] *Where?* is noticed before *What?* This automatic processing of spatial arrangements serves to provide us with critical information regarding how to move in space and interact with objects.

The automatic, deep processing of spatial layout is at the core of one of the oldest known memory improvement techniques: the *method of loci*. Ancient orators would imagine vivid objects or persons to represent different points in their speeches and then "place them" each at a different location along a well-known path or in a familiar house using their imagination. To remember their speech, then, they merely had to imagine themselves walking through the space again and seeing the imagined reminders along the way. This memory technique is excellent for remembering a number of items in a particular order.

That space is automatically encoded in a way closely related to bodily movement has not escaped the notice of landscape and structural architects. The layout of space impacts us nonconsciously before it does consciously. No wonder, then, that the architects of the structures at southern Turkey's Göbekli Tepe, possibly the world's oldest discovered dedicated site of worship (approximately nine thousand years old), used carefully arranged, semisubterranean, imposing monoliths to attack worshippers' emotional,

fast-processing conceptual system with feelings of what? Small-
ness? Sublimity? Being in the presence of something powerful
and uncanny? Being in the subterranean belly or womb of anthro-
pomorphized nature? Using space to trigger particular content-
rich feelings in worship occasions has continued, as the medieval
Gothic cathedrals and mosques attest.

Likewise, it might be that pilgrimages and spiritual walks capitalize on natural configurations of space to act on participants unconsciously or to give them memory cues of spiritual leaders' life or
teachings via associating particular events or ideas with particular spatial locations. Pilgrims will be able to recall a long, complex
sequence of ideas by rewalking the route in their imagination à la
method of loci.

THE WHAT: CONCEPTUALIZING THE OBJECTS[3]

After establishing the "Where," our minds eagerly move onto the
"What." We make sense of the world by identifying objects or things
in the world. Indeed, linguistic evidence suggests that nouns (indicators of persons and things, in particular) are the most common
words acquired early in life. This identification of objects is both
visual and tactile, using hands and mouth. These objects are immediately categorized and reasoned about in terms of sets of expectations appropriate to their category membership. The classification
of objects into such categories is sometimes called *intuitive ontology*, and the classes are called *intuitive ontologies*.[4]

Basic objects can be thought of as falling in one or more of five
basic categories: *Spatial Entities*, *Solid Objects*, *Living Things* (that
do not appear to move themselves), *Animates*, and *Persons*. (Solid
Objects include an important subclass, *Artifacts*, human-made
objects.)

These five *ontological categories* are distinguished by characteristic sets of expectations or assumptions. The key expectation sets
here are *Spatiality*, *Physicality*, *Biology*, *Animacy*, and *Mentality*.

These expectation sets are *not* ontological categories, but different combinations of their activation characterize intuitive ontological categories. Expectations cluster into these five sets because of common activations and causal relations among these set members.

One additional expectation set, *Universals*, is tacit in essentially all causal reasoning and does not differentiate among the ontological categories. Universals are expectations that apply to all reasoning in any causal domain. They include such assumptions as time moves in one direction, laws and regularities are constant from moment to moment, and causes precede effects. If such expectations are not operational in a baby, learning causal correspondences and building up the other expectation sets would be impossible.[5]

Two expectation sets are generally conflated in experimental research. An intuition concerning the *Spatiality* of objects—that all objects have a single location in space and time—is presumed in discussions of *Physicality*. In addition to visibility (under normal conditions) and tangibility, the Physicality expectation set includes at least the intuitive expectations of *solidity, cohesion, continuity*, and *contact*.[6] Solidity entails that solid objects do not readily pass directly through each other or occupy the same space at the same time as each other: an apple cannot be in exactly the same place as an orange at the same time without one or the other being displaced. Cohesion refers to objects moving as connected wholes: if you grab one end of a banana, you expect that the whole banana will move with it instead of disintegrating. Continuity bears on movement as well. It captures the idea that objects do not teleport, but objects move from point A to point B by traversing the intermediate space. Finally, objects move because of contact. For an object at rest to begin moving, it must be launched through contact. For it to change course or stop abruptly, contact is necessary. This set of intuitive expectations is sometimes called *naïve physics* or *folk mechanics* (because of pertinence to movement) and appears to be part of reasoning during infancy. Clear evidence for Physicality in humans exists within the first few months of life and appears robust in adult nonhuman primates.[7] Later in the first year, babies also acquire the expectation that solid objects must be supported or they will fall.[8]

Many of these Physicality expectations presume *Spatiality*, that an object has only a single location in space and time. Nevertheless, Spatiality is distinguishable as a specific expectation set from object Physicality. A cloud is not a bounded physical object, but is in one place. If you divide a cloud, you get two clouds each with a location. Spatiality expectations apply to clouds, shadows, fires, and conglomerates such as a pile of sand (and perhaps minds), but these examples do not meet the intuitive assumptions I refer to as Physicality.

Biology (more typically called *folk biology*) includes the intuitive expectations *growth and development* (that living things grow and change),[9] *vulnerability to death* (that living things' bodies can permanently stop working),[10] *like-begets-like* (e.g., dogs give birth to puppies not kittens),[11] *natural composition* (living things are made of natural materials such as guts instead of artificial parts such as metal gears),[12] *vitalism*,[13] and *essentialism*. *Vitalism* here is not a reflectively worked out and culturally particular metaphysical notion, but simply the idea that internal parts or substances sustain life. Even those of us who would reject vitalism reflectively will typically find intuitive the idea that something "departs" at death and that some "vital force" powers our bodies and makes them alive instead of dead and living beings instead of nonliving collections of matter. Cultural ideas of vitalism or animating spirits likely gain intuitive plausibility by activation of this nonreflective expectation. *Essentialism* refers to the intuition that all of these other biological properties arise out of a single, unseen, kind-specific "essence" that generates and accounts for the physically observable features. Again, these intuitions are nonreflective and appear to be natural and not tied to a particular cultural context. Indeed, we may reflectively reject essentialism (the idea that kinds such as species have an invisible, shared essence) and vitalism (that living kinds have a

life force), but our nonreflective beliefs in these biological properties will continue to shape our thought. Biology might be the latest
developing intuitive expectation set with most of its expectations
emerging around age three to five years.[14]

Animacy adds to Biology the expectation that a thing is self-
moving.[15] That is, it can act in or on its environment and not merely
be acted upon. Being able to move oneself from one location to
another in space is referred to as *self-propelledness*. This concept
also captures the ability to change its appearance or make noise.
For instance, a frog puffing up its throat or croaking count as self-
propelledness even if the frog does not move from its lily pad. Self-
propelledness is insufficient as a marker of animacy unless the
self-propelled behavior is perceived as constituting goal-directed
action. The behavior might, for instance, be construed as aiming
to communicate, avoiding something, threatening, or moving to
a particular location (not just moving aimlessly). These Animacy
intuitions are in place in babies before their first birthdays.[16]

THE WHO:
CONCEPTUALIZING MINDED OBJECTS

An object with *Mentality* extends Animacy to include a conscious
mind and specific assumptions about how mental states motivate
action (often called *folk psychology* or *theory of mind*). The mental
being's activity is guided and shaped by percepts, beliefs, desires,
emotions, and perhaps personality. For instance, a mental being
has percepts that inform beliefs about desires, will act to satisfy
desires, satisfied desires result in positive emotions, and so forth. I
will give Mentality more attention in the next chapter.

Though some might disagree and wish to add to these five expectation sets, collapse them (e.g., combining Animacy with Mentality
or Spatiality with Physicality), or reduce their number (e.g., omit
Biology), I suggest these five because of their general support in
the cognitive developmental literature, their apparent independence in developmental course, and their general mapping onto

what appear to be reasonable proper domains of the natural world throughout human existence.[17]

Perhaps my most unorthodox division is paring Spatiality off of Physicality. As mentioned above, I give Spatiality independence because of its relevance for reasoning about a distinct domain: nonmassive but *Spatial Entities* such as shadows, clouds, conglomerates (e.g., pile of leaves), and flames. These Spatial Entities have locations but do not activate the Physicality expectations of a Solid Object. I am further motivated to divide Spatiality and Physicality into distinct expectation sets by psychologist Paul Bloom's work on *intuitive dualism* that suggests minds are intuitively represented as nonphysical things that might, nevertheless, have spatial properties such as a specifiable location.[18] Developmentalists frequently collapse Animacy with Biology or Animacy with Mentality, but these collapses gloss some important distinctions.[19]

Selective activation among these five expectation sets (Spatiality, Physicality, Biology, Animacy, and Mentality) creates five intuitive ontological categories: Spatial Entities, Solid Objects, Living Things, Animates, and Persons—an intuitive ontology.[20]

: Spatial Entities: If a thing activates Universals and Spatiality but no other expectation set, its intuitive ontological category is Spatial Entities (e.g., clouds and shadows).

: Solid Objects: If a thing activates Universals, Spatiality, and Physicality but no other expectation sets, its intuitive ontological category is Solid Objects. Solid Objects includes both artifacts (all human-made objects such as chairs, shoes, pencils) and natural nonliving objects (e.g., stones, icebergs).

: Living Things: An object activating Universals, Spatiality, Physicality, and Biology (but not Animacy) is a Living Thing. People classify trees, flowers, mushrooms, sea sponges, and many other (apparently) nonmoving biological kinds into Living Things.

: Animates: Animates are produced by the activation of Universals, Spatiality, Physicality, and Animacy (but not Mentality). Biology activation might be optional. The category

Animates might typically include animals that appear to propel themselves such as sharks, snails, beetles, and bunnies, but in some situations might include nonanimals such as complex, motorized machines.

: Persons: Activation of Universals, Animacy, Spatiality, and Mentality produces Persons, capturing human beings and perhaps (depending upon how they are conceptualized) some animals such as chimpanzees and the family dog. Exactly which animals are intuitively granted full-blown minds, albeit slightly different than humans', is unknown and likely quite variable.[21] Persons may also be Living Things and Physical Objects.

These intuitive categorizations do not necessarily map onto scientific or philosophically defensible divides, or even how ordinary people would categorize the same objects across all contexts, but reflect the natural, nonreflective way in which objects are classed (see Figure 1).

Intuitively, minds can be bodiless. That we do not automatically assume that Persons and Animates have the biological and physical properties of animals is a departure from some previous discussions of intuitive ontology.[22] Nevertheless, I find support for this departure in the recent research on the development of theory of mind and teleological reasoning in children. We now have a growing body of evidence that from infancy children distinguish the causal properties relevant to agents and minds and those relevant to physical objects.[23] Infants expect objects that propel themselves in an apparently purposeful or goal-directed fashion to continue to behave in a purposeful fashion even if violating basic expectations of mechanical movement.[24] Importantly, these expectations may be triggered in infants and adults by two-dimensional spots— stimuli that do not resemble three-dimensional objects let alone human beings.[25] These findings suggest that reasoning about Animacy and Mentality does not presume later-developing Biology— as spots are unlikely to be construed as Living Things—or perhaps even standard object Physicality. Together with research demon-

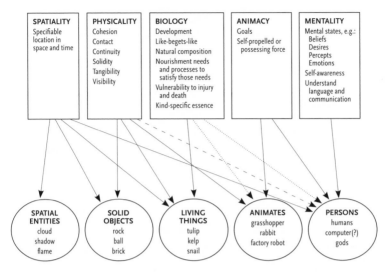

FIGURE 1.

How Activation of Expectation Sets Compromise Intuitive Ontologies

Arrows indicate the relationship between expectation sets and intuitive ontologies. Dotted lines represent that Biology need not but may be active for Animates and Persons. Dashed line represents that, provided intuitive dualism is correct, Persons need not include an activation of Physicality.

strating how readily preschool-aged children reason with disembodied imaginary friends,[26] these data hint that Mentality and perhaps even Animacy expectations may operate without a solid, bounded physical object as the target. For young children, minds do not need physical bodies.[27]

Universals, Spatiality, Physicality, Biology, Animacy, and Mentality do not exhaust intuitive causal reasoning applied to things in the world. Teleo-functional reasoning—thinking about objects in terms of design and purpose—is an intuitive conceptual stance that may be applied to many different types of things in the world.[28] Some evidence exists that Artifacts may be discriminated from other Solid Objects by virtue of their activation of functional expectations concerning human use—what could I use it for?[29] Animals and their parts are likewise readily reasoned about in terms of their functions as a whole or the function of their parts. I return below to teleo-functional reasoning and its connection to creationism and teleological arguments for gods.

COUNTERINTUITIVE IDEAS

In the cognitive science of religion (CSR) area, ideas are considered *counterintuitive* if they run counter to the expectations that intuitive ontologies generate. These ideas may be counterintuitive in two basic ways: either by breaching expectations, or by transferring expectations from one ontological category to another. A *breach*, for instance, might be a cow that can walk through walls. Cows, as Animates and Living Things, activate Physicality, and since physical objects cannot pass through other solid physical objects, the solidity expectation has been breached. A talking elm tree would be a counterintuitive *transfer*. The Mentality expectations set has been transferred to a kind that does not normally have these properties. Of course many properties, such as being purple, are not specified by these intuitive expectation sets for either cows or elm trees. Being purple, then, might be strange in these cases, but is not technically counterintuitive.

One may sensibly talk about ideas as varying in degree of counterintuitiveness. A talking elm tree is counterintuitive, but basic Mentality as applied to a tree does not present extreme conceptual difficulties. A talking elm tree that is also intangible (breaching Physicality), has offspring that are oaks (breaching Biology), is in two different locations simultaneously (breaching Spatiality), vanishes during odd hours of the day (breaching Universals), and has no desires (breaching the transferred Mentality) would be highly counterintuitive, and hence, difficult to conceptualize.

An immediate implication for religious and theological thought is that theological ideas that are too counterintuitive—too deviant from natural content-specific cognition—will be a struggle for people to maintain consistently and accurately. Difficulties will be greater when forced to use counterintuitive concepts under time demands or *cognitive load* such as doing more than one thing at a time. In fact, the difference between performance in a slowed-down, low-demand, "off-line" context and a speeded or high-demand, "on-line" context is frequently taken by cognitive scientists as a measure of the difficulty of the cognitive task. If you cannot perform a task under demand, it must not be easy for your cognitive systems. If you can perform a task even under distraction or without great conscious attention, it must be relatively easy for you. The novice driver cannot hold a conversation and drive, but as expertise improves (the driver acquires practiced naturalness for the task), then additional task demands can be added such as speed, music, and conversation. The more reflective beliefs deviate from nonreflective beliefs, the more difficult it is to use them in high-demand, real-time situations. Similar lessons apply to theological thought, a point I return to in chapter 8.

Content-specific natural cognition creates intuitive ontologies that then inform how we understand the furniture of the world around us. This same equipment anchors our religious thought. If a religious idea is largely intuitive—that is, closely according with what our minds naturally assume—then that idea may be easily used in real-time, on-line thinking. It will present no onerous conceptual burden. Theological ideas that deviate too greatly will be difficult to use in many day-to-day situations. These counterintuitive ideas will consume more attention and more chunks of working memory to use and will be, consequently, more cumbersome for generating inferences, predictions, and explanations. They will be more difficult to remember and communicate, a point I return to in chapter 6.

Further, given the relationship between nonreflective and reflective beliefs described in chapter 3, it follows that largely intuitive theological notions will be more likely to be acquired as reflective beliefs.[30] One such largely intuitive theological belief might be belief in some kind of creator, as explained below.

WHAT FOR?
HOW REASONING ABOUT PURPOSES
ENCOURAGES BELIEF IN A CREATOR

From infancy we continually try to make sense of what goes on around us. One strategy in making sense of things is to look for how things might be purposeful or designed. So useful is this strategy that sometimes it gets overused, what psychologist Deborah Kelemen calls *promiscuous teleology*.[31] Kelemen found that seven- and eight-year-olds preferred teleological explanations for the features of various animals and natural nonliving objects. For instance, when shown a picture of a pointy rock and asked, "Why do you think the rocks were so pointy?" children in these studies favored purposeful, functional explanations such as "They were pointy so that animals wouldn't sit on them and smash them," over physical explanations such as "They were pointy because bits of stuff piled up on top of one another for a long time."[32] In another set of experiments, Kelemen presented children with a disagreement between two fictitious characters, Ben and Jane. Ben and Jane disagreed over whether various things are "made for something" including natural things such as clouds, icebergs, tigers, and body parts. Surprisingly, these four- to five-year-old American children were just as likely to agree that natural objects and living things were *made for* something as artifacts. About three-quarters of children's answers favored a functional "made for" answer—a rate far beyond what adults in their communities would condone. Given the nature of these questions and examples, arguing that children were simply taught these kinds of explanations for what tigers are for is a stretch. Surely American parents don't teach that tigers and trees are made for something with the same conviction or frequency with teaching that machines and jeans are made for something. Children seemed very drawn to answers that suggested a purpose or function for the natural things' existence.

In a similar vein, Kelemen and collaborator Cara DiYanni asked six- and seven-year-old British children about the origins of a number of natural and artificial things. The experimenter first asked children open-ended questions in the form "Why did the first ever flood occur?" and "Why did the first ever bird exist?" In keeping with their tendency to find purposefulness in the natural world, these children offered teleological answers more than any other type of answer for natural objects, animals, and artifacts. Only for natural events did they favor physical explanations (for instance, the first thunderstorm occurred because "two clouds bashed together").[33] When subsequently asked to choose the original cause of the first ever flood, river, bird, monkey, and so forth, and forced to choose among "Someone made it," "Something made it," or "It just happened," children chose "Someone" answers most of the time (especially for animals). Children who gave purpose-based answers for origins were more likely to link this teleological explanation to intentional action.

Preschoolers, then, are inclined to see the world as purposefully designed *and* tend to see an intelligent, intentional agent as behind this natural design. But who is the intentional agent behind the purposeful design of the natural world? It is not hard to see that these natural conceptual tendencies would make children receptive to the idea of a god or spirits who have caused the natural world to have the features it has.

Importantly, studies suggest that we do not simply outgrow the tendency to see purpose in the world but have to learn to override it. Kelemen has recently demonstrated experimentally that adults—even scientifically trained ones—carry a bias to favor purpose-based explanations into adulthood. Kelemen and Evelyn Rosset asked adults to evaluate various explanations for natural things and their particular features (such as the long neck on a giraffe).[34] Among the explanations were scientifically "good" explanations (not invoking design or purpose but only natural processes) and other explanations that included both purpose-based explanations and strange ones on the order of polar bears being white because the sun bleaches their fur. When they had plenty of time to consider their answers, adults often rejected the teleological explanations. Evolution has no purpose, direction, or design, we are taught, so such explanations were often classified as "bad" along with sun-bleaching as the cause of white polar bears. But when the experimenters forced adults to answer quickly, these college students began accepting the teleological explanations as "good" while their accuracy in (correctly) rejecting other "bad" explanations actually improved (possibly because they didn't have time to second-guess themselves). Even without time pressure, uneducated adults answer similarly to children in these teleo-functional reasoning tasks.[35] This tendency to see the world in teleo-functional terms does not appear to be something we simply outgrow. Perhaps we can only learn to tamp it down.

Perhaps it is this persistent, early-developing intuition that there is design and purpose behind everything we see in nature that makes it hard to dislodge the idea that even evolution by natural selection needs an intentional being behind it all or at least the intermittent help of an intelligent designer to make the account satisfying.[36] Our gut tells us that positing a designer for the design is right. From early childhood our brains encourage us to think this way. Even among staunchly committed antidesign evolutionists, the language of design and purpose appears unavoidable. As Nobel Prize–winning biologist Francis Crick wrote, "Biologists must constantly keep in mind that what they see was not designed, but rather evolved."[37] The natural cognition of our minds drives us to wonder who is behind the evident design and purpose in nature. Who is the grand designer? Is it a god? No wonder then that arguments from design (teleological arguments) for the existence of at least one creator God have such a long pedigree. Their intuitiveness derives from natural, content-specific cognition.[38]

CHAPTER 5
How We Conceive of Humans

ALLEGEDLY THERE IS a very predictable time during which Britain must import power from continental Europe: just after the BBC soap opera *EastEnders* ends and millions of viewers all at once go and put on their high-wattage electric kettles to make tea. Whether the impact on power draw is true or not, the powerful draw of soap operas and other dramatic films, television, and stories on human attention is indisputable. This attraction reveals something important about human nature.

Humans are fundamentally social animals that have conspicuously large networks of social relations and personal interactions. Unsurprisingly, then, we have considerable natural cognitive resources for conceptualizing other humans, an exercise dubbed *folk anthropology*.[1] In fact, some evolutionary anthropologists argue that the impetus leading to the evolution of such large brains in humans was the need to richly conceptualize other humans and our social relations with and among them. Can I trust that person to cooperate with me? Who knows what about whom? Who is loyal to whom? Who knows that I know what so-and-so did?[2]

Below I synthesize what various lines of research suggest about how we naturally conceptualize the fundamental properties of humans. Our natural cognition tells us that humans have biological, physical bodies that house minds. Further, we naturally regard ourselves and others as animated by some kind of vital force (or "spirit") and as individuated by a person-specific essence (or "soul"). We also feel we can judge whether our actions are moral or not because we perceive them as consciously and freely chosen to some degree. I offer that these various intuitive components of a human could be the nonreflective wellspring of various cultural elaborations about the nature of humans, including *theological anthropology*—the study of human nature by the lights of a particular theological system. I conclude that the cognitive science that I review here does not necessarily give us reasons to believe in the reality of conscious human minds, free will, souls, or spirits, but neither does it undercut belief in them.

THEORY OF MIND IN HUMANS

Even before babies are talking, they distinguish humans from other things in the world. Fresh from the birth canal, they selectively attend to human faces in their environment and even imitate some basic facial expressions.[3] Later in their first year, they produce more vocalizations in the presence of people than other objects and begin pointing and gesturing to direct others' attention. Babies carefully watch parents' eye-gaze direction and look to see where they are looking. When another person points, babies look to see where the person is pointing. These might seem like banal and trivial accomplishments, but upon these natural foundations a rich representation of human beings as minded, intentional actors is built.

Some of these foundations are rare or even entirely absent in other species. Consider *declarative pointing*—gesturing to direct another's attention. It might be that no other animal naturally produces such behaviors or is naturally sensitive to them. Even chimpanzees, very clever social animals, do not appear to use declarative pointing and require enormous socialization by humans to even begin to follow the pointing gesture to a target instead of merely looking at the pointer's fingertip. Similarly, humans make distinctively heavy use of eye-gaze to anticipate the actions of another or even to infer mental states: if someone looks at that object in a sustained manner, she might want it. Other social animals naturally shy away from looking each other in the eyes.[4]

What is widely regarded as the most important difference between humans and other animals with regard to social capacities is our robust attribution of conscious mental states to infer, predict, and explain actions. "Nick wants them to think that Sheila does not like them" is a readily understandable statement about mental states about mental states about mental states. By age five or six, most humans find such mental states relations easy to understand, but we have no evidence that any other species has such a capacity. In the jargon of cognitive science, regarding others as having minds and mental states, and understanding how mental states relate to each other and to actions is called *theory of mind* or *folk psychology*.[5]

The basics of a normal adult human's theory of mind are the following. People have conscious mental states that include beliefs, desires (wants), emotions, memories, and percepts. Action is driven by desires and modulated through percepts and beliefs. For instance, if I want coffee, I will act to get coffee based upon my beliefs about how to best go about getting coffee. These beliefs are informed by relevant perceptual experiences: seeing the coffee in the cupboard leads me to form a belief that the coffee is in the cupboard; if I cannot see in the cupboard, I might not know that the coffee is there. Emotional states arise through satisfaction or frustration of desires: if I want coffee, and successfully get coffee, I will feel positive emotion (happy); but if I want coffee and cannot get coffee, I will feel negative emotion (sad or frustrated). Adults understand that beliefs need not reflect real states of affairs in the world, but can be about possible or false states of affairs (as in believing that my keys are in my pocket when I actually left them in the door, again). Beliefs can also be about beliefs (or even about beliefs about beliefs about beliefs), what is called *metarepresentation* (representations of representations or thoughts about thoughts, as in wondering whether what I am thinking is true). That is, beliefs are representational instead of strictly veridical and may be false. Note that the presumption that humans have consciousness and the ability to act freely are presumptions of our natural theory of mind.[6]

I present these relations among mental states and actions as a set of rules because cognitive scientists widely regard thinking about minds as characterized by rulelike regularities or theories, hence the label *theory* of mind. These theories are analogous to scientific theories in that they have been built up through experiences: experiences with one's own mental states and through observing and interacting with others. These "theories" are then used to predict or explain others' mental states and actions. If they fail to do a good job, they are revised.

Not all of folk psychology is theorylike, however. In some cases, such as when a rule or "theory" has not been adequately built up for a particular situation, we may use *simulation* to reason about others' mental states. That is, we imagine what we would think or feel ourselves if we were in the other person's situation, and then use the result of this simulation to postulate what the other is thinking or feeling. To illustrate, the adolescent male who has just begun dating adventures might have no "theory" to account for why his girlfriend is suddenly angry with him after he went out with friends on a Friday night instead of with her. He could develop an appropriate theory through instruction from wiser informants or by running a simulation: *putting myself in her situation, why might I feel angry?* If successful, the next time around, he won't have to simulate. Simulation requires privileged access to our own internal states—I need to know my own thoughts and feelings. Such access itself might have to develop during childhood, and even as adults we sometimes are at a loss regarding our own mental states.[7]

Nevertheless, our ability to monitor our own mental states (however limited) arguably supports our natural conviction that we (and by analogy, others) have the ability to willfully choose actions. I have the subjective experience that when I will to move my hand to pick up a pen, most of the time my hand responds shortly thereafter by moving. Over a lifetime this tight (but not perfect) correspondence is reinforced again and again. The evidence that we can freely and willfully choose to act in many situations is overpowering. These (apparently) willed actions can include thought acts. If I want to remember what I had for breakfast, I pause, think, and there is the answer (at least most of the time). If I want to calculate thirteen times seven, I can think about it and figure it out "in my head." If our natural causal cognition includes the presumptions that causes closely precede effects—and we have reason to think it does—then we could empirically build up the idea that our thoughts causally control our bodies, if such empirical evidence is even necessary. Either way, our natural cognition provides us with the nonreflective belief that we are free actors who can willfully influence our own thoughts and behavior. I return to whether these nonreflective beliefs bear upon reflective beliefs about free will below.

Theory of Mind in Nonhuman Animals

Whether or not other animals have theory of mind is hotly disputed, with definitive evidence being very difficult to muster. Part of the challenge is that mental states (and in this case, mental states about mental states) have to be measured through observable behaviors. In humans we have verbal behaviors that aid this study, but in other animals we do not.

For instance, with humans we can create a scenario such as the following classic experimental task: A child sees Emma place chocolate in a red cupboard and then leave the room. Michael enters the room and moves the chocolate to a different, blue cupboard. Emma returns in search of her chocolate. Where will Emma look first: the red cupboard, the blue cupboard, or a third, yellow cupboard? Three-year-olds have difficulty saying that Emma will look in the location where she first placed it: the red cupboard. As they know it is in the blue cupboard, and as people act to satisfy their desires, they seem to regard it as most reasonable to say that Emma will search the blue cupboard for the chocolate. Three-year-olds seem to have difficulty consciously reflecting on others' thoughts—particularly if those thoughts deviate from their own or from reality (as the child sees it). By age five or six, most children understand that Emma will look in the red cupboard because she has a false belief about the location of the chocolate. Emma did not see where Michael put the chocolate and so she thinks the chocolate is still in the red cupboard. Children by this age have a representational theory of mind. They can understand others' thoughts as representations of possible states of affairs that may be false.

Because we cannot ask other animals "Where will Emma first look for the chocolate?" it is difficult to unambiguously demonstrate how chimpanzees, dogs, or elephants think about mental states (if at all). A review of this comparative cognition literature would be beyond the scope of this book, and so at this point I will simply offer a fairly conservative interpretation of the literature for the present discussion: we have no compelling evidence that any other species have the kind of full-blown representational theory of mind we see humans evincing from the fifth or sixth year in life (or perhaps much earlier). Chimpanzees might attribute mental states to others and even try to change others' behaviors by disrupting their perceptual access. For instance, chimpanzees have been known to hide food so that another does not take it as if they understand that seeing leads to certain actions. What is not clear is whether chimpanzees regard seeing as leading to beliefs that then lead to actions. Even granting this theory of mind achievement, we are far from convincing evidence that chimpanzees think that other chimpanzees have thoughts about others' thoughts.[8] Does chimpanzee Tim think that chimp Skylar knows that chimp Sierra wants Skylar's food? Perhaps, but probably not. We do know, however, that most five- and six-year-old humans perform this sort of higher-order theory of mind without difficulty.

THEORY OF MIND AND COLLECTIVE RELIGION

In the next chapter I will take up how gods are conceptualized more directly, but here I want to make an observation regarding how theory of mind capacities enable shared thought about gods. Being able to think about others' mental states about mental states appears to be a prerequisite for the kind of collective relational engagement we see in many religions. Many religions involve more than individuals relating to a god. Rather, they involve more than one person being aware of each other's mutual attitudes toward a god or gods. In participating in a group ritual, we signal to each other that we all believe that the god demands propitiation, for instance. I have to be able to think that you know that I think the god wants us to perform this ritual, and so do you. We are aware of our *joint attention* on the god. This kind of joint attention might be distinctively human and undergird our ability to flexibly acquire and use language and develop cultural systems that cumulatively build and develop over time.[9]

Further, such advanced theory of mind facility appears to be required to imagine joint activities with a god instead of merely viewing a god instrumentally. In many cultures people interact with spirits, ancestors, or gods to protect from famine or to end illness or bring rain or luck. Gods are treated much like automatic bank machines: push the right buttons and good stuff comes out; but you do have to put stuff (offerings, sacrifices, prayers, etc.) in every once in a while. Reflecting on the mental states of the gods is not strictly necessary, let alone wondering how the god thinks about my thoughts. In devotional traditions, however, one may wonder about what a god thinks about what one is thinking, or consider how the god and oneself might interact collaboratively to bring about a commonly desired state of affairs. Such relational religious thought requires more advanced theory of mind skills than we are likely to find in any other species or even in toddlers.

These observations raise possible theological speculations about the kinds of relationships different animals could have with a god, depending upon their conceptual equipment. Animals without emotional states and only biological drives (e.g., oysters and earthworms) might only be capable of being objects of a god's attention but not be able to have relational interaction. Animals with emotional states but inability to consciously reflect on those states might be able to have some degree of relational attachment to a god (if they somehow are aware of the god's existence). I have in mind here something akin to the way baby birds attach to or *imprint* on their parents and feel security in their presence. Unaware of their own internal states in any reflective sense, such animals might feel anxiety, pain, or pleasure, but not have existential concerns about such states. Genuine joy or suffering might not be possible.[10] More complex animals that can reflect on their own mental states might be able to know that they feel an attachment to a god or not. Perhaps intelligent, socially adept animals such as dogs, elephants, dolphins, and chimpanzees have the requisite cognition for this sort of relationship.[11] Adding the ability to attribute mental states to others would introduce the possibility of wondering what the god wants as well as trying to please or anger the god. Here we would have something like a rudimentary individual relationship with a god. Finally, the capacity to have thoughts about thoughts—to exercise metarepresentation—would enable the animal to both recognize that others have a relationship with the same god and see the god as a collaborator in joint activities. It seems that only humans have this potential for collaborative relationship and collective relationship with a god.[12]

PERSONS AS OBJECTS *AND* MENTALISTIC AGENTS[13]

In the previous chapter I left open the possibility that our intuitive ontological categories Animates and Persons do not necessarily entail the assumption that they will be presumed also to be solid physical objects or living things. When it comes to reasoning about humans, however, our understanding of humans as minded must be conjoined with humans as physical objects and living things. It might be that this is a nontrivial conceptual accomplishment.

From early in the first year of life, infants expect solid objects to follow continuous pathways through space, to cohere, and to not merge with other solid objects or pass through them. These same properties apply to humans. Infants further appreciate that one solid object cannot influence another from a distance, but must contact it in order to make it move, stop moving, or change course. This principle does not apply to Animates or Persons, however, including humans. If the Physicality expectation set is jointly activated and develops as a whole, it might be a challenge for us to except one rule of the set. Do infants understand that agents, though they are also physical objects, can stop and start of their own accord and can influence other agents from a distance? It seems so. A series of studies suggests that infants distinguish between agents (Persons) and nonagents and successfully suspend the contact principle when reasoning about agents. Indeed, violation of the contact principle (that objects must be contacted in order to be launched) is a strong indicator that the object in question is a self-propelled agent.[14] Nevertheless, some developmental psychologists have suggested that our early emerging ability to distinguish persons from other things produces an interesting cognitive byproduct: mind-body dualism.[15]

These cognitive developmentalists, most prominently Paul Bloom, note that the relevant natural cognition for reasoning about physical objects (such as bodies) and that for reasoning about minds have different evolutionary and developmental courses. Other species (such as monkeys) appear to use similar principles of Physicality but lack Mentality (theory of mind). These different cognitive mechanisms are activated by different stimuli, particularly different forms of motion. They further yield different kinds of outputs:

explanations and expectations in terms of physical causality on one hand and in terms of psychological causality on the other. Bloom has argued that the autonomous functioning of these systems, and their exclusive focus on either physical or psychological causality, renders a type of nonreflective mind-body dualism cognitively natural. The default stance is to see bodily and mental phenomena as occupying separate causal domains. Learning when and how these two domains interact is a culturally and individually variable developmental accomplishment. This *intuitive dualism* arguably helps explain the cross-cultural recurrence of various notions of mental disembodiment as in soul flight, out-of-body experiences, the persistence of minded ghosts or spirits after death, and even forms of spirit possession. These ideas might be only a modest elaboration upon a cognitively natural core.

PERSONS AS LIVING THINGS

Many persons, including human beings, are not just minds trapped in physical containers. Adults and young children alike understand human bodies as living, activating the Biology expectation set. As sketched in the previous chapter, evidence suggests that children's developing understandings of Living Things—including humans—are framed within a *vitalistic causality*.[16] Living things have a vital power that is fuelled by the ingestion of food, water, and/or clean air. This vital power drives life, growth and development, movement, and health. Further biological expectations spring from a tacit species-typical essentialism.

Nevertheless, children and adults distinguish biological phenomena from physical and mental phenomena, attributing different sorts of causes to events in each domain.[17] They appear to encounter conceptual difficulty in reasoning about phenomena that straddle these boundaries, such as bodily changes due to psychological causes or biological causes for psychological conditions—evidence that supports Bloom's contention that in some sense our cognitive equipment encourages us to be mind-body dualists. For instance, stigmata, a condition in which thoughts or feelings appear to trigger remarkable bodily changes such as tissue damage on limbs, has commonly been regarded as a supernatural sign because it so radically violates our intuitive notions about what mental states apparently can do to bodies.

Likewise, regarding someone's abusive behavior toward another as a biological matter, no different in kind from someone being unusually drowsy, generally offends our sensibilities, even though both drowsiness and abusiveness might prove to be explainable in terms of a biological abnormality in neurotransmitter absorption (for instance). Similarly, recent research with 130 mental health professionals with thorough professional training in the biological bases of behavioral pathology revealed that they still use a mind-body distinction when reasoning about clinical cases. They perceive some mental illnesses as more or less psychological and some as more or less biological. From a physical monist perspective, all are equally biological. Further, compared with those deemed "more biological," "more psychological" disorders were associated with higher attributions of intentionality, controllability, responsibility, and blameworthiness on the part of the patient for illness-related behaviors.[18] Indeed, the current fascination that laypeople and scholars alike express over brain-imaging studies that show which part of the brain is most excited during a range of psychological tasks could betray a certain tacit dualistic thinking as well.

Why do we find it so awesome that part of the brain is active when we think particular kinds of thoughts? If we really had a fully integrated view of the relationship between the biology of the brain and psychological processes, such studies (to the nonspecialist, at least) would likely be greeted with only a ho-hum: why should the nonspecialist care just which part of the brain "lights up" when we do mathematics versus reading? Surely we already regarded the brain as active during both, recognize that math and reading are

importantly different, and expect that our brain wouldn't be identical performing the two tasks any more than our muscles would be
identically busy when dancing versus swimming.[19]

One key component of natural folk biology, vitalism, might provide the nonreflective timber from which various reflective cultural
beliefs are built, such as animating spirits, life-forces, the Chinese
Qi, and other beliefs about unseen internal energies that animate
humans (and sometimes other things). Judaism and Christianity
share the notion that the breath or spirit of God is an animating and
energizing force transforming inert matter into living things. Note
that often spirit (as opposed to mind or soul) is often conceptualized as something that one can have in varying degrees or intensity. To illustrate, in 2 Kings 2:9 Elisha asked for a double portion
of Elijah's spirit. A "double portion" of Elijah's mind or soul would
have been a peculiar request indeed, suggesting that these various
immaterial aspects of humans are undergirded by different causal
cognition.[20]

Persons as Individuals

A treatment of how we naturally conceptualize humans would
be incomplete without recognizing that we do not simply think
about humans as exemplars of a general class of beings but as distinct individuals. It might be okay to think of all potatoes, oak trees,
or starlings the same way, but it would be disastrous when thinking about humans. Babies are not just interested in finding faces in
their environment. They want to find Mom's face. Another important aspect of folk anthropology, then, concerns representing the
identity of individual persons. The ability to trace the identity of
an individual over space and time is present from infancy.[21] Developmental psychologists Rebekah Richert and Paul Harris have
suggested that Western adults and children represent individual
people as having an invariant *person-essence* that confers stable
identity across processes of growth and aging, and even biological

death.[22] This person-essentialism might recruit some of the same intuitions as species-essentialism: we each have an unseen internal something that gives rise to our distinguishing physical and behavioral features. In the case of a species-essence, the essence accounts for stability in species membership across changes in appearance and lifespan. For individual humans, the person-essence anchors individual identity across changes and causes individuating features to be present. Research in this area is in its infancy, but if on the right track, could be pivotal in accounting for the cross-cultural recurrence of concepts such as "soul," which carry some psychological properties but emphasize individuating features such as preferences, personality, and autobiographical memories as opposed to the basic theory of mind concerns. Reviewing concepts from cross-cultural ethnographic accounts that closely parallel Western concepts of "mind" and "soul," Richert and Harris suggest that the mind-soul distinction "is not tied to Christian or Western traditions alone but is widespread, if not universal."[23] Perhaps these various soul-like concepts are cultural elaborations of the same natural cognitive core. Nonreflective beliefs about there being a nonphysical something in us that anchors and sustains our identity might underpin the idea of an immaterial soul that is distinguishable and potentially separable from the body.[24]

Moral Persons

The naturalness of viewing humans as freely acting, conscious beings that choose to act in one way or another opens up the possibility of construing humans and their actions in terms of normative considerations: what makes for a right or wrong action, or a good or bad person.

The view that humans have naturally occurring *moral intuitions* with general cross-culturally recurrent themes has become a staple claim of sociobiology and evolutionary psychology.[25] Whether moral intuitions can be distinguished from other normative thinking, and whether moral reasoning is undergirded by a distinctive set of cognitive mechanisms are questions under current exploration. Similarly, the scope of moral intuitions, whether they apply to one's in-group, to all of humanity, or even to nonhuman animals, remains contested as well. It is too soon to handicap the outcome of these studies. Nevertheless, a recurring theme is that humans seem to naturally converge upon a common set of intuitions that structure moral thought. For instance, a strong candidate for a cross-culturally recurrent moral intuition is that it is wrong to harm a nonconsenting member of one's group (barring other considerations). Likewise, it seems that the intentions behind an action bear upon the degree to which one is morally culpable of the outcomes of the action: I am more culpable of wrong if I intended to do wrong. From an evolutionary perspective, the core argument is that individuals with moral inclinations (even if they do not always act in accordance with them) will outcompete the wholly immoral for survival and reproduction. It is not an adaptive strategy to be completely selfish, cheating, stealing, fighting, and murdering. Such behavior would discourage others from cooperating or trusting such an individual and lead to them having less access to the resources and other benefits of large group living.[26] Aside from the content of natural moral intuitions (what counts as right or wrong and why), it seems that a recurrent nonreflective belief is that at least a subset of our norms are fixed and reflect some truth beyond mere convention or the ordinance of those in authority. Perhaps the naturalness of these moral intuitions gives them the impression (correctly or not) that they go much deeper than the transient whims of society.

Long before contemporary cognitive and evolutionary scientists began converging on a similar point, thinkers suggested that some kind of moral code lies within each of us.[27] In his book *The Abolition of Man*, C. S. Lewis argued for a set of moral intuitions common to all peoples, which he called the *Tao*.[28] Writing as a scholar of letters, he builds his case from the remarkable convergence among the world's wisdom literatures. I suggest that if this convergence is genuine (and I suspect it is), it is because the wise minds that compile, select, edit, and affirm the wisdom of each age and culture have common natural intuitions that anchor evaluations of what is good and virtuous. That is, natural cognition provides nonreflective moral beliefs that may be modified or elaborated through cultural situation and innovation but nonetheless shine through the cross-cultural variability.[29]

Implications of Natural Conceptualizations of Humans

As noted earlier, content-specific cognition anchors reflective beliefs in important ways, particularly when it comes to widespread culturally shared ideas. Natural cognition produces nonreflective beliefs that serve as starting points for reflective belief formation and transmission. If an idea resonates with nonreflective beliefs, it will more likely become adopted as a reflective belief. The same principles apply here: nonreflective beliefs about the constitution and nature of humans will tend to become reflective beliefs. Put another way, for an idea to be cross-culturally recurrent—successfully entertained by many minds across time and place—it will have to seem largely intuitive, and this feeling of being "intuitive" will be because it is built from natural cognitive timber.

We would expect, then, for reflective cultural thought about the features of humans to congeal upon ideas that are largely natural. Candidates suggested above are:[30]

: Bodies: humans have bodies that are bounded physical objects having ordinary physical properties, but are also animate, living things made of natural stuff, growing and developing over time, and threatened by bodily death.

: Minds: humans have minds with consciousness, desires, emotions, free will, percepts, and thoughts. This mind is potentially separable from the body. Largely intuitive cultural elaborations include the possibility that this mind can persist after death.

: Spirits: humans have some kind of spirit or vital force that animates them. This force is fuelled by food, water, air, and possibly other external sources such as sunshine. Because of its intuitive connection to external inputs, culturally or theologically this force might be regarded as implanted by a divine being or as part of a similar force or substance shared with other living things.

: Souls: further, humans are individuated by a person-essence that makes them each a unique individual, and the same individual over time and over physical changes. The person-essence may be culturally or theologically elaborated into the idea of a soul. Because of its conceptual independence from the physical body, regarding it as existing before or after death presents no great conceptual difficulty.

: Moral beings: humans, in part by virtue of their ability to willfully and freely act, are moral beings whose specific actions and action orientations can be evaluated in terms of rightness or wrongness. We would expect, from this cognitive perspective, for theological and philosophical reflections down through the ages and across cultures to share common themes when analyzing what constitutes virtue and virtuous behavior.

If these natural tendencies indeed exist, we would expect widespread reflective cultural ideas to be variations on these themes—and this includes theological treatments of human nature—an area called *theological anthropology*. Given special cultural conditions and resources, theological anthropology is able to stretch the tethers to these cognitive natural anchors and produce much less natural and more counterintuitive ideas about the nature of humans. The further it does so, however, the more ideas will seem alien to the average person. I return to these issues in chapters 8 and 9.

Most individuals' reflective beliefs about humans, however, will be largely a product of these naturally arising nonreflective beliefs.

So believing that people have conscious minds with free will and are able to determine their own actions based upon beliefs and desires arises as an ordinary function of natural cognition at work. Does this imply that such beliefs are unjustified?

Are We Justified in Thinking That Humans Have Free, Conscious Minds?

For some reason it is tempting, when someone gives an explanation for why people tend to believe something for us, to conclude that the belief in question, therefore, must be false or at least poorly supported because we know why they believe it. It is easy to imagine the following type of exchange:

"Why do people believe in an immortal soul?"

"Well, because they have natural cognitive mechanisms that yield nonreflective beliefs in something like a soul that makes the idea of a soul seem sensible."

"Ah, so that's why. I guess there is no good reason to think that there are souls. It's just a trick played on us by our minds."

This line of reasoning—that the identification of a belief's causal ancestry in nonreflective cognitive processes undermines particular instances of the type's truth or justification—is problematic, but exactly why is not necessarily obvious. Here I want to make some comments showing why this is problematic reasoning and actually reach an opposite conclusion: if our cognitive systems naturally produce a particular type of belief, we are justified in believing it until sufficient reasons amass to the contrary. That is, we should treat these natural, intuitively sourced beliefs as innocent until proven guilty, an epistemological stance championed most famously by philosopher Thomas Reid.[31]

As discussed at the end of chapter 3, the origins of reflective beliefs in natural cognition need not have any bearing on the truth of the beliefs. As embodied beings, all of our beliefs are going to have at least partial, probabilistic natural causes, whether the beliefs are true or false. The same lesson applies here: just because belief in others' minds (including thoughts and consciousness) and in human free will, some kind of soul, or an animating "spirit" (for instance) has a basis in natural cognition does not entail that these beliefs are false or true. We *naturally* regard cricket balls as unable to pass through solid walls, which is true; and also naturally regard rainbows as having bands of color, which is false. The cognitive naturalness of a reflective belief does not easily pick out true from false beliefs.

Placing the truth of a belief aside, one might still be concerned that rooting our common reflective beliefs in conscious minds, souls, and so forth in the deliverances of our natural cognition implies that we are unjustified in holding these beliefs. The general principle in operation here appears to be that if our natural intuitions make us think something is the case that might or not be the case, then we are not justified in believing it to be the case (whether or not it is the case). By way of illustration, here is such an argument against justified belief in free will along these lines. Similar argument might be constructed for the existence of "conscious mind," "thoughts," "feelings," "souls," or the like.

1. The source of reflective beliefs in free will is nonreflective beliefs in free will.
2. To be a justified belief, a thing's actual existence must make us believe it exists (directly or indirectly).
3. Instead of the actual existence of free will making us believe it exists, a nonreflective belief in free will makes us reflectively believe in free will.
4. Therefore, reflective beliefs in free will are not justified.

The strength of such an argument comes from the assumption that beliefs about a thing's existence are linked to the actual thing itself.[32] For instance, if I am out running and I see some sheep in a field, I am justified in believing that there are sheep in the field because the sheep actually being there makes me think they are there. Exactly how the sheep cause me to believe they are there might be unclear, but I have the sense that somehow a link between the sheep and the belief in them is important. It would be strange to suspect that I would (reflectively) believe that there were sheep in the field whether or not they were there. And this is the rub with the case of free will beliefs (or belief in consciousness, souls, and the rest): it seems that the source of my reflective belief (the nonreflective beliefs or intuitions) do not co-vary with the truth of the belief. Free will could be false and I still have the nonreflective belief in free will. The source and the belief appear to not have the appropriate link. Consider a different case. I am out running and a gas leak causes me to hallucinate and think that there are sheep in the field (when there are not). Now I am not justified in my belief because my belief in sheep is not connected to actual sheep in the field, but to something completely different: hallucinogenic gas. The claim against justified belief in free will is that our nonreflective beliefs in free will are a source of reflective beliefs in free will comparable to the gas leak: they encourage belief in something whether or not the something actually exists.

As sensible as (I hope) this argument against justified reflective belief in free will based on nonreflective belief sounds, I fear it misses the mark for at least two reasons. First, the operative principle regarding a link between the source and the belief might not apply in the case of free will even if it does apply to sheep in a field. Second, even if the right link is necessary, it might be that such a link is actually present in the case of free will.

I am sympathetic to premise (2) in many cases: to be justified in believing in the existence of things like sheep, the thing's actual existence must make us believe it exists (through perceptual contact, via testimony presumed to be informed by perceptual contact, etc.).

Nevertheless, this principle is less obviously applicable in the case of belief in free will (or in conscious minds, thoughts, and the rest). The sheep case is importantly disanalogous. The

hallucination-producing gas is meant to be analogous to nonreflective beliefs insofar as both are causes or sources for reflective
beliefs (in sheep and in free will, respectively). The problem is that
the gas and the sheep, on one hand, and nonreflective belief on the
other, are causes in two different senses. The gas and the sheep are
both external factors that stimulate the belief-forming cognitive
system to produce a belief. In contrast, the nonreflective belief in
free will *is* part of the belief-forming cognitive system. It is not an
external source or cause at all. It is far from obvious that the same
rules therefore apply for the connection between nonreflective and
reflective beliefs.

Even if we grant that the same principle expressed in (2) *does*
apply in the case of believing in free will, it is not obvious that nonreflective beliefs really are unlinked from reflective beliefs. The concern over justification of beliefs in free will was premised on a lack
of the right connection, but it might be that, as both free will and
nonreflective belief in free will are features of a single mind, they
might be connected in nonobvious ways. Perhaps we would not
believe that we had free will if we did not have it. The point is easier
to make with reference to the belief in conscious minds. It might
very well be that I would not have the nonreflective belief that I
have a conscious mind unless I had a conscious mind indeed, and
only have it because I do. Certainly it seems likely that becoming
aware of the intuition (i.e., nonreflective belief) that I have a conscious mind requires that I do have consciousness. Perhaps when
it comes to connecting nonreflective beliefs to reflective beliefs,
because we are dealing with different aspects of the belief-making
cognitive system and not unrelated things in the external world, we
cannot presume that nonreflective beliefs are disconnected from
the content of the beliefs they produce.

These considerations give me some confidence that we are justified in holding reflective beliefs about our internal states such as
free will and having a conscious mind with nothing more than our
nonreflective beliefs as a source (unless sufficient reasons arise to

reject them). Belief in free will may have additional encouragement in the repeated pairing of experiences of will apparently causing action. The extension to other humans having free will, however, requires an extra step. Others' free will, conscious mind, thoughts, feeling, and the like are not *my* internal states. Nevertheless, I see us as justified in believing that others have these properties. Our natural cognition produces nonreflective beliefs in others' free, conscious minds that become our reflective beliefs. Here justification is preserved because if we are justified in believing ourselves to have free, conscious minds, and we regard others as being relevantly similar to ourselves (e.g., behave in similar ways, are made of similar stuff, have similar forms, etc.), then, until we have evidence to the contrary, we are justified in assuming that other members of the class *humans* will be similar to the one (ourselves) for which we have justified belief in its free, conscious mind.

Allow me another thought. It appears to be a case of special pleading if these reflective beliefs in free will and attribution of mind, thoughts, and consciousness to others cannot be justified, at least in part, by appeal to intuitions, but other arguments (including those against their justification) may appeal to such intuitions. Intuitions—nonreflective beliefs—about whether an argument seems good, whether the evidence is strong enough, and the like— are critical for much (if not all) of our knowledge. At some point, appeal to my natural intuitions is required. But if I am not justified in an appeal to natural intuitions, I cannot be justified in even the belief that appealing to natural intuitions leads to unjustified beliefs.

Here I am only gesturing toward the types of problems requiring philosophical attention. My position is a commonsense realist position, of the sort defended by eighteenth-century Scottish philosopher Thomas Reid and his disciples. Reid recognized, accurately, that many of our cognitive faculties produce beliefs immediately—that is, without the support of evidence or argument. Although Reid wholeheartedly endorsed reason as a legitimate belief-producing faculty, he rejected the idea that it is the only legitimate and justified belief-producing faculty. We have many cognitive faculties and activities that produce beliefs, not just reflective disaffected reasoning. Reid calls all of these faculties, taken together, "common sense." As we cannot form beliefs without use of these cognitive systems (that generate nonreflective beliefs), we are entitled to treating them as trustworthy. Contemporary philosopher Nicholas Wolterstorff affirms Reid's intuitions and develops them into a criterion of rationality. Wolterstorff contends:

> A person is rationally justified in believing a certain proposition which he does believe unless he has adequate reason to cease from believing it. Our beliefs are rational unless we have reason for refraining; they are not nonrational unless we have reason for believing. They are innocent until proved guilty, not guilty until proved innocent.[33]

Until I have reason to think otherwise, I trust my cognitive faculties and regard their deliverances in nonreflective beliefs as true and justified. If some nonreflective beliefs conflict others or other reasoned considerations reveal inconsistencies or incoherence, then they might have to be amended. As the human possession of conscious minds with free will is a deliverance of natural cognition, the burden of proof is on those who deny conscious minds and free will. I have not yet seen compelling evidence meeting this burden, and even Daniel Wegner, who is regarded as a leading scientific challenger to the existence of free will, conceded after a review of the scientific evidence, "Does all this mean that conscious thought does not cause action? It does not mean this at all."[34] Rather, to date, clever experiments only show that in some situations people can have the illusion of conscious will even when the action was partly or wholly independent of their conscious experience of willing—a fascinating finding nonetheless.[35]

Even if my line of thought is correct, it does not follow that conscious human minds with free will *do* exist, only that one is justified in believing that they do exist. That is, the cognitive science that I have reviewed here is not *by itself* inconsistent with believing in the existence of conscious human minds and free will and the like.[36]

I have taken the time to point out the sorts of philosophical questions that applying cognitive science to beliefs about human nature raises because the same types of questions will arise as a result of the next chapter. Observations from the preceding chapters provide the framework for a cognitive science of religious beliefs.

CHAPTER 6

How We Conceive of the Divine

WHEN VISITING INDIA, one cannot miss the colorful diversity of shrines and temples devoted to the various gods. You will find images of multiarmed human forms—elephant-headed Ganesha, the monkey-god Hanuman, the god Vishnu in the form of a fish or a boar, and hundreds of others. These various images correspond to as many (or more) different conceptions of the divine—and this is only in Hindu India and only considering those beings that are objects of worship and not countless demons, spirits, fairies, and other superhuman beings. If we consider all of the superhuman concepts from the world over, how can any general patterns be drawn?

My argument in this chapter is that a cognitive scientific perspective can provide descriptive and explanatory insights into how humans conceptualize the divine the way we tend to do, and why. I begin by summarizing one common account from cognitive science of religion (CSR) for why concepts of gods are common around the world. I then offer some observations about why some god concepts are conceptually effective for injecting meaning into life's events. I end the chapter with some brief comments on whether cognitive explanations for why people tend to believe in gods undercut justification for these beliefs.

WHAT IS A GOD?

One of the difficulties in studying how people think of gods is even identifying what counts as *god, divine, superhuman,* or *supernatural.*

All of these terms are contested, and their use will reflect a particular perspective or theoretical framework. Rather than try to define *gods* from a theological perspective—a perspective that is bound to be disagreeable to someone from a different theological vantage point—here I will treat *gods* and related terms from a cognitive scientific perspective.

Gods, here, will refer to:

: counterintuitive intentional agents,
: that a group of people reflectively believes exists,
: that have a type of existence or action (past, present, or future) that can, in principle, be detected by people,
: and whose existence motivates some difference in human behavior as a consequence.

Recall from chapter 4 that being counterintuitive is having a property that violates (either through breach or transfer) the expectations of an intuitive ontology. A living cow with metal internal parts is counterintuitive because the expectation of having organic innards is intuitively applicable to Living Things, and this expectation is breached here. A tree that listens to people's conversations is counterintuitive because the expectation set Mentality has been transferred to an ontological category to which it does not belong. *Counterintuitive*, then, as a technical term motivated by current understanding of natural human conceptual systems, maps roughly onto how people often use the terms *supernatural* or *superhuman* without running aground on the problem of specifying what is natural and what is "super" or above humans. (What if the divine is part of nature? What if a god is decidedly subhuman in some respect?) Such a definition of a god, as it appeals to cross-culturally recurrent features of human cognition, avoids the problem of being nonapplicable to other times or places.

Gods, as defined in this way, are certainly not the only concepts that have occupied theologians or thinkers concerned with the ultimate concerns, the meaning of life, or spiritual pursuits. If one wants to see Paul Tillich's idea of God as an abstract "ground of our being"[1] or variants on the theme that God is some kind of impersonal force much more like that portrayed in the *Star Wars* movies than that in the Bible, then the cognitive approach I am advocating will disappoint. From this cognitive perspective, such nonagentive ways of viewing "God" or "the divine" do not fall into the same category with Allah, Shiva, or Zeus as conceived by ordinary devotees.

Perhaps surprisingly or disconcertingly, demons, ghosts, ancestors, and other traditional religious beings are gods under this framework. Whether a god is good or bad, powerful or feeble, all knowing or laughably fallible, or worthy of devotion or scorn does not factor into this definition of gods. I regard this inclusiveness as a strength. Ancestor-spirits and nature-spirits just might be the most common focus of rituals and other "religious" activity in traditional small-scale societies, and their echoes are present in even the most "complex," urbanized societies in the form of ghosts and saints. An account of belief in gods that marginalizes these as "superstition" is unduly narrow.

A key question before the cognitive scientist of religion is to account for why gods are so recurrent across cultures. Whenever a particular type of idea or practice is widely recurrent across cultures, the human scientist should want to know why this is so. Simply answering "Because gods exist" is an insufficient answer. Quarks might exist but that does not mean quark-concepts are widespread across time and space. It might be that fairies do not exist and yet beliefs in such beings have stretched from China to Ireland. Whether or not something exists is a different question than why people believe that something exists. Cognitive scientists study such seemingly banal questions as "Why do people believe there is a three-dimensional world around them?" without resorting to "Because there is." Even if the actual existence of a three-dimensional world is patently obvious to us, there is still a cognitive problem regarding just how we come to find belief in such a world patently obvious.

A second important question is why do some of these gods become connected with belief systems or theologies concerning meaning and ultimate concerns? Fairies might meet the definition of a god and they might be widely recurrent, but they do not figure centrally in theological treatments of why humans are here, how they should understand themselves, and how they should live their lives. Why not? Why are some gods better candidates for providing meaning, and becoming focal in religions, than others?

Why Gods?

Gods are common because of the operation of ordinary natural cognitive systems we use to make sense of the world and especially minded agents. The concert of various content-specific systems facilitates our belief in gods. Previously I noted how we humans are eager to make sense of the world around us and have a number of early developing natural ways to do so. If something bears the marks of a bounded, physical object, then the Physicality and Spatiality expectation sets kick in, providing inferences, explanations, and predictions for the object's properties and movement. What if something does not appear to move in a way easily explained in terms of ordinary mechanics? As described in chapter 5, we eagerly seek out intentional agents—particularly other humans—in the environment. Persons such as humans violate Physicality in some important ways, and this partitioning of things that wholly conform to Physicality from those that do not is a conceptual act that even infants engage in. Persons play by different rules than ordinary objects, and babies know this. Persons and their causal properties can account for events and states of affairs that the rules of Physicality cannot. As reviewed in chapter 4, Kelemen's research on design reasoning shows that children often regard *someone* as a more sensible cause of natural states of affairs (such as features of mountains and camels) than some mechanical process.[2]

We have other natural causal strategies available, including essentialist and vitalistic reasoning that come from the Biology expectation set. Nevertheless, given persons' (apparent) potential ability to explain a broad range of events and states that are not obviously the result of these other forms of intuitive causal reasoning, and given the importance of person-based causation in human social life, we have a strong natural propensity to resort to person-based causal explanations when other forms of intuitive causal reasoning fail.

This natural tendency to resort to person-based conceptualization of events, states, and things might be an instance of *error management*. Humans and other animals have limited and fallible decision-making abilities that will at least occasionally lead to making errors as in failing to detect food at hand or regarding something as edible when it isn't; or being scared of a harmless object or failing to notice a dangerous predator nearby. Because errors will happen, in many cases it would be advantageous for an organism to err in one direction instead of the other depending upon which kind of mistake is more costly for the organism. For instance, the cost of mistaking a poisonous mushroom for an edible mushroom could far outweigh the benefit of finding lots of edible mushrooms. This observation applied to human cognitive systems entails that humans will have some tendencies that are tuned in a particular "safer" direction.[3] Anthropologist Stewart Guthrie has argued that the human perceptual and conceptual tendency to see human-like agents and agency everywhere—even in situations we later recant—is one such better-safe-than-sorry tuning.[4] I have labeled this cognitive system *HADD* for *hypersensitive agency detection device*.[5] Evidence that humans have such a device is strong.[6]

Cognitive scientists have demonstrated repeatedly that, from infancy, movement that looks self-propelled and goal-directed activates thinking about objects as agents, and further can trigger attribution of mental states, beliefs, desires, and sometimes even personality and social roles. Famously, psychologists Fritz Heider and Marianne Simmel showed American female college students a film of geometric shapes moving in and out and around a broken rectangle and then asked them to recall what they saw. Instead of producing simple factual descriptions such as, "The large triangle moved toward the circle and stopped just to its right. The large triangle then moved out of the rectangle and toward the smaller triangle and circle . . . ," observers mostly described the movement using personification—for instance, describing the smaller triangle and the circle as friends and the larger triangle as their enemy, and them wanting to escape, and the large triangle becoming angry.[7] This and subsequent studies illustrate that our perceptual and conceptual systems readily attribute minded agency with little provocation—even in conditions in which we reflectively think that such attribution is in error.[8] That is, we have an agency detection system that produces false positives (or at least we reflectively believe it to do so). Guthrie has argued that this tendency to find humanlike agency even where it does not actually exist is a primary generator of belief in gods. We have *HADD experiences*, experiences in which we detect agency for which the type of agency is unclear, and then sometimes regard them as evidence of a god or gods. Our natural cognitive systems find minded agency even where there is not any, and are likewise attracted to intentional explanations for natural events and states of affairs. Gods, by these lights, are false positives.[9]

Even if one is uncomfortable with Guthrie's decidedly dismissive approach concerning the possible existence of one or many gods, his general point is helpful. Our natural cognition readily applies purposive and mentalistic construals to a broad range of objects, states, and events even given only ambiguous evidence that mental agency is in fact at play. If one has been exposed to a god concept—and recall that in principle gods' activities are detectable in the world—one's agency detection system has a good likelihood of detecting evidence of the god's activity. Similarly, given this agency detection system that is more forgiving of false positives than failures of detection, one will occasionally encounter events or conditions that *seem* to cry out for an explanation in terms of the activity of an intentional agent and a regular human or animal will clearly be insufficient. Such events might occasionally lead to the postulation of a god (or support the existence of a known god).

To illustrate, recently when I arrived at home and prepared to open my back garden gate, the door slowly swung open just in front of me, without me contacting it—not a normal occurrence! While it opened, I assumed that some*one* on the other side heard me coming and opened it for me, but when it was fully open, I saw no one who could have opened it. I checked behind the gate and saw no one. Strange. My agency detection system registered agency (I had a HADD experience). I assumed a human agent was present, but then no human agent was present. Who did it? We probably all have such experiences. Most of the time we shrug it off, but perhaps occasionally such experiences reinforce beliefs in ghosts, spirits, and the like.

Similarly, as Kelemen's work suggests, we seem to have a conceptual bias to see natural things in terms of their function or purpose, and have a tendency to connect this apparent purpose to the activity of someone—an intentional agent or person. Finding purpose in the natural world and eagerly attaching purpose to intentional agency would provide impetus for believing in beings that can account for the apparent purpose or design in the natural world. As humans and animals are rarely good candidates, conceptual space is open for gods to fill this role.

Taking Guthrie's and Kelemen's work together, we see that humans have natural, intuitive impetus for postulating gods. Events and things in the world appear purposeful, designed, or otherwise the product of minded, intentional activity. It has been speculated that events of unusual fortune or misfortune likewise provide motivation to consider the existence and activities of gods. When some improbable event happens that seems meaningful, we might readily assume someone, perhaps a divine someone, is responsible.[10]

Such thinking could be reinforced by moral intuitions as well. Psychologists have discovered some evidence that we easily think about the world as operating on some kind of reciprocity principle, what is called *just world reasoning*.[11] If someone does something morally wrong, something bad is more likely to befall him. But why? One way of theologically elaborating this intuition is to postulate a punishing and rewarding force such as karma, as we see in many Asian religions. Alternatively, a fairly intuitive account would be that someone knows about the wrongdoing and punishes it. As gods might know even what is done in secret, and can use natural forces and things to reward or punish, gods may serve an explanatory role in these cases of unusual fortune or misfortune. Even gods that have little concern about human interactions may be vengeful when humans trespass against them.

The natural tendency to see agency around us, to see purpose in the world, to demand explanation for uncommon fortune or misfortune, and to connect fortune or misfortune to reward and punishment may conspire to make gods readily understandable and provide impetus for entertaining their existence and activities. One further set of considerations deserves mention as well.

How Dead People Become Gods

Many if not most of the world's gods (broadly construed) bear some relation to deceased humans. Ancestor-spirits and ghosts were, at one time, humans. In small-scale and traditional societies, warding off ghosts and malevolent spirits, propitiating the ancestors, or garnering the support of (deceased) saints often takes on far greater importance in regular practice than concerns about creators or cosmic deities. What might account for this cross-cultural recurrence?

At this point the answer is largely speculative. If we accept that our natural cognitive equipment makes us intuitive dualists as Paul Bloom has suggested (and discussed in chapter 5), then the idea that an immaterial something—mind, body, spirit, or some combination thereof—is left behind after death is not radically counterintuitive. Even if such dualism is not an intuitive default but is merely an easily accommodated idea, the point remains that mind- and soul-related ideas are not difficult to decouple from bodily reasoning, and the fact that someone's body has stopped working need not conceptually turn off reasoning about the person's thoughts, feelings, desires, and other properties. Further, as Pascal Boyer has noted, with someone intimate, we know a lot about their tastes, desires, preferences, personalities, and the like; and upon death these mind-based properties remain untouched. Our theory of mind, informed by such information, continues generating inferences and predictions even after someone has died.[12] Add to these considerations the occasional, emotionally gripping experiences related to the deceased, such as dreams, hallucinations, or strange sounds, which trip our enthusiastic agency detection system (HADD), and you have a recipe for supposing that the recently deceased is still active without his or her body. Indeed, the distinct sense that someone passed away is still somehow present is not uncommon even among people who explicitly reject belief in ghosts and spirits of the dead.[13] As the dead no longer have visible, physical bodies, they may satisfy the search for an intentional agent in the many cases in which our agency detection system detects agency but it is clear a visible human or animal could not have been responsible (HADD experiences). It follows that little cultural encouragement is needed to develop the idea that some form of the dead is still around and active among the living in some cases.[14]

MINIMALLY COUNTERINTUITIVE IDEAS AND CULTURAL TRANSMISSION

Thus far I have been stressing the content-specific natural cognition that likely encourages thinking about gods and entertaining their existence and activity. If these dynamics characterize many people's automatic thinking in ordinary human contexts, we would expect that ideas about gods would be readily generated by individuals (if only in a piecemeal fashion) and transmitted from person to person, perhaps gaining elaboration. As god concepts have a strong intuitive foundation, conforming well to nonreflective beliefs, they will be strong candidates for reflective beliefs as well. Recall from chapter 3, strong accessibility breeds believability.

Though I have been stressing intuitive impetus, a god concept need not be wholly intuitive but might deviate a bit from the expectation sets sketched in chapter 4. As long as a concept is not *too* counterintuitive, the concept need not suffer in terms of how easy it is to conceptualize, remember, and communicate. Consider a spirit that can read minds. Mind reading might be counterintuitive, but a disembodied mind having the additional feature of being able to know what people are thinking is not particularly cumbersome. It is only modestly counterintuitive and so is easy to think and talk about. Some experimental research shows that concepts that are only slightly counterintuitive are as or more memorable and transmittable than wholly intuitive ones.[15] If so, then their good potential for being communicated will increase with how often they are talked and thought about. Thus, they will be more frequently encountered and, in turn, become more familiar and accessible, leading to believability. Being mostly intuitive and just slightly counterintuitive poses no special problem for a religious concept and may actually be an asset.

Not all god concepts are only slightly counterintuitive, however. Many have features that deviate radically from natural expectations and are highly counterintuitive. Consider the idea of a god that knows all, has no location whatsoever, exists in a different time (or no time at all), and yet, can interact with the world. This approximates a view of the divine that we see in some theological treatments in Judaism, Islam, Hinduism, and Christianity. What then? Such concepts are likely to require special cultural scaffolding to aid their transmission: special artifacts, institutions, practices, or other devices that help people learn and use these more complex concepts.[16] I return to this problem in chapter 8.

GODS AND MEANING MAKING

Some Westerners think of gods in terms of their ability to give existential meaning to life, to account for why we are here, what makes life worth living, and how we should conceive of ourselves in relation to other humans, the rest of nature, and the cosmos. Though some gods might help with the big existential questions, perhaps most are more modest in their meaning-making. Why are my chickens laying poorly? Why was this fishing trip so successful? How can I get the spouse that I want?

As noted previously, intentional beings (Persons) can help explain and predict a broad range of phenomena either as proximate or more distant causes. As concepts, they possess what Pascal Boyer has called *inferential potential*, the ability to generate a broad range of ideas, inferences, explanations, and predictions about issues that matter to people. That is, a concept with inferential potential has the potential to enable people to *infer* or draw conclusions across a broad range of concerns.[17] Appealing to the activity of an average person (let alone a super person) can account for a greater variety of things than appealing to the average rock, shrub, or beetle. Not all person concepts—human or gods—have the same inferential potential, however. We naturally learn about human causal limitations and thus understand, for instance, that positing human activity cannot make meaning from a freak thunderstorm that destroys my crops. Humans have a restricted range of things they can do and, thus, can explain.

Boyer has argued that gods—particularly the ones that attract a lot of attention and behavioral investment—are those whose counterintuitive property or properties give them greater and broader inferential potential in domains of human concern. For instance, by virtue of being invisible, being able to read minds, or seeing all, a god can have access to strategic information about who plans to do what to whom, and may act on that information or share it. Different counterintuitive properties, such as failing to exist on Wednesdays or only knowing languages that cannot be used, yields little gain in inferential potential. Such beings will be unable to importantly bear upon human concerns or experiences. They are not terribly interesting or worth talking about, and so will be less accessible, and hence, less believable. Consequently, such beings will usually fail to persist as shared ideas and will rarely (if ever) become recognized as gods.[18]

Even successful gods vary in the ability to make meaning. Some local forest spirits might be very powerful and inferentially important when it comes to reasoning about what goes on in a particular part of the forest, but completely irrelevant when drawing inferences about domestic affairs, whereas the opposite would be true of domestic spirits. Gods vary in the meaning they can help make. Those with broadest ranges of activity—both spatially and in terms of kinds of things they can and cannot do—will generally have the greatest ability to serve as meaning-makers. A cosmic creator who can act in essentially any domain of life has more meaning-making reach than the ghost haunting the house on the corner and, therefore, is more likely to come to mind, be talked about, and be accessible and believable (all else being equal).

I raise these observations concerning how gods are recruited to make meaning because, from a Western perspective, it is commonly assumed that gods are all about meaning and that all gods are equal in this regard. Westerners sometimes talk about religions as fundamentally existential meaning-making systems. The suggestion is that those "spirits" or "ghosts" that do not serve this function are not really a part of religion, but are merely part of local superstition and should not be called *gods*. In terms of conceptual properties, however, a clear dichotomy does not exist.

REASONS TO DOUBT THE EXISTENCE OF GODS?

Gods come in dazzling diversity, from ancestor spirits to cosmic creators, but amidst this diversity we can see that a small number of conceptual factors make an idea more likely to become entertained and believed in as a god. A strong god candidate is a modestly counterintuitive intentional agent or person, because such persons have great inferential potential while not being too complex or difficult to understand and communicate. Successful gods will also tend to produce actions that are detectable in the world, either through our agency detection system, or because they account for apparent design and purpose in the natural world. Beings that may be invoked as morally interested, and perhaps accounting for fortune and misfortune in terms of reward and punishment, might be especially successful. In short, successful god concepts need to be able to make meaning of life's events in relatively intuitive, straightforward ways. Observing these features of gods are not new. The novel contribution of cognitive science is that we can now better explain why these features are important for gods and why they tend to congeal.

How we conceive of the divine is shaped by the natural cognitive equipment we have, but by no means does this entail that beliefs in gods are mistaken or suspect on this basis. Merely providing a scientific account of such beliefs should not be taken as casting doubt upon their truth.

Previously I argued that identifying that a belief has a natural cognitive basis does not bear upon whether it is true, but may justify someone in holding such a belief to be true until sufficient reasons to the contrary arise. That is, when it comes to naturally derived beliefs, we may treat them as "innocent until proven guilty." I believe the same principles apply here to belief about gods. Insofar as beliefs in the existence of gods are fairly direct, natural outcomes of ordinary human cognition, they may be regarded as justified until reasons arise to reject them.[19]

For instance, our natural tendency to see design and purpose in the natural world, and regard that design and purpose as the product of intentional agency seems to be cognitively natural and, hence, innocent until proven guilty. Likewise, in many situations our agency detection system tells us that someone has acted and we are justified in this belief until we have good reasons to reject it. Note, however, that identifying the particular someone responsible for the perceived design in the natural world or as the agent whose action has been detected requires inferences beyond the immediate deliverances of natural cognition. The more inferential the steps, the less obviously justified such beliefs are. That is, intuitive religious ideas have stronger grounds for justified belief (all else being equal) than theological reflections and elaborations upon these beliefs. This conclusion is ironic in that theologians often regard themselves as in the business of sharpening and refining religious instincts and intuitions much in the same way that philosophers intellectually sharpen and refine other classes of intuitions. Perhaps theologians do refine religious thought and consequently produce better intellectual products than what we receive through simple natural cognition. Nevertheless, such theological concepts may bear a greater burden of proof than simpler claims such as "That tree was deliberately brought about in some way by someone" by virtue of being less natural.

In this vein, philosophers have begun exploring whether doubt is cast upon religious beliefs or whether they are encouraged by cognitive explanations of religion.[20] Here I only want to dispense with three common arguments against belief in gods that arise in the context of cognitive explanations.[21]

One objection is that if belief in gods is produced by natural cognition, then they are not based on relevant evidence, and hence, are dubious. I believe my argument from the previous chapter covers this objection but even if not, it is an error to infer that natural cognition being part of belief formation precludes the use of evidence in the case of believing in gods. The account presented above clearly points to the role of agency detection and inferring design and purpose from *observations* of the world around us. Surely this constitutes one sort of relevant (even if insufficient) evidence. It might be that people accurately "read" intentional agency from the text of the natural world.

Alternatively, one might argue that perhaps our natural cognition does prompt us to believe in gods using evidence, but is simply unreliable in this regard. Our cognitive equipment might be fine for finding human agency with bodies and the like, but it produces belief in beings that do not exist such as ghosts and fairies and so it cannot be trusted when applied to gods. The difficulty with such a line is that it assumes that we *know* that there are no disembodied or invisible agents, so when our cognitive systems detect one, they do so in error. Such an argument is what is known as "assuming facts not in evidence" in American legal terminology or "question begging" in philosophical jargon. You cannot use the (alleged) fact that invisible agents do not exist as support for the claim that the cognitive system in question is error-prone and so undermines belief in invisible agents. You have assumed what you are setting out to reject.

Similarly, consider a household scale upon which we weigh things. I might suspect that it gives bad readings for any number of reasons, but I cannot determine that it is in fact error-prone without independently determining the weight of an object and then showing that the scale does not give its true weight. Just dropping a bag of potatoes on the scale and saying, "See, the scale says 10 kilos. That's not right. This scale is no good," would only be convincing if we knew already that the sack of potatoes does not in fact weigh 10 kilos. If our cognitive systems "weigh" our experiences and conclude that there is at least one god out there, we cannot take this conclusion as evidence that the cognitive systems are mistaken unless we have independent reason to think there are no gods. Indeed, normally we would regard such a "weighing" as evidence that there is indeed at least one god.

A third objection is a rejoinder to the first two. One may concede that the cognitive faculties that encourage belief in gods use inputs from the world around, and that we must leave open the possibility that at least one god exists, but these faculties result in many divergent beliefs in various sorts of gods. This divergence suggests error in the belief-forming mechanism, at least as applied to gods, and gives us reason to hold suspect the beliefs it produces. This more formidable objection still ignores an important point: natural cognition converges on the existence of at least one and possibly many gods. The precise character of the gods in question might vary, but it would be a mistake to take this variation as reason to reject justified belief in some kind of god. Imagine three people are out for a walk in the woods and they each think they see an animal in a distant thicket. One says it is a deer. One claims it is a fox. The third believes it to be a bird. Clearly, the belief-forming mechanisms in question are imprecise in this context, but should we conclude that they are not justified in believing they saw an animal of some sort?

Color perception provides another helpful analogy. Our cognitive system naturally gives us impressions about what color(s) various things are, but this fact does not preclude that there are disagreements in particular cases. A tropical fish might be described variously as red, fuchsia, magenta, pink, violet, or purple (just to name a few) depending upon the individuals' personal history, eyesight, and expertise. One person might even see no color at all (on this occasion) because he is among the roughly 7 percent of American males who are color-blind.[22] We would surely be in error to suppose that the lone person who sees the tropical fish and believes it to be violet does not have a justified belief on the basis of having an error-prone cognitive device. Likewise, people might disagree on the details of the gods in question, and a minority might fail to detect any gods at all, but it does not follow that those who believe in the existence of gods are unjustified in such beliefs. Many of these beliefs are likely to be false upon further, reasoned considerations, but as with belief in free will, souls, and consciousness, the naturalness of belief in gods should be taken as grounds for giving such beliefs the benefit of the doubt.

CHAPTER 7

Cognition and Experiencing Religion

IMAGINE THAT SOMEONE, out of the blue, offered you an opportunity to take a trip to the international space station at no cost to you, no strings attached. You would get to go into space and orbit the earth in the adventure of a lifetime. Would you feel excited? Elated? Anxious? Scared sick? No doubt most of us would feel a jumble of feelings that we would have to pick through, consider, reflect on, and then come to some conscious reflection on what it is we were feeling. This feeling too would likely change depending on information we receive that is relevant to the trip, such as testimonies from others about how amazing being in space is, or about how zero gravity wreaks havoc on your physiology. This information would be used to modify how you feel. This case illustrates how important cognitive appraisals are to filling in our experience of emotional states.

From basic emotions to ecstatic mystical encounters with the divine, experiences are structured and informed by our cognitive systems, including the systems trafficking in conceptual information. Experiencing—religious or otherwise—does not simply happen to us: we actively participate in it.

We might think of *religious experiences* as when people have a mystical encounter with the divine, but as most religious people know, many experiences can have religious significance, including regular worship, meditation, prayer, rituals, retreats, pilgrimages, scripture reading, acts of service, taking moral stands, and countless other acts and events. An experience might be religiously meaningful without altered states of consciousness or visions. The most common religious experiences are associated with ordinary religious practices and expression. Hence, here I leave *experience* broad and briefly discuss how cognitive science is beginning to aid our understanding of religious experiencing in a handful of specific illustrative areas: religious rituals and ceremonies, scripture reading, petitionary prayer, and spirit possession. First, I offer some comments on how experiences generally—from ordinary emotions and perception of the world to religious ones—are structured by cognitive content to build the case that it is conceptual information that makes an experience religious or not.

COGNITION AND ORDINARY EXPERIENCING

Even when it comes to fairly ordinary emotional experiences, our conceptual equipment plays a key role. Once, I was standing just off stage waiting to give a lecture and found myself shaking. As I do not usually shake before speaking, I inferred that I was feeling particularly nervous. Then I took a few steps and discovered I was not shaking anymore. I took a few steps back to where I had been standing and I started shaking again. I repeated this procedure with the same results and discovered that I had been standing on a part of the floor that was vibrating from the building's air-handling system. I laughed at myself and no longer felt the least bit nervous. This instance illustrates a well-established finding from the psychology of emotions: we often determine our emotions from our physiological states (which can be manipulated by too much coffee, alcohol, or vibrating floors) *and* conceptual appraisal, which is influenced by our environment. Unconsciously I had thought, "I'm shaking. I'm about to speak in front of a crowd of strangers. Nervousness is a common emotion in such cases. I must be nervous." That is, many emotional experiences are part what our body *feels* and part how our conceptual cognition interprets or labels the feelings. Combining these two components often happens automatically and without conscious awareness.[1]

Similarly, our content-specific cognition fleshes out our otherwise skeletal perceptual experience of the world around us. We have the *illusion* of a complete representation of the world around us, particularly in familiar environments, because we know what should be there. We only have to attend to enough details about the environment to trigger the right conceptual information, then our knowledge automatically and nonconsciously fills in the blanks to provide us with the rich perceptual experience.

I raise these cases of emotion and perception to emphasize the point that any experience, however mundane, draws upon what we already think to create the experience. No experience is simply imposed upon us. In the case of more ambiguous experiences that are open to many different interpretations, such as dreams or visions, the point is all the more apt, and we have no reason to think that religious experiences are any different. It might seem that we contribute nothing to such experiences because we do not consciously will to understand them one way or another, but not having a sense of agency in the experience does not mean it is wholly foisted upon us without being importantly influenced by the contents of our minds.

Even if we accept that gods or spirits are communicating directly to a person's mind in a mystical vision, the gods are still communicating to an embodied mind with certain natural and expertise-based cognitive proclivities that will necessarily shape that communication.

It follows, therefore, that to fully understand religious experiences—from unusual peak mystical experiences to the more mundane—we need to understand something about the cognitive systems that interpret the images and feelings associated with such experiences. Indeed, such an approach suggests that speaking about "religious experiences" at all is problematic. It might be more appropriate to consider how experiences become deemed *religious*—imbued with meaning connected to gods.

EXPERIENCING AN EVENT AS RELIGIOUS

What kind of experiences are people likely to deem religious? As regarded as evidence of divine action or otherwise meaningfully connected to gods? To begin, events not readily explained by natural, nonreflective causal cognition—particularly intuitive biology and physics—would be strong candidates for experiences deemed religious. People do not (typically) see the behavior of billiard balls moving in regular, predictable ways as possessing religious meaning. Such events don't scream out for any religious meaning making because they conform to our ordinary expectations concerning the movement of bounded physical objects. Similarly, if gods readily are associated with unusual events of great fortune or misfortune and such events tend to be imbued with moral overtones, then we might expect that events that seem morally relevant are likely to be experienced as religious. Of course, objects, patterns, or arrangements that start the agency detection system and cannot be attributed to human or animal agency will tend to be regarded as caused by religious agency and potentially meaningful (provided they fit with how the posited religious agents act).

Even physical events such as being on a bridge when it collapses or *not* being struck by a falling tree branch could be construed as events worthy of religious reflections. Cases of great fortune and misfortune might bypass normal causal reasoning as they focus one's attention on the timing of the event or the particular person involved rather than the general causal mechanism. Consider the account of the Israelites crossing the Jordan River into Canaan:

> So when the people broke camp to cross the Jordan, the priests carrying the ark of the covenant went ahead of them. Now the Jordan is at flood stage all during harvest.

Yet as soon as the priests who carried the ark reached the Jordan and their feet touched the water's edge, the water from upstream stopped flowing. It piled up in a heap a great distance away, at a town called Adam in the vicinity of Zarethan, while the water flowing down to the Sea of the Arabah (that is, the Dead Sea) was completely cut off. So the people crossed over opposite Jericho. (Josh. 3:14–16, NIV)

Cambridge material scientist Colin Humphreys has suggested that this event could have been caused by mudslides upriver at what was Adam in Zarethan, causing the water to "pile up," an event that has been known to temporarily block the Jordan River at times subsequent to this famous crossing. Nevertheless, it is easy to see, as Humphreys suggests, how the event would be construed as miraculous because of its improbable timing, *not* because it did not have a natural or even intuitive proximate cause.[2] The particular timing—why did the river stop flowing when we wanted to cross and entered it carrying the Ark of the Covenant?—is not readily answered by ordinary, natural physical or biological reasoning.

Once someone has adopted certain religious beliefs about the existence and activity of various gods, if these conceptual schemas are made salient for some reason, this conceptual information is likely to guide our perception of events. For instance, when I was about eight years old, an unusual cold front moved through Southern California in May, bringing with it a small chance of snow in the mountains, including the area where I lived. Wanting to have a snow day off of school, I prayed earnestly for enough snow to lead to a cancellation. Two feet of snow fell on Mother's Day Sunday. There was no school the next day. Without the conceptual framing of my prayers, my family and I probably would have regarded this as not much more than a freak storm. As it was, I was convinced that this was answered prayer.

The snow prayer story illustrates that when we are looking for events and experiences with religious significance, we are more likely to find them. Because of how the event was anticipated by a particular conceptual scheme, it was experienced in a very different way than it might otherwise have been experienced. My agency detection system had detected divine action in this situation. Because of the framing in terms of ordinary communication—if we make a request of a person (not necessarily a human person), we are more attentive to a potential reply—I saw the subsequent improbable event as an answer to that request. This story is an example of how conceptual information can frame, and thereby shape how we think about events or ideas.

Just because our mind is naturally oriented to see the divine in some situations does not mean that a god is not really acting. When we turn our attention to things or search them out, we are more apt to notice them, and this would apply to both illusions we might have but also the genuine article. Sometimes we fail to understand—or even hear—someone talking to us because we did not realize the person was talking to us. We had not tuned our attention to the available message. Maybe, in some cases, that is the situation with experiencing some events as permeated with religious significance: if your expectations are not appropriate, you miss it. Of course it is possible that we sometimes see things the way we want to see things and not in a fair way.

Such cognitively motivated predictions about what gets attributed to divine action or imbued with religious significance accords fairly well with the small amount of psychological research on the topic. Religious attributions were found to be more likely to be made by individuals who are religious, unsurprisingly,[3] but also when events were important or life altering—for instance, when events were related to medical or health-related needs.[4] Likewise, when events involve morally relevant harm, they are more likely to be attributed religious significance.[5]

That experiences deemed religious will tend to be more common when expectations are framed by prayer, meditation, or other religious practice suggests the intriguing possibility that participation in religious practices creates more opportunities to be affirmed in religious convictions, thereby reinforcing motivation and conviction in the value of such practices. The Hindu might perform a puja because he believes, but he might also believe because he does the puja. The Catholic might participate in Mass because she believes, but she might also believe because she participates in Mass. Not only, then, is religious practice structured by how we think, how we think can be impacted by religious practice.

Religious Practices Undergirded by Ordinary Cognition

Because of the importance of religious practices in framing and encouraging experiences regarded as religiously important, I turn now to the cognitive science of religious practices: rituals, use of scripture, prayer, and spirit possession.

Religious Rituals

Our natural content-specific cognition appears to inform whether we experience a religious ritual as effective or not, whether a god is acting in human affairs, and the degree of centrality to one's tradition. The amount of arousal or emotionality is, in part, a function of whether rituals are performed with great stimulation for the senses, "smells and bells" or *sensory pageantry,* but the decision to really do it up appears to be driven by cognitive considerations. I have in mind here the scholarly work of comparative religion scholar E. Thomas Lawson and philosopher Robert McCauley on ritual form.[6]

Like other cognitive treatments of religion, Lawson and McCauley have tried to see how much explanatory mileage they can get from appealing to ordinary psychological dynamics when considering religious rituals. Their *ritual form theory* begins by circumscribing its focus as those observable actions that bring about some kind of change and reference at least one god (in the sense used above) in the action. That is, someone acts in some observable way upon some object to prompt the gods (or use a god's power) to bring about some sort of change.[7] Ritual cleansings, weddings, and sacrifices commonly fit this description of a religious ritual. Lawson and McCauley assume that as actions, these "religious rituals" are conceptualized using the same cognitive equipment as is used for any other action. Consequently, across religious traditions and cultures some commonalities in how religious rituals are understood and experienced would be expected by virtue of the common cognitive equipment.

Lawson and McCauley specifically predict that the particular *form* of the ritual—independent of reputed meanings—will generate intuitions and feelings regarding a number of features of the ritual. Ritual form here refers primarily to a small number of considerations. First, does the ritual have a suitable agent performing the ritual? As deliberate intentional actions, a religious ritual must be performed by a suitable agent for it to be regarded as efficacious. For instance, in Catholicism, ritual blessings with holy water are common, either with a priest or with oneself as the agent. One can imagine that a holy-water-sprinkling machine could distribute water just as well as a human functionally, but as the machine is not an intentional agent, Lawson and McCauley's theory predicts that the average Catholic would be suspicious of the ritual's efficaciousness if blessings were so automated.

A second consideration is the particular type of ritual form the religious ritual takes, specifically whether or not the ritual is what they call a special agent ritual (SAR). Recall that for a ritual to be religious, it must include reference to a god in the action. This reference or connection can occur in one of three ways. First, a representative of the god could be the agent of the ritual action. For instance, when a rabbi circumcises a baby, the rabbi acts as a representative of God and is the agent of the action. Alternatively, the god could be referenced in connection with an instrument. When Catholics cross themselves with holy water, the water has a special connection to God (because of a previous ritual in which it was blessed by a representative of God). In Lawson and McCauley's terminology, when the most direct connection to the god is through a ritual instrument, the ritual is a special instrument ritual (SIR). The third option is for the patient or object of the ritual—the thing being acted upon—to have the most immediate connection with a god.[8] When Hindus bathe an image of a god, the god is the recipient of the action or the patient in the ritual. This ritual, then, is a special patient ritual (SPR). Rituals are either SARs, SIRs, or SPRs—special agent, special instrument, or special patient rituals. We are not consciously aware of this classification when observing or engaged in a ritual, but nonconsciously this classification bears upon our experience of the ritual and the ritual's stability or change over time.[9]

Lawson and McCauley predict that special agent rituals (SARs) will have additional different features or generate different expectations than the other two types (SIRs and SPRs). Most simply, the divide is between rituals in which the god (via a representative) is acting versus those in which the god (or the god's representative) is being acted upon (SPRs) or acted by means of (SIRs). We arguably have different intuitions about what it looks like when gods act in contrast to humans acting upon or through them. When the gods act, what they do is superpermanent, say Lawson and McCauley. Consequently, you do not need to do the ritual repeatedly. Once is enough. Note that weddings and rites of passage (such as baptisms or Bar Mitzvahs) are typically conducted once, and they usually have the form of a special agent ritual. It also follows from superpermanence that if we want to undo something that has been achieved ritually (such as a marriage through a wedding ritual), we might need to ritually undo it. That is, the god needs to undo its own handiwork. "What therefore God hath joined together, let not man put asunder." SARs *may* be ritually reversed as in a divorce ceremony, defrocking, or excommunication—which typically take the form of SARs.

In contrast, SPRs and SIRs may be repeated an indefinite number of times and it would be silly to ritually reverse them. Consider a sacrifice. I give a god some meat. As the god is the patient of the action, it is a special patient ritual (SPR) and is, hence, repeatable and nonreversible. I can give the same god the same sort of meat weekly for the rest of my life to accomplish the same thing, but I cannot take a sacrifice back. I don't need to specify a religious tradition here, as I trust your intuitions on this matter are the same as mine (and Lawson and McCauley's).

Further, Lawson and McCauley note that in special agent rituals, a god is acting in a one-off way. This is a big deal! For such a ritual to be convincing in this regard—changing someone from a girl to a woman, from damned to saved, from single to married, or from commoner to king—observers and the participants in particular need to *feel* that the god is acting in this moment. How is that accomplished? Through *sensory pageantry*—the sights, sounds, smells, and other adornments that provoke emotional arousal. Dramatic clothing, the anxiety produced by speaking in front of a crowd, immersion in chilly water, or even beatings, cuttings, and scarification conspire to elevate emotional response primarily in the participants and secondarily in the audience. Given the verbal and enacted cues related to the activity of the divine, and the ability for physiological arousal to be labelled or relabelled depending upon such conceptual cues, everyone involved is likely to experience something special, unusual, and superhuman happening in such religious rituals. In contrast, special patients and special instruments tend to be relatively less dramatic and less emotional affairs for the participants with lower degrees of sensory pageantry.

The claim made here is not that people necessarily consciously think, "Hmm, we need to convince everyone that these two people are really married. Let's make sure there are lots of smells and bells to gin up emotions." Rather, people have intuitions (or natural nonreflective beliefs) that one-off events should be marked in unusual ways and such observances then have higher degrees of emotional arousal, which in turn creates a greater motivational impact and experience of gods acting. Because of this sense of religious impact, such rituals are likely to be repeated by others in a similar fashion. Rituals that had little emotional impact would just *feel* insufficient and would be less likely to be reconstructed similarly by others. What Lawson and McCauley offer, then, is a cultural evolutionary model of how SARs tend to feature relatively high degrees of sensory pageantry, based upon guiding intuitions derived from fairly banal cognitive processes.

They further offer that because of their ability to make participants and audiences alike experience the activity of a god in a ritual, it is important to a religious tradition to have frequent exercise of SARs. Religious communities that lack such rituals will (typically) find declining motivation and commitment. The challenge, however, is that SARs, by virtue of being nonrepeatable, will be lower in frequency than special instrument and special patient rituals (SIRs and SPRs). A church can conduct Mass every few days but only so many people can be baptized, confirmed, married, or ordained.

Lawson and McCauley's work remains underexplored empirically, but initial experimental and ethnographic results are generally supportive.[10] If their ritual form theory bears out, it would prove a major explanatory achievement because it captures so many performance-related features of religious rituals without appeal to cultural particulars.

Hazard Precaution and Ritualized Behaviors

Considerable evidence exists that people easily form emotional aversions toward potential carriers of pathogens or other contaminants. One of the early findings that precipitated the rise of cognitive science was that people readily form strong aversions to foods. For instance, once when I was a child on a road trip up to Grandma's house for the holidays, we stopped to have lunch and

I ate a cheeseburger. Soon thereafter I got carsick and evacuated the contents of my stomach. The consequence was that I felt sick just thinking about cheeseburgers for the next six years. I wouldn't dare eat one. My motion sickness tricked my cognitive system into associating cheeseburgers with nausea. My father-in-law once ate some bad canned spaghetti and decades later will still not touch any spaghetti (a point of frustration for his Italian American wife). This narrowly circumscribed area in which strong associations are formed through a single pairing clearly supports the idea that we have natural tendencies to form some kinds of associations over others.

Pascal Boyer and Pierre Liénard have proposed that these associations and a number of related emotional, conceptual, and behavioral tendencies result from an evolved *hazard precaution system* that has been selected for its ability to keep people away from unseen potential harms such as predators, pathogens, and contaminants.[11] Cultural rituals, they argue, piggyback on this system as is evinced by both the common features of such ritualized actions and also the recurrent themes surrounding these rituals such as cleanliness and purification, establishing sacred spaces, and fending off unseen threats. Many cultural rituals bear similarities to personal "rituals" found in mothers-to-be, parents of young children, children at different stages of development, and people with obsessive-compulsive disorder (OCD). Features of these ritualized behaviors include preoccupation with the need to perform the action, emotional concern for action precision, and unnecessary repetition. Boyer and Liénard argue that certain cultural problems such as protecting oneself from unseen malignant spirits, or the "contaminating" effect of "unclean" out-group members or sinners mimic the natural input conditions for this hazard precaution system and thereby shape the actions used to address the problem and feelings about the action. Failure to perform the action correctly produces anxiety. One might feel disgust until the ritual is performed.[12]

Empirically, much work remains to be done on this hazard precaution theory, but if it is on the right track, it can help account for why some religious practices and ideas are difficult to uproot. For instance, it might be very easy for people to understand what ritually created sacred space is (free from contamination). Hence, the idea that the altar space at the front of a church or the pulpit is special and not to be invaded by those who have not been ordained will be attractive even to people, such as many Protestant Christians, who affirm a theology that does not mark off a distinct priesthood. Similarly, it might be largely natural to see food consumption or eating practices as readily merged with spiritual contamination.

Consequently, cultural elaborations on these tendencies are easy to manifest and can be difficult to uproot. Food taboos (such as Jewish kosher restrictions) are common throughout the world. Reformers trying to unsettle such taboos will likely face stiff resistance. If pork, for instance, is spiritually contaminating (as Hindus, Jews, and Muslims agree), a visceral reaction against eating it may be acquired and appropriated into a religious domain. Even if a religious authority says it is okay to eat, the idea is likely to be met with revulsion. When St. Peter was told in a vision relayed in Acts chapter 10 to "arise, Peter, kill and eat" unclean animals, he likely felt not just intellectual reluctance but disgust too. Emotional reactions inform our conceptual appraisals—indeed, it is often difficult or meaningless to distinguish the two.[13]

Reading Scripture

Brian Malley has provided the only book-length treatment of scripture reading from a CSR perspective.[14] Drawing upon Dan Sperber and Deirdre Wilson's cognitive relevance theory of communication,[15] Malley does a careful ethnographic and analytic treatment of a Baptist community in the United States with an emphasis on how they conceptualize and use scripture. He reports that their reading of the Bible is experienced differently than the reading of other texts. Instead of reading for prosaic information or entertainment, these Christians tend to approach the Bible as a mode of communication from God to them. They assume that every page includes potential meaning for their immediate situation and circumstance, and so they read it slower, with greater rereading and dwelling upon particular words and phrases than what would be expected in another text. We would expect such a difference to be common across religions in which texts are regarded as revelatory messages from the divine, and it seems that this is actually the case.

Petitionary Prayer

As is the case with ritual, insofar as gods are conceptualized using similar theory of mind assumptions that we use to conceptualize humans, we would expect that *prayer*, verbal communication with gods, to likewise bear similarities to how we communicate with other humans. Prayer will tend to be informed by natural cognition, particularly spontaneous prayer.

Prayer research from cognitive scientific perspectives is in its infancy, but one study I conducted some years ago illustrates how ordinary cognition might influence how people pray and think about prayer and other spontaneous religious activities even apart or in contradiction with theological instruction.[16] In this study concerning *petitionary prayer*, making requests to a god, I focused on Protestant, Evangelical Christians because of their tendency to encourage prayer for anything, no matter how big or small, an openness to God acting in miraculous ways, and the rarity of theological instruction concerning the particular modes of action God prefers (if any). Without salient theological instruction to interfere, we might expect natural cognition to fill in the gaps and shape the sort of petitions people make to God. What kinds of things do they think God is likely to do for them?

Previous research had shown that people have difficulty holding in working memory all of God's counterintuitive properties (such as being in multiple places at once) when conducting real-time tasks, and resorting, instead, to a more humanlike, limited representation of God.[17] If a similar dynamic were at play during spontaneous prayer, we would expect requests to God to conform to what a more humanlike god would be able to do. When I lose my keys, I could ask God to act psychologically (e.g., remind me where I left them or help me see where they are) or I could ask God to act physically (e.g., having them materialize on my desk). Either course of action is possible for an all-powerful God. Nevertheless, if God is more easily conceptualized as a person with a single, distant location, we might expect the psychological act to be preferred since psychological and social causation can take place at a distance, whereas mechanistic causation cannot. It might be more cognitively difficult to conceptualize God to act mechanistically or biologically on people or things right here right now. To test for any such preferences, I analyzed prayer journals and asked young adults to judge their most likely prayer strategy in a number of hypothetical situations. I found a tendency for these young adults to pray for God to act through psychological or social causation more than through biological or physical causation even if either type of request was equally acceptable from a reflective theological perspective, and even, if granted, they would bring about an equally suitable solution to the problem.[18]

Spirit Possession

Emma Cohen conducted ethnographic fieldwork among Afro-Brazilian spiritualists in northern Brazil. In this group, going into a spirit-possession trance in which one's own agency is supplanted by that of a spirit or ancestor is commonplace. Cohen observed grown adults acting like a baby, a snake, or a dolphin. She saw women acting like long-deceased men, and men acting like ancestral women.

Cohen was interested in how these spiritualists experienced the possession episodes, either as observers or as participants.[19] Her observations and interviews revealed an interesting gulf between what was taught by the *pai-de-santo*, the expert leader, and what was understood by the laypeople. Over and over again, the laypeople reported a clean dissociation between themselves acting in their bodies and when a possessing spirit acted. Typically they regarded themselves as either unconscious or simply passively watching their body being manipulated by the spirit during the trance. The *pai-de-santo*, however, taught that the spirit of the host and the possessing spirit merged during each episode to form a unique individual for that time. He used metaphors such as blending water from the Amazon with lemon juice. Why this difference between what was taught (a fusion of spirits) and what was received (a displacement)?

Follow-up experimental and cross-cultural research has led Cohen and me to argue that these spiritualists are, as Paul Bloom has suggested, naturally mind-body dualists, and further, that the most natural way of reasoning about mind-body relations is in terms of a one-mind–one-body principle: only one will or agency can direct a body at a single time. More than one person "fusing" or "merging" is too counterintuitive to be readily understood, remembered, and used consistently by the laity.[20] Consequently, they have adopted a "theologically incorrect" view of spirit possession and that view subsequently shapes their experience of being possessed and observing others being possessed.

When in a possession trance, the spiritualists assume that every action is caused by the possessing spirit and so this is indeed what they experience. Such feelings that our bodies are being manipulated by forces outside of our control is open to all of us, even when not in an altered state of consciousness. For instance, perhaps you have had a reflex reaction of moving a limb or withdrawing a hand so quickly that you did not realize what had happened until after it was over. You did not *will* to move your limb. It moved on its own. Daniel Wegner and others have documented laboratory situations in which this feeling of acting without volitional control can be induced.[21] Clearly there are times at which we act without the *experience* of being in command of our own bodies. In these spirit-possession trances, this same principle is taken to an extreme, and because the conceptual framing is that a spirit is acting on the host's body, that is precisely what they experience as happening.[22]

Much more scientific research into the cognitive dynamics of each of these areas of religious practice is needed, but research to date illustrates the potential fruitfulness of such investigations. It is often assumed that religious experience is a unique class of experiences that impose themselves upon our unsuspecting conceptual frames. To the contrary, cognitive science teaches us clearly that experiences—from the most basic emotional states to ecstatic mystical encounters with the divine—are informed and framed by our cognitive architecture. How we experience our physiological states and the world around us, including events we regard as religious, are importantly shaped by conceptual information of which we might not even be aware. Likewise, religious expression, as in ritual contexts or in personal prayer, necessarily draws upon cognitive regularities that then shape those forms of religious expression. On the flip side, religious experiences and practices, especially those conducted with great frequency or of great emotional intensity, hold the potential of reshaping our cognition, reframing how we understand subsequent events, leading us to see the hand of God erroneously, or perhaps helping us see divine action that we might otherwise have missed.

CHAPTER 8
From Natural Religion to Theology

IN THE FIRST six chapters I tried to build the case that human minds have a number of natural features that importantly shape the sorts of ideas we are likely to entertain and believe. In particular, content-specific cognitive systems, such as those responsible for reasoning about the properties and movement of physical objects, those concerned with living things, and those driven to find and reason about intentional agency help us make sense of the world we inhabit. This content-specific cognition that is critical for making sense of the world around us cooperates to make us receptive to many religious beliefs, including the existence of gods. Consequently, people the world over entertain religious beliefs and act upon these beliefs to form religions. Chapter 7 concerned some of the ways in which, similar to beliefs, natural cognition informs religious experiences and practices. For my purposes, *religion* refers to the collection of beliefs related to the existence of one or more gods, and the activities that are motivated by these beliefs.

The natural cognitive tendencies that help generate and support religious thought become elaborated in divergent ways— sometimes in ways that depart radically from the natural cognitive anchors, resulting in theologies. The cognitive dynamics surrounding this divergence is the topic of this chapter.

NATURAL RELIGION

Cognitive linguists have suggested that our natural cognitive systems inform and constrain our acquisition and use of language.[1]

Because of the anchoring effect of natural cognition, only a tiny range of the theoretically possible universe of languages is actualized. For children to pick up and use a language easily and fluently, it must be a natural language. Of course, for these same reasons, the languages we encounter are natural languages: Arabic, Cantonese, English, Hindi, and Spanish are all natural languages. If a language started deviating too far from the natural cognitive anchors, it would be pruned back to natural language. In contrast, the various computer-programming languages that have been invented are unnatural, artificial languages, for which our minds do not have any comparable receptivity, which is why they require special education and training to use, and even experts never reach the fluency of natural language.

Analogously, natural cognition creates receptivity to what might be called *natural religion*. Natural religion is the cultural expression of numerous natural tendencies that I have described in previous chapters (especially chapter 6), which encourage belief in gods and related concepts and practices. Like natural language, natural religion has an intuitive core supported by naturally occurring non-reflective beliefs. Further, as in language, religious expression that conforms closely to the parameters of natural language will be easily acquired by children (and adults), readily understood and talked about, and will tend to be widespread across individuals and cultures. But also as in language, the anchoring effect of natural religion allows for variability. As formal study of language can increase one's linguistic expression beyond what is simply natural (such as in complex linguistic constructions, extremely large vocabularies, and facility with figurative language), so too religious expression can extend beyond the most basic features of natural religion.[2] Nevertheless, knowing the features of natural religion will help explain why people tend to adopt the religious ideas and practices they do, and to anticipate challenges in changing people's religious thought and action—for instance, through theological instruction.

Natural religion is like an anchor with actual religious expression being comparable to the anchored boat. Under ordinary conditions, the boat will tend to float right above the anchor, but wind, currents, or the paddling efforts of someone in the boat could move it in various directions and distances away from the anchor. So too with religious expression: typically, religious expression will float above the anchor that is natural religion, and only deviate under culturally variable conditions, some of them particular to the environment (like wind and currents) and some of them due to special human efforts (like the paddling).

Unlike the scientific study of language, the study of natural religion remains in its infancy, but I tentatively offer some of its features that I regard as mutually supporting each other's intuitive plausibility. Research into children's acquisition of religious ideas and cross-cultural comparisons suggest that natural religion includes several assumptions or nonreflective beliefs:

1. Elements of the natural world such as rocks, trees, mountains, and animals are purposefully and intentionally designed by someone(s), who must therefore have superhuman power.[3]

2. Things happen in the world that unseen agents cause. These agents are not human or animal.[4]

3. Humans have internal components (such as a mind, soul, and/or spirit) that are distinguishable from the body.[5]

4. Moral norms are unchangeable (even by gods).[6]

5. Immoral behavior leads to misfortune; moral behavior to fortune.[7]

6. Ritualized behaviors such as marking off special spaces or ritual cleansings can protect from unseen hazards (including those caused by gods).[8]

7. Some component(s) of humans that has agency (such as souls or minds) may continue to exist without earthly bodies after death (thereby becoming ancestors or gods).[9]

8. Gods (as defined in chapter 6) exist with thoughts, wants, perspectives, and free will to act.[10]

9. Gods may be invisible and immortal, but they are not outside of space and time.[11]

10. Gods can and do interact with the natural world and people, perhaps especially those that are ancestors of the living, and hence, have an interest in the living. This interaction with the world accounts for perceived agency and purpose in the world that cannot be accounted for by human or animal activity.[12]

11. Gods generally know things that humans do not (they can be superknowing, superperceiving, or both), perhaps particularly things that are important for human social interactions.[13]

12. Gods, because of their access to relevant information and special powers, may be responsible for instances of fortune or misfortune; they can reward or punish human actions.[14]

13. Because of their superhuman power, when gods act, they act permanently, and so when they act in religious rituals, the religious ritual need not be repeated.[15]

This natural religion subsequently becomes specified, amplified, or even contradicted in particular cultural settings—what we often call *theology*—not unlike how we learn the particulars of our native language. For instance, in Christianity, Islam, and Judaism, the ideas represented in 1 and 8—that a god or gods purposefully ordered the world—are elaborated into the notion of a supreme cosmic creator. Further steps might include specifying properties of the creator, such as being nonspatial or nontemporal, or a Trinity (in Christianity, one God in three persons). Note that with each level of amplification or elaboration, these ideas often move further away from natural religion.

Another example pertains to the nature of humans and what happens after death. Natural religion grants that some component of humans can continue to exist and act after death (from 3 and 7 above). Such a notion can remain fairly vague, as was arguably the case for the ancient Hebrews. Alternatively, the nature of existence after death can be amplified into ideas about ghosts or ancestor spirits, which we see in much of the world. Patterns of reincarnation (as in Hinduism and Buddhism) or bodily resurrection (seen in strains of Judaism and in Christianity, for instance) might be less natural elaborations. Unsurprisingly, then, these would be the sorts of doctrines that excite considerable reflective specification and also disagreement.

Note that these illustrative elaborations are harder to understand and more cumbersome to express than the core supplied by natural religion. The idea of a superagent that made the world is easier to understand than the eternal, omnipresent, immaterial Trinity that Christians profess. We have reason to believe that being superknowing, superpowerful, superperceiving, and immortal are relatively natural attributes for a god. We have no such assurance that being outside of time, having no spatial location, and being able to attend to an infinite number of things simultaneously are very cognitively natural.

THEOLOGICAL CORRECTNESS

The more complex that theological ideas are—that is, the more they deviate from the ordinary cognition that undergirds natural religion—the more effort that will be required to teach them and maintain them.

Consider Muslim theologian Mohammad Zia Ullah's conception of God:

> God is infinite, pervasive, and man finite and limited to a locality. Man cannot comprehend God as he can other things.... God is without limits, without dimensions.... How can a limitless, infinite being be contained in the mind of a limited being like man?[16]

Comparably, Christian theologian Gordon Spykman, in discussing the biblical view of God, explains that God and the world are two uniquely distinct realities. The difference between them is not merely quantitative but qualitative. God is not simply more of what we are. There is an essential discontinuity, not just a share of difference, nor a gradual more-or-less distinction, as though God has only a "running head start" on us. God is absolutely sovereign, "the Other," not simply "Another."[17]

Though someone might sincerely believe that God is the unknowable, indescribable, wholly transcendent otherness that is really outside of time and existing in an infinite number of dimensions of reality, such concepts of God are difficult to use to solve problems, generate inferences, and make predictions, especially in the course of normal events—in *real-time* thinking.

Spend time around believers in God—the God with no location, no humanlike form, outside of time that many Christians, Jews, Muslims, and some Hindus affirm—and you might hear them say things like, "When I went through that ordeal, I felt like God was walking right beside me," or "Sometimes when I pray, I imagine myself embraced in God's arms." This sort of language suggests a conception of God far more humanlike and far less abstract than what theologians produce and believers affirm. These might just be relational metaphors, figures of speech meant to convey a feeling or image, but not indicative of how people *really* think about God. Nevertheless, adults—even theologically savvy ones—do not always seem to *use* these sophisticated theological concepts all the time.

To try to clarify the relationship among various conceptions of God, collaborators and I conducted several experiments. In these experiments we contrasted what adults *said* they believed about God with how they thought about God in a less reflective, real-time situation—understanding stories.[18]

Stories present a wonderful opportunity for uncovering what readers or listeners bring to the stories themselves, a means of indirectly tapping their thoughts and intuitions. The reason stories are so effective in this way is that stories are always incomplete. They have gaps that we often do not even notice. No storyteller can relay all the details in a story. Cognitive psychologists have shown that we automatically fill in the gaps in stories to the point that we actually misremember the original story as being more complete than it was. That is, we use our current knowledge to complete what was presented, leading to *intrusion errors*, remembering things as being in the story that were not actually there. For instance, in one set of experiments by Marcia Johnson and colleagues,[19] participants heard: "John was trying to fix the birdhouse. He was pounding the nail when his father came out to watch him and to help him do the work." Subsequently, a large portion of the listeners confidently agreed that the following sentence was one of the sentences they heard: "John was *using the hammer* to fix the birdhouse when his father came out to watch him and to help him do the work" (emphasis mine). Notice that in the original sentences, no hammer was mentioned. Listeners who know that nails are typically "pounded" with hammers naturally inserted the presence of a hammer in their memory of the sentences.

My collaborators and I capitalized on this tendency for the hearer to automatically fill in the gaps to create an indirect measure for people's ideas about God.[20] We constructed a number of stories that included God as a character, but we carefully left gaps for our audience to fill. For instance, one story read:

> A boy was swimming alone in a swift and rocky river. The boy got his left leg caught between two large, gray rocks and couldn't get out. Branches of trees kept bumping into him as they hurried past. He thought he was going to drown and so he began to struggle and pray. Though God was answering another prayer in another part of the world when the boy started praying, before long God responded by pushing one of the rocks so the boy could get his leg out. The boy struggled to the riverbank and fell over, exhausted.[21]

What idea of God do listeners or readers use to make sense of the story? Is it the same as what they say they believe about God?

To answer these questions, we asked memory questions after participating adults listened to the stories. To illustrate, one item read, "God had just finished answering another prayer when God helped the boy." (Was that in the story? Yes or no?) If participants understood God as someone that can attend to any number of things at once, the story is ambiguous in this regard, in which case the answer is no. God might have been continuing to answer the prayer of another *while* saving the boy. Alternatively, if thinking about God as omnipresent and able to answer any number of prayers simultaneously is too counterintuitive, then the story might be misremembered as saying that God *finished* answering the first prayer and *then* saved the boy.

Using stories and questions like these, intrusion errors revealed that our participants used a very *anthropomorphic* (humanlike) understanding of God to make sense of the stories. There is something hard about understanding the story with an all-present, all-powerful, nonanthropomorphic God. At least when trying to *use* our ideas of God in these kinds of tasks, a more humanlike concept of God seems easier, more natural.[22] Across all groups— believers or nonbelievers, Christians, Hindus, or Jews—everyone showed the same pattern of intrusion errors. They understood God as humanlike in the stories, but denied that they believed God to be humanlike in the same ways when asked directly. In the stories they incorrectly remembered God as being in one place, but when asked directly, they claimed God was everywhere or nowhere. They incorrectly remembered God as doing one thing at a time, but claimed God could do any number of things at once when asked directly. The God in the stories could be interrupted, could have vision blocked, and could fail to hear something because of competing noise. Participants explicitly denied all of these limitations on God in a direct questionnaire.

After presenting this once in a public lecture, a fellow psychologist who happened to be the wife of an Orthodox rabbi asked me, "What did you expect?" How else would people think about God under these conditions? Of course we need to use a simpler, more familiar idea of God sometimes. These experimental results demonstrate that in a sense adults might actually have two (or more) different sets of ideas about God: one set is the fancier theological set about an all-present, all-knowing, and radically different kind of being that comes up in reflective situations, and the other set is the one that looks much more like a human and is easier to use in real-time situations. That a difference between these two conceptions exists is called *theological correctness*. Like political correctness, when our intellectual guard is up, we use the ideas we know we are supposed to use—different ideas than those that come naturally. The further religious ideas deviate from natural religion, the harder they are to use in real-time situations.

Theological Incorrectness

Cognitive scientists have shown that natural, content-specific cognition can interfere with science education. Ideas in physics that run counter to natural cognition are often misunderstood or misapplied. For instance, when presented with an illustration of a ball passing through a curved tube, science-educated adults often predict that it will continue on a curved path when it leaves the tube instead of assuming a straight course, as would actually be the case.[23] Other areas of physics, biology, and psychology conflict with our natural content-specific cognition and are thereby difficult for people to learn.[24] Similarly, attempts to teach theological concepts that deviate too far from natural religion run the risk of confusion and misinterpretation. Boyer refers to this tendency as the *tragedy of the theologian*, and religion scholar Jason Slone calls it *theological incorrectness* because it is a corollary of theological correctness.[25]

Slone has described many cases of theological incorrectness

caused by the restrictive influence of natural cognition on the successful uptake of theological concepts. For instance, Buddhist reasoning about karma as a causal force is complex for solving real-life problems because of the effect of living in communities. Is a negative event the result of bad karma I have brought about, someone else has caused, or both of us, or neither of us? Slone argues that doing precise karmic calculations rapidly becomes untenable, and so Buddhists commonly degrade karma to luck.[26] Alternatively, sometimes ideas of karma from versions of Hinduism and Buddhism, which may be taught formally as an impersonal force, get reasoned about as if karma were an intentional agent. Karma likes some things and not others and acts to reward or punish.[27]

Another illustration Slone develops is how to square the status of individual free will with traditional predestination within Calvinist theology. Theologians might offer intellectual ways to bring the idea that God determines who does and does not become a Christian together with the idea that humans freely choose whether or not to accept the Gospel of Jesus Christ, but the apparent mutual incompatibility, and the counterintuitiveness of humans not being free in this regard, lead people to positions that theologians might regard as distortions.[28] These cases illustrate that while general religious thought and action have largely natural cognitive foundations, theology does not typically have anything like the same naturalness.[29]

RELIGION IS NOT THEOLOGY

CSR typically distinguishes between religious thought and theological thought. There is a difference between what people tend to believe in an automatic, day-to-day sort of way, and what they believe when they stop to reflect and systematically figure out what they do and do not believe. Some ideas, such as the particular sense in which Krishna might be Vishnu but not exactly the same, or how exactly karma works, or what precisely happens to a Mormon after death are the sorts of issues that theologians rigorously ponder and argue about in hopes of getting things right. Theologians have spent and spend enormous amounts of attention and energy on trying to work out the reasonableness of different propositions regarding God (or gods) and related matters. They draw upon historical considerations (including archaeological findings), linguistics, philosophy, textual studies, and modern science to reach their conclusions. Most individual believers do not engage in such theological exercises but are content to live religiously. To be religious is not to be a theologian or vice versa.

A similar distinction between folk ideas and formal, reflective beliefs appears in other domains. For instance, as an English speaker, you know that "The pine hates listening to Mozart" is strange but grammatical, whereas "The hates to Mozart listening pine" is nonsense. This folk language capacity, however, is distinguishable from the sorts of reflective knowledge about language that adult specialists acquire in studying language. A linguist might be able to tell us more precisely the relationship among various parts of speech in English, and why it is that the first utterance above is well formed but the second is not, and tell us about various other specialized knowledge—none of which is necessary to successfully use the English language to hold a conversation, get directions, or tell stories. Regarding language, then, we can distinguish between folk knowledge of language and linguistics.

Likewise, though developmental psychologists sometimes draw parallels between the way children learn about the natural world and the way scientists do,[30] a large difference exists between folk understandings of the natural world and scientific ones. Science, linguistics, and theology on the one hand, and folk knowledge, language, and religion on the other differ in degree of conscious reflection, effort, and commonness. The first group contains examples of relatively rarified thought that not all people engage in or care about. Because these kinds of thought take time and effort, they have not developed in all cultural contexts, let alone in all individ uals. These observations imply that you can have knowledge about the natural world, language, or religion without having much if any knowledge that might be called *science, linguistics,* or *theology.*[31]

Deviating from Natural Religion

The hard-earned theological ideas that thinkers develop tend to gravitate toward natural religion when shared with the laypeople, or even when put into real-time use by the theological experts. Aside from the just slightly or minimally counterintuitive ideas that have strong inferential potential, the more counterintuitive an idea is—the more it deviates from natural cognition and natural religion—the more special, nonuniversal resources will be necessary to successfully communicate it, for people to use it, and for it to withstand distortion and become common expertise. The special resources I refer to here are sometimes called *cultural scaffolding*— peculiar features of the cultural environment that support building ideas and practices far removed from the sure foundation of natural cognition. Cultural scaffolding works by providing memory aids such as external information storage (e.g., in writing), cues for retrieving information (e.g., illustrations, artifacts, and buildings for particular activities), or distributing responsibility for elements of ideas or complex tasks across individuals. For instance, in conducting a complex religious ceremony with several embedded rituals (such as one might find in more elaborate weddings), it might be that no one person simply remembers each component, but can re-create the complex ceremony through a combination of division of labor and reference to written or illustrated instructions.[32]

Successful theological traditions have developed just this cultural scaffolding to make complex ideas more accessible. A portion of religious activities includes teaching, preaching, or instructive components in which religious ideas are communicated. These institutionalized practices are one part of the cultural scaffolding. Likewise, the use of written texts (scripture) and sermons, common features in many religions, is the clearest example of cultural scaffolding that aid in transmitting relatively unnatural theological ideas.

Modes of Religiosity

Cognitive anthropologist Harvey Whitehouse has argued that religious communities tend to gravitate toward two strategies as options for communicating less than cognitively optimal ideas and practices,[33] and the two strategies yield religious communities with very different characteristics.[34] In the *doctrinal mode of religiosity,* heavy repetition of doctrinal material takes center stage. In the *imagistic mode of religiosity,* haunting images of pivotal ritual experiences serve as religious touchstones.

One strategy for communicating complex material is heavy repetition. Religious traditions that have weekly or even daily practices in which religious ideas are communicated have a device for helping to transmit and maintain a common body of beliefs and practices that mark out a community's members. Whitehouse calls the type of religious expression built on such repetitive communication the *doctrinal mode of religiosity.* Much of contemporary Christianity and Islam bear this profile. The doctrinal mode triggers the development of *semantic memory* (memory for the meanings of ideas) for large bodies of doctrine. Complex ideas and intricate ceremonies are scaffolded by heavy repetition and doctrinal specialists who work to maintain right doctrine and practice. The resulting religious communities tend to be bound together by common bodies of ideas and hierarchical power structures. Because having the right commitments to ideas (and related practices) mark out the religious community, the communities can be very large and the religions can spread rapidly.

In contrast, in the *imagistic mode of religiosity,* religious ideas, identities, and practices are importantly focused on rarely performed, emotionally evocative rites such as initiations, often featuring trial and trauma. As illustrated by the initiation rites of the Baktaman in New Guinea or the "sun dance" of the North American Sioux,[35] participants in rites might suffer hunger, thirst, exposure, beatings, burnings, and scarification. Whitehouse argues that whereas the doctrinal mode triggers the development of semantic memory, the rites of the imagistic mode spawn *episodic memories*: personal, auto-biographical memories about these special events that are comprised of vivid images, more than semantic content, including who were co-initiates and what they ritualistically endured. Drawing upon regular psychological dynamics, Whitehouse argues that survivors of such rites are haunted by the images of the event, prompting them to spontaneous exegetical reflection about the meaning of the event. This deep thinking, over the course of a lifetime, can produce highly counterintuitive ideas that would have been difficult to communicate through direct verbal teaching. Convergence in thus produced "revelations" would be difficult to achieve as each individual produces their own meanings. Identification with the group, then, arises not through a common body of shared doctrines but through having gone through a similar trial and having reflections on the same images. Participants in these rites feel a deep sense of identification with their co-initiates.[36] Because they have relational bonds by common rites, such religious traditions tend to be relatively small and spread slowly, if at all. As doctrinal policing is unnecessary for community coherence, religions characterized by the imagistic mode tend to be nonhierarchical.[37]

Using Context Biases

What we learn through testimony or through behavioral imitation is importantly influenced by social context biases. We model our thought and behaviors on others based upon what we perceive most others to think and do (conformity bias), favor prestigious individuals for role models (prestige bias), and prefer to ape those whom we see as similar to ourselves or whom we want to be (similarity bias). We would expect these dynamics to be operable in religious and theological communication as well. People will be more inclined to invest in the counterintuitive, nonnatural ideas that appear to be embraced by most others, and particularly those of prestigious individuals they regard as similar to themselves in important ways.

These observations suggest that the common practice in Christian circles, for instance, of using charismatic young adults to teach their youth in groups is strategically sensible. Teens are likely to regard such youth leaders as people they want to be like (similarity), and to credit their greater maturity and position of authority with at least some prestige. The group education environment can capitalize on conformity biases. In contrast, missionization efforts in which a nonprestigious layperson is sent into a foreign culture (little similarity) and try to convert people away from consensus religious ideas and practices will likely face greater challenges. A project for *missiologists* (those who study missions and their methods) would be to harvest such insights from cognitive science for practical applications, and in turn, put cognitive science to use in testing existing methods. Perhaps missiologists, conversely, have insights that will improve the knowledge base in cognitive science.

BUILDING ON CONTENT BIASES

Some theological ideas will always be a struggle to maintain, as they are difficult, massively counterintuitive ideas. For instance, Buddhism's highest "sphere of existence," the sphere of formlessness, with its levels of "infinite consciousness" and "neither perception nor nonperception" will always be difficult ideas to communicate, grasp, and use.[38] Those ideas and practices that build closely upon natural religion and avoid ideas that are too counterintuitive, lacking inferential potential, or unable to make sense of common concerns of humans will have more likelihood of successful communication and use. Theological ideas that help interpret experiences of agency detection for which humans or animals are not the apparent cause (HADD experiences), explain the perceived order and purpose in the world around, interpret striking fortune and misfortune, bear upon moral evaluations and judgments, and can help make sense of human death and the afterlife, stand on better footing than esoteric concerns.

That some theological ideas deviate from natural religion and will be relatively difficult to transmit does not mean necessarily that the theological ideas are not valuable or true. A more thorough treatment of the possible relationship between cognitive science and doing theology is the topic of the final chapter.

CHAPTER 9
Cognitive Science and Natural Theology

ONE DAY AFTER LUNCH I was having coffee in my Oxford college's senior common room, and a theologian friend challenged me about this book: "What have I been missing all my life? What does cognitive science have to tell me that I desperately need to know as a theologian?" My short answer is this: cognitive science is rapidly gaining prominence in shaping how people think about themselves and the world, and the theologian who ignores it voluntarily surrenders a useful tool for her scholarly or pastoral vocation, and risks limiting her relevance to the contemporary world. As cosmologist and Catholic priest Michael Heller writes concerning the sciences generally, sciences (in part) shape prevailing images of the world and theologians remain ignorant of them at their peril:

> First, speaking and thinking within a certain image of the world is unavoidable. The world image is present in the entire cultural climate and intellectual atmosphere of the epoch, and because theology is a part of this climate and this atmosphere, it cannot avoid speaking and thinking in terms of the current world image. . . . Second, if a theologian avoids using the actual image of the world, he very often implicitly makes use of an ancient outdated picture of it. . . . Third, if a theologian uses the outdated world image (openly or implicitly), his pastoral efficiency is very limited.[1]

Heller's argument might be overstated when it comes to some relatively narrow areas of science that do not have broad reach into fundamental human concerns or life's big questions. Cognitive science is by no means one of these sciences.

In this final chapter I attempt to make clearer where some fruitful connections between cognitive science and theology lie. This is necessarily only a brief sampling, a shopwindow for possibilities within. My presentation is organized by two chief ways in which the sciences (broadly) have been brought into contact with theology, what I am calling *universal natural theology* and *confessional natural theology*.

Traditionally, *natural theology* is the attempt to use reason, self-evident truths, and evidence from the natural world to say something about gods or the transcendent, such as to demonstrate that God exists, and to demonstrate what properties God has. Special revelation, via prophecy or scripture, is out-of-bounds for this kind of natural theology because its grand vision is to produce strong reasons for theistic belief that all rational people *universally* would be inclined to accept.[2] Cognitive science—and particularly the cognitive science of religion—only bears indirectly on this *universal natural theology*. I will sketch some connections in the first part of this chapter.

An alternative, more contemporary version of natural theology, *confessional natural theology*, begins with some basic theological premises from a particular theological tradition already in hand, and then uses reason and insights from the naturalistic study of the world to augment, amplify, or disambiguate those theological premises. For instance, one might begin with the idea that there exists at least one god, and accept a body of special revelation about that god (such as a collection of scriptures), but then use scientific and philosophical tools to add precision and breadth to those "revealed" insights. For instance, arguing for a Christian natural theology, Alister McGrath writes:

Contrary to the Enlightenment's aspirations for a universal natural theology, based on common human reason and experience of nature, we hold that a Christian natural theology is grounded in and informed by a characteristic Christian theological foundation. A Christian understanding of nature is the intellectual prerequisite for a natural theology which discloses the Christian God.[3]

COGNITIVE SCIENCE AND UNIVERSAL NATURAL THEOLOGY

The most basic way in which cognitive science might matter to universal natural theology is if it produces results that make religious beliefs suspect or untenable. Some scientists regard this as already the case. Richard Dawkins, representatively, muses: "One especially intriguing possibility mentioned by [Daniel] Dennett is that the irrationality of religion is a byproduct of a particular built-in irrationality mechanism in the brain."[4] By showing the ignoble, nondivine, natural origins of religious belief, one has (allegedly) shown that belief in God is irrational. Likewise, Jesse Bering, a cognitive scientist of religion, writes:

So it would appear that having a theory of mind was so useful for our ancestors in explaining and predicting other people's behaviors that it has completely flooded our evolved social brains. . . . What if I were to tell you that God's mental states, too, were all in your mind? That God . . . was in fact a psychological illusion, a sort of evolved blemish etched onto the core cognitive substrate of your brain? It may feel as if there is something grander out there . . . watching, knowing, caring. Perhaps even judging. But, in fact, that's just your overactive theory of mind. In reality, there is only the air you breathe.[5]

Are Dawkins and Bering correct? Is cognitive science a threat to theological beliefs?

Is Cognitive Science a Threat to Theological Claims?

If we want to know whether findings from cognitive science are irreconcilable with any and all theological claims, the answer appears to be no. Philosophers have begun to consider such matters,[6] and though it is early days, the growing consensus does not side with such a blanket rejection of the existence of gods and other religious ideas. From my brief presentations in earlier chapters, I hope it is not hard to see why.

Compare the specific cognitive systems that encourage religious beliefs to a radio. A group of people is on an island with the radio. Sometimes transient, nonobvious signals get detected and processed to reveal to some possessors of the radio that there is an unseen, intelligent, intentional being out there somewhere causing the signals. Some people use the radio but haven't formed the belief that someone is out there. Perhaps they did not tune the radio properly or there was some environmental interference jumbling the message reception. Maybe the transmitter isn't "out there" but is hidden on the island, and the people are just catching snippets of their own speech. Or maybe the transmitter "out there" is running a recording of someone long since gone. In any case, discovering how the radio works does not matter to whether there really is an unseen someone "out there" broadcasting. Maybe there is, and maybe there isn't. Similarly, it is not obvious that specifying the cognitive equipment relevant for forming beliefs in gods, souls, the afterlife, and other religious concepts importantly impacts whether one is justified in holding such beliefs.

Likewise, consider a species of blind bat.[7] Their perceptual systems were tuned by natural selection to detect flying insects, prevent midair collisions with each other, avoid trees and other obstacles, and find places to sleep. Hence, humans might be only marginally apparent in their world, perhaps as some kind of awesome and terrifying giant insects with superbat powers to build trees and mountains, and wantonly kill bats. Some of these bats could "believe in" the existence of humans, whereas others regard humans as nothing more than small trees or shrubs, large insects with no special properties, or as illusions. Suppose these bats were to discover how their perceptual systems worked, without reference to the actual existence of humans. Perhaps they discovered that their perceptual systems sometimes provide them with automatic, non-reflective beliefs that then become reflective beliefs (unless good reasons arise not to reflectively accept them), *and* that their perceptual systems were tuned by natural selection to err on the side of insect detection. As a result, things that seem to move about on their own can trigger the "hypersensitive insect detection device." Their cognitive systems were not "designed" for detecting humans, but for detecting insects, obstacles, and other bats. With better understanding of their cognitive equipment, would the bats have good reason to question their beliefs that humans exist? Clearly not.

A scientific explanation of how human cognitive systems form beliefs in gods only "explains away" gods if you already believe they don't exist. For believers, such explanations just specify the means by which actual gods are perceived and understood (or misunderstood).

Findings from cognitive science would be much more troubling for religious beliefs (or any other types of beliefs about things in the world) if they bore no connection to the external world. It is difficult to justify belief in purple bunnies on a planet somewhere in another universe when you have absolutely no access to information relevant to the purple bunnies' existence. Such is not the case here. People do have access to information about the features and happenings of the world and use these as part of the process that arrives at the existence of gods. If conditions in the world were different, we might expect beliefs to be different.

Beliefs about gods, souls, and the rest would likewise be more suspect if it were discovered that *no matter* the information available, the mind used it to arrive deterministically at such beliefs. If 100 percent of humans believed in the existence of an immortal human soul, for instance, and cognitive science was able to demonstrate that we have cognitive systems that unswervingly make us believe in immortal souls, then we might have reason to doubt their actual existence. We might not be right in saying there are definitely *not* immortal souls, but only that our reason for believing in them (namely our strong intuition produced by cognitive mechanisms) would be seriously damaged: the causal connection between actual immortal souls and our beliefs in them would be suspect. Even if things were different in the world, our cognition would bully us into belief. Ironically, then, the fact that no religious belief is completely universal and uncontroversial affords religious beliefs some protection from being "explained away" by cognitive science.

The apparent immunity of core religious ideas from being undercut by cognitive science does not apply to all specific theological claims.[8] Suppose a theology taught that human minds have boundless potential and are fully shaped by their social environments. Or suppose a theology argued that a sense of what is right and wrong is only accessible through undergoing a special childhood ritual. Theologies often contain claims about the nature of human thought, moral sensibilities, and the like. Many of these are empirical claims that fall in the domain of cognitive science and are, hence, open to empirical challenges. To illustrate, in some meditative traditions, introspection is given privileged status as a reliable way to access the inner workings of the human mind. This position is difficult (though perhaps not impossible) to reconcile with research from cognitive science that shows the limited or even misleading character of introspection—we typically have rather poor access to our own minds, one reason for the emergence of psychological science.[9] Likewise, a theology that teaches that people have no natural ideas about the divine but are fully dependent upon special revelation or theological teaching would seem to be imperiled by findings from the cognitive science of religion.[10] The flipside is that some theological claims, such as that humans naturally share a set of moral intuitions or some hazy sense of the divine (or *sensus divinitatis*), would gain qualified support from cognitive science, a point returned to below in relation to confessional natural theology. A theological understanding of humans, or *theological anthropology*, needs to square with facts revealed by the human sciences, including cognitive science.[11]

Compatibility of Cognitive Science and Theism

Perhaps the greatest promise for cognitive science to support universal natural theology is regarding arguments from internal coherence or compatibility: can a set of theological claims and the findings from cognitive science be true at the same time? Like any other scientific findings, those from cognitive science might be more compatible with a theistic worldview than a nontheistic worldview or vice versa. Findings from cosmology that suggest "fine-tuning" of the universe or from biology that suggest "convergent evolution" (i.e., that evolution appears to naturally gravitate toward some arrangements over others) might be more compatible with theism than with atheism.[12] Similarly, it could be that some findings from cognitive science are more compatible with theism or with atheism.

One great debate in the science-religion area is whether evolution by natural selection is a challenge for theism, supports theism, or is neutral. For instance, philosopher Alvin Plantinga has argued that the probability of our minds being reliable for producing true beliefs is *lower* given natural selection with no God, than natural selection with God.[13] Further, he argues that given the ordinary dynamics of natural selection in a world lacking God, the probability of having a reliable mind is either quite low or is impossible to evaluate. In either case, one is not justified in regarding one's own mind as reliable and so should not even trust it when it delivers ideas such as "There is no God" and "Evolution by natural selection is true." If Plantinga is correct, the conjunction of natural selection and atheism is self-defeating. God, however, could have designed the world such that natural selection produced in us reliable minds. In this way, Plantinga sees natural selection as more compatible with a god than with complete atheism.

I raise Plantinga's particular argument because it concerns not just the compatibility of evolution and God, but of evolved *minds*—belief-forming systems—and God. Plantinga's argument depends upon a disconnect between the activities of the belief-formation activities of minds and physical actions relevant to survival, an important issue at the nexus of evolution and cognitive science: to what degree do survival and reproduction depend upon true reflective beliefs? Standardly, natural selection is "blind" to beliefs. If you behave in a way that makes you successfully survive and reproduce, it does not matter if you have true beliefs about the composition of stars, how to factor a quadratic equation, or whether or not humans have souls. Less exotically, every day in your back garden millions of animals—from nematodes to spiders and slugs—are successfully surviving and reproducing without having reflective beliefs at all, let alone *true* reflective beliefs.

But isn't it the case that because human's actions *are* dependent upon their reflective beliefs, natural selection does "care" what we believe? Plantinga argues that we have no such guarantee from *atheistic* natural selection, and to make his case he hints toward cognitive science. Some cognitive scientists argue that our beliefs do not cause actions, but that our actions and our corresponding beliefs are both caused by brain activity. Beliefs don't cause anything. Plantinga writes:

> And the same can be said for conscious belief: if "behavior, however complex, is governed entirely by biochemistry," there seems to be no room for conscious belief to become involved in the causal story, . . . it will be causally inert. Furthermore, if this possibility were, in fact, actual, then evolution would not have been able to mold and

shape our beliefs, or belief-producing structures, weed-
ing out falsehood and encouraging truth; for our beliefs
would be, so to speak, *invisible* to evolution. Which
beliefs (if any) an organism had under this scenario
would be merely accidental as far as evolution is concerned. It wouldn't make any difference to behavior or
fitness what beliefs our cognitive mechanisms had produced because (under this scenario) those beliefs play
no role in the production or explanation of behavior.[14]

Whether adaptive actions do entail true (or even approximately
true) beliefs is in part an empirical matter for which the cognitive
sciences might weigh in.[15]

For instance, let's suppose that research in cognitive science does
provide evidence to suspect that humans do not consistently have
free will to control their actions, including their mental actions.
Rather, what we experience as conscious will is a correlate of brain
activity that actually causes the thought or action in question.[16]
Such findings appear pertinent to Plantinga's argument. If our conscious beliefs do not cause actions (or at least, many do not and we
do not know which ones do and do not), on what basis do we have
confidence that we can have true beliefs? Certainly we would not
be able to trust them on the pragmatic basis of their having successfully motivated useful or adaptive action. If natural selection cannot help give us confidence in our beliefs, a god might be needed to
serve as guarantor for the reliability of our conscious states: we can
trust them because their ultimate source is rational and has made
us to have generally trustworthy faculties. Perhaps, then {theism +
the illusion of conscious free will + justified true beliefs} is a more
coherent set of beliefs than {materialism + the illusion of conscious
free will + justified true beliefs}.[17]

Similarly, cognitive science suggests that because of processing limitations, we must inevitably make some mistakes of perception, thought, and judgment. Hence, human minds are tuned

through selective pressure to avoid some kinds of costly errors at the expense of making less costly errors. This balance is termed *error management*.[18] The fact that natural selection has resulted in minds that make systematic errors appears to undermine our confidence in our minds as reliable for both theists and atheists. But error management also serves to demonstrate that the connection between true beliefs and adaptive behavior is far from straightforward: sometimes false beliefs lead to more adaptive behaviors than true beliefs. These findings also might fortify Plantiga's argument for the relatively better coherence of natural selection, God, and reliable minds versus natural selection, no-God, and reliable minds.[19]

Shifting the Burden of Proof

In previous chapters I demonstrated sympathy with the epistemological stance of Thomas Reid and his followers in the school known as reformed epistemology. In answering Enlightenment skepticism, Reid argued that the automatic deliverances of our cognitive faculties—not just our reasoning faculty—should be given the benefit of the doubt, and their deliverances should be treated as true and justified until sufficient reasons mounted to supplant them. That is, instead of providing proof or evidence for every belief before holding it, beliefs produced automatically by our cognitive faculties—those reflective beliefs that are simply adapted nonreflective beliefs—are justified until being sufficiently challenged.[20] I find Reid's epistemology attractive because it preserves ordinary, commonsense trust of our minds, *and* because Reid anticipated how minds really work. We do automatically form beliefs through the deliverances of our cognitive faculties—independent of conscious reasoning—and we really do automatically regard such beliefs as true (under typical conditions). As Reid argued, it is impossible to *not* do so consistently, and so we cannot be obliged to do so. Reid only did not know just how content-rich our natural cognition is.

If one adopts such a Reidian commonsense stance, a consequence is that discovering the content of nonreflective beliefs might shift the burden of proof in some disagreements. If our ordinary, natural cognitive systems provide us with nonreflective beliefs along the lines of natural religion (see chapter 8), then, until reasons arise that we should regard these beliefs as suspect, they are justified beliefs. It is for the opponent to show that there is a considerable probability that they are false and not for the possessor to first show that they are true. These justified beliefs, then, appear to be those listed on pages 132–33.

I emphasize that I am *not* saying that cognitive science shows that natural religion *is* true or that cognitive science, by itself, justifies holding natural religion as true. Rather, cognitive science (particularly, CSR) *plus* a particular epistemology justifies holding natural religion as true *until* problems with these beliefs are demonstrated—and simply identifying a natural cause for them is insufficient.

Note too that this changing burden of proof does not only fall upon antitheists or those who wish to dissuade others from religious beliefs, but also on apologists, reformers, and theologians wishing to advance alternatives to natural religion. Their less natural, more reasoned theologies do not automatically enjoy the presumption of "innocent until proven guilty" because they are not (necessarily) closely tied to the automatic deliverances of our cognitive systems. Believing that some kind of god exists might be automatically justified, but believing in a specific theologically enhanced god (such as Allah, Diyoos, or Shiva) would require additional justification.

Cosmological Arguments for a Creator

Traditional natural theology has produced many arguments in support of the existence of some kind of god. One class with a very long pedigree is cosmological arguments, those that infer the existence of a creator God from the existence of the cosmos. Cosmological arguments are variations on the following:

: All contingent (not necessary) entities have causes.

: The universe is one such entity.

: Therefore, it has a cause.

: The cause must be an uncaused (necessary) entity that could plausibly bring about the existence of the universe.

: That entity is called God.

For such an argument to be compelling, we need to believe that the universe is sufficiently like other entities that, like baby chickens or lampshades, it too needs a cause to explain its existence, and a god of some sort is such a satisfactory cause.

Though subjected to criticisms throughout the centuries, cosmological arguments have not disappeared. Why not? Philosophers Johan De Smedt and Helen De Cruz argue that cosmological arguments are intuitively appealing because they build upon natural cognition. After surveying relevant research with babies, young children, and adults, they summarize:

> It seems that the causal reasoning that lies at the basis of the cosmological argument is *not* an arbitrary act of the mind, but rather a way of reasoning that is both obvious and intuitive to humans: we readily infer generative causes for events, we routinely deal with unique states of affairs, we habitually infer unobservable causal mechanisms, and we have a preference for deterministic causes.[21]

Further, De Smedt and De Cruz observe that because theistic cosmological arguments try to take you from the universe having a cause to the cause being God (an intentional agent or person), for these arguments to be persuasive, people need to have the intuition that intentional agents are reasonable efficient causes. Here too cognitive science provides relevant evidence for just these intuitions. Even thirteen-month-olds appear to regard an intentional agent (one that does not resemble a human or animal) as capable of bringing about order, whereas a similar nonagent is not capable. Babies look longer (as if surprised) when a rolling ball appears to neatly stack a heap of blocks compared with when the ball turns the neat stack into a jumble. When the ball has eyes and a mouth on it and scoots toward the blocks (like an agent) instead of rolling, then babies do not regard the two events differently.[22]

We naturally regard agents as good causes for perceived order or purpose, and appear to have the causal reasoning tools to regard the universe as the sort of thing in need of a causal explanation. Add to these natural tendencies the observed propensity to believe in at least one god, and cosmological arguments have an intuitive ring about them. According to De Smedt and De Cruz, this intuitiveness supports judgments of internal coherence: the idea of a God is a satisfying explanation for the existence of the cosmos.

Interestingly, if one adopts a Reidian epistemology, the conclusions we can draw from De Smedt and De Cruz's analysis might be stronger still. If, as De Smedt and De Cruz argue, all of the relevant intuitions for cosmological arguments are automatic deliverances of our cognitive equipment, we should extend to them the benefit of the doubt. These intuitions have a high *prima facie* probability of being true. The burden of proof is on those wishing to reject the intuitions. Hence, critics of cosmological arguments must do more than assert that they see no reason why the universe needs a cause, or even offer an alternative causal explanation for the universe's origin. They need to offer arguments that sufficiently unseat the natural intuitions that it both needs a cause and that a god is a satisfying cause.[23]

Teleological Arguments

I have presented De Smedt and De Cruz's treatment of cosmological arguments at some length because similar considerations apply to teleological arguments for the existence of a god. *Teleological arguments* or arguments from design begin with the observation that the natural world appears orderly or designed and infers

a designer to account for this perceived design. Like the cosmological argument, teleological arguments have a long pedigree and
still receive attention. From the discussion above, it should be evident why. We naturally possess intuitions that the world is ram-
pant with apparent order, design, and purpose, and that an agent
(or agents) best account for this order, design, and purpose. The
ability to account for much of this perceived design by appeal to
natural selection does not completely remove the intuitive appeal
of teleological arguments because the apparent design extends to
nonbiological features of the world and cosmos, and to processes—
such as natural selection itself—that are invoked in the sciences as
explanatory mechanisms.[24]

As with cosmological arguments, if one adopts a Reidian epistemology, the key premises of a teleological argument receive the
benefit of the doubt and are granted high credence (before other
considerations). That the natural world evinces design, that an
agent is the most reasonable cause for the design, and that a god
is a good candidate for this role do not require more evidence to
be rationally accepted. Instead, sufficient evidence is needed to
uproot such intuitions.

On the Persuasiveness of Religious Arguments

One of the failures of universal natural theology has been its inability to persuade. Those arguing against theism seem to be unable
to move theists, and vice versa. Philosopher Jennifer Faust has
recently argued that this failure to persuade is because people
come to such arguments already inclined to believe the conclusion
(for or against a god), and consequently assign accordingly low or
high credence to one or more premises.[25] If I already am inclined
to believe there is a creator God, I think an assertion such as "The
apparent design in the natural world requires a designer" is a good
premise. If I am inclined to believe there is no god, then I regard as
implausible a premise such as "The cause of the universe is a person." In a sense, theists and nontheists automatically (and perhaps

unconsciously) "put their thumb on the scale" when evaluating such arguments.

If Faust has captured the psychology of arguments from universal natural theology well, then I offer a friendly amendment based on the findings from CSR and their applications to cosmological and teleological arguments: it is only nontheists who adjust the credence of the key premises in these arguments to better accord with the desired conclusion. That is, nontheists try to support their belief that a god does not exist by presuming the premises in such arguments (e.g., that the universe requires a sufficient cause) are weak; whereas theists are apt to simply maintain the higher truth probabilities delivered by natural cognition. If, as De Smedt and De Cruz argue, the pivotal premises jibe with natural cognition, then initially regarding them with high credence is the default stance, and an open-minded, noncommitted person will tend to regard them as sensible. It is the nontheist, then, who has changed the default judgments on these premises (perhaps for good reasons, perhaps not). If these observations are correct, it follows that theists find these arguments persuasive because of natural dispositions—in a sense, they *are* persuasive—but nontheists find them unconvincing because they have already reached an alternative conclusion.[26]

COGNITIVE SCIENCE AND CONFESSIONAL NATURAL THEOLOGY

Confessional natural theology can be understood as an attempt to augment, disambiguate, and amplify theological claims of a given religious tradition by consideration of facts gleaned from the natural world, particularly the sciences.[27] Like other sciences, cognitive science provides insights about the natural world. Unlike most other sciences that have been fodder for confessional natural theology, cognitive science also bears upon human nature and how humans form religious beliefs themselves. For this reason, cognitive science possesses great promise to have a broad impact on confessional natural theology. The limits are only the current state of the art and the creativity of scholars.

In the previous chapter I offered some suggestions for using cognitive science to inform the successful transmission of theological ideas. Here I offer a brief sampling of various other areas in which cognitive science generally, and CSR in particular, could contribute to new and existing questions in theology.

On the Nature of Humans

CSR provides evidence that humans have natural propensities toward believing in some kind of god. A rudimentary sense of the divine, called a *sensus divinitatis* in Calvinist theology, appears to be not only natural but early developing.[28] But such a notion, that children have receptivity to thinking about the divine, appears in many theological traditions. In Islam, children are regarded as born with some kind of belief in Allah. In Hinduism, children can have better understanding of Brahman than adults because they have been with the divine more recently and have not yet been corrupted by the world. CSR provides support for the basic thrust of these related theological notions, but perhaps CSR could also help determine which of the competing conceptions of this natural *sensus divinitatis* is likely to be accurate.

For instance, in the Calvinist tradition within Christianity alone, at least two different views have been prominently defended: John Calvin's and Alvin Plantinga's.[29] Calvin's *sensus divinitatis* is divinely "implanted in all men" (I. iii. 1), and the conviction that there is some god "is naturally inborn in us all, and is fixed deep within, as it were in the very marrow" (I. iii. 3).[30] Though in all of us, it only yields an inchoate sense of God. Plantinga's conception, however, is more of a disposition to be convicted of God's existence in certain widely realized situations such as beholding the awesome beauty of a sunset, or feeling humbled by an act of forgiveness.[31] Who is right? So far, evidence can be marshaled for and against aspects of both perspectives. Additional research, guided by postulated models of the *sensus divinitatis* from Calvinism and comparable constructs from other religious traditions, could help resolve these sorts of disagreements.

Similarly, it is not uncommon for theologies to comment on the condition of people's natural access to moral truths. Due to biblical passages such as Romans 2, Christians commonly regard everyone—regardless of culture—as having some access to genuine morality:

> Indeed, when Gentiles [non-Jews], who do not have the law, do by nature things required by the law, they are a law for themselves, even though they do not have the law. They show that the requirements of the law are written on their hearts, their consciences also bearing witness, and their thoughts sometimes accusing them and at other times even defending them. (Rom. 2:14–15, NIV)

As suggested in chapter 5, such claims have great potential to be substantiated and amplified by cognitive science. What moral intuitions do humans have in common? We might also wonder about the evolution and development of moral intuitions. When did they arise in our ancestry? When do they appear in children? At stake could be the species and age boundaries of moral culpability.

On Revelation

Suppose you are a god and you want to reveal yourself—your properties, character, and will—to humans. Suppose that some of your properties will be difficult for humans to understand or even be ineffable at points. The whole truth would be more challenging for humans to understand than quantum physics, advanced calculus, and neuroscience all rolled into one. Then how do you reveal yourself?

One strategy would be to stick to the essentials, particularly early in human evolution, and only reveal complex ideas when people have the cultural scaffolding available to support the comprehension, use, and transmission of these difficult ideas. From such a strategy we would expect to see cumulative revelation throughout the ages, not because the god is changing or what the god wants to reveal is necessarily changing. Rather, when humans could produce symbolic artifacts, they could use these as memory aids and cognitive prosthetics, enabling them to grasp and use more complex ideas. As writing systems, mathematical systems, and specialist schools of study developed, even more capacity for shared sophisticated ideas became possible.

These thoughts concerning revelation are not new observations. What cognitive science adds is firmer criteria for what counts as complex—for any normal human regardless of culture—and what kinds of ideas can be encouraged by what kinds of cultural scaffolding. The implication for theologians interested in the nature of revelation and theological development is that cognitive science has resources for both explaining patterns of theological development in the past (by appeal to cognitive structures interacting with forms of cultural scaffolding as they appeared), and predicting where theological thought might be going in the future.

Concerning Scripture

Scriptures and their use play a prominent role in literate religious traditions. Scripture is regarded as an act of communication: either from prophets or historians to a people long ago, or a message from God or an enlightened teacher to people at all times. As communication, scripture might be profitably understood by cognitive scientific approaches to communication. One such approach is Dan Sperber and Deirdre Wilson's *relevance theory*.

The theory draws its name from a central principle, the principle of relevance. In a communicative exchange, people expect *relevance*: that what is being communicated consists of information that is worth processing, that I can use. Relevance has degrees that may be described in terms of a cost-benefit relationship. The most *relevant* propositions in a given discourse are those that (1) have the greatest cognitive impact in the context, and (2) are the easiest to process. In Sperber and Wilson's words, relevance is geared to "the processing of information which is likely to bring about the greatest contribution to the mind's general cognitive goals at the smallest processing cost."[32] If a communicator fails to deliver information at a fair cognitive cost for the degree of cognitive impact, we will find the exchange frustrating, as when someone rabbits on without getting to the point, or when the amount of new and useful information is much less valuable than the time and energy required to extract the information.

Applying such insights to scripture, we might expect (in general) that canonical texts are those that, for one reason or another, had or continue to have high relevance. As anthropologist Brian Malley has noted in his application of relevance theory to Bible use, however, the authorship of and special authority afforded scriptures elevate the expectation of cognitive impact, making readers more willing to invest cognitive resources. We would therefore expect scriptures to be read very differently—slower, with more pauses and rereading of sections—than comparable nonsacred texts.[33] We might expect too that favorite passages are predictable based on relevance calculations including how cultural context, personal situation, and expertise might change the relevance calculus.

Further, interpretation practices could be impacted by relevance dynamics. For instance, passages that require considerable investment may be regarded as having more valuable information (cognitive impact) than a simpler presentation of the same content—an instance of dissonance reduction.[34] (It must have been difficult for a reason. . . . Ah, it contains profound truths!) Distortions in interpretation would tend to be in the direction of improving the relevance of the passage—either by finding more meaning than was actually communicated, or by opting for a simple interpretation that reduced cognitive load. Of course, these are only informed speculations and the application of cognitive science to uses of scripture has just begun, principally in the area of solving translation problems.[35]

Religious Teaching

In contrast to natural religion, the complex theological belief systems we see today are relatively difficult to understand and embrace. Consequently, theology must be explicitly taught. As teaching is a form of communication, we can address it using relevance theory of communication. Combining relevance theory with observations from chapter 8 concerning transmitting theological ideas produces a ready prediction: theological ideas that deviate too greatly from natural religion will require greater cognitive investment, and so if the cognitive payoff is not perceived as sufficient for the investment, the communication will tend to fail. Teaching relatively unnatural, massively counterintuitive ideas will require additional cultural scaffolding to reduce the cognitive cost; and the return on the investment needs to be clear and substantial.

As I discuss at greater length elsewhere, cognitive science can already begin suggesting effective strategies for cultivating religious thought and practice in children, building upon their natural propensities.[36] Children might be more receptive to ideas about divine attributes such as being superknowing, superpowerful, and immortal than is often supposed, but religious teachings need to be useful for children (and adults) to make sense of their experiences and be connected in practical ways to day-to-day thinking and acting, instead of cloistered away in special places, on special days, and regarding special topics.

On Decision-Making in Religious Leadership

Religious leaders often have to make decisions about the focus, organization, and officially orchestrated actions of their communities. Leaders have to decide what places of worship will look like, how rituals will be conducted, and what teachings need center stage. Making such decisions will partly be based on theological reflections, precedence, and wisdom gleaned through experience. Often these decisions require some appreciation of the psychology of the people involved. If we hang that painting, how will it make people feel? If the worship service has this element, how will it change what people think about? CSR provides tools for making better-informed decisions.

For instance, due to the spread of swine flu, in the summer of 2009 the Archbishops of Canterbury and York recommended that Anglicans no longer share a common cup for observing Holy Communion for fear of spreading the illness. Apparently recognizing the potential unpopularity of such a suggestion, alternative arrangements were offered for those insistent upon taking both the bread and the wine: a priest (with sanitized hands) would dip a wafer in the chalice before handing it to those taking communion.[37] In discussing this arrangement with churchgoers, many I spoke to regarded the idea of "semicommunion" as offensive—no matter that in other times and places wine was withheld from the masses. Historical or theological justification does not necessarily trump people's intuitions and, hence, their experience of a ritual observance. A scientifically informed understanding of the relevant human cognition in these situations could help religious leaders anticipate the reaction of laity and plan accordingly.

Similarly, a student studying anthropology in my department at Oxford was a West African Catholic priest concerned with the desire of some West African Roman Catholics to substitute millet bread and millet beer for wheat or barley bread and wine in Holy Communion. One consideration in this case was how people regarded this central ritual and the possible substitution: an empirical, cognitive question. How people understand their religious practices and react to proposed changes and substitutions certainly falls within the purview of CSR,[38] and findings could help religious leaders make judicious decisions in cases such as these. Based on cognitive considerations, McCauley and Lawson predict under what conditions changing elements of religious rituals (e.g., substituting sand for water in a ritual cleansing) will tend to be regarded as changing or not changing the meaning of the ritual. In such a central ritual as Holy Communion—central because of the immediacy of God in the elements—it is unsurprising that a substitution would be resisted. To allow a substitution would be to change the body and blood of Jesus. In this case, cognitive considerations converged with the Vatican's stance.

Cognitive scientists of religion, working collaboratively with theologians, might produce findings relevant to other matters of practice. For instance, McCauley and Lawson have argued, based on cognitive considerations and case studies, that religious communities with an imbalance of ritual types (especially not enough emotional, high-pageantry, special agent rituals) will struggle to maintain motivation and run the risk of being outcompeted by other religious groups.[39] Perhaps downplaying traditional rites of passage, which are typically special agent rituals, has negative motivational consequences for religious individuals and communities.

As with many of these topics sketched above, many possible ways in which religious leaders and communities could make use of cognitive science (and CSR in particular) have not yet been explored. A closer relationship between scientists and religious communities could put religious leaders on safer footing when it comes to making decisions that will have psychological and social consequences.

Conclusion

Contrary to what scientific triumphalists boast, science has no monopoly on knowledge or truth. Nevertheless, modern science has proven itself a fruitful means of gaining new insights about the empirical world, including human thought and behavior. Cognitive science—the science of the mind, stretching from cognitive neuroscience and computer science to philosophy of mind—is an exciting new science that dives into some of life's big questions such as the nature of humans; the relationship between minds and bodies; whether we have free will; why we think; feel, and experience what we do; and how our minds accommodate thinking about the divine. Cognitive science is growing in shaping how people understand the world—particularly the human world. The theologian who fails to appreciate the contributions of cognitive science will rapidly find himself or herself trafficking in outmoded ways of thinking and unable to connect with the concerns of contemporary audiences. Such a theologian will also self-impose an unnecessarily scholarly handicap.

The challenge for the theologian, then, quoting Heller is to "responsibly discern what . . . comes from a solid theory, what forms a scientific hypothesis, and what is an element of a current intellectual fashion rather than that of science. Of course, this puts a heavy burden on the theologian. . . ."[40] I hope this book has helped lighten this burden by providing an introduction to reasonably reliable findings and guideposts for promising engagement.

This treatment of the connections among cognitive science, religion, and theology might seem like a mere tease. Certainly, many more and more rigorous and sophisticated connections could be made. As I warned at the beginning of this book, this short book is something of an invitation to the area, a challenge for others to build upon what I have presented here. Collaborations among cognitive scientists of all flavors (anthropologists, computer scientists, linguists, philosophers, and psychologists) with religion and theology scholars will be needed to actualize the potential of this area. It is not just theologians who can learn from cognitive science, but theologians can help guide cognitive science into important new problems and challenge hasty and facile conclusions about what such sciences explain or explain away.

Hopefully, if I have done my job, I have provided enough of an introduction that readers not previously familiar with cognitive science can see the promise of this scientific area for elucidating problems in the study of religion, help account for the recurrence and resilience of religion that we see today, and provide practical tools for religious leaders and teachers, as well as adding new grist to the mill of theologians. Like most disciplines involved in the "science-religion dialogue," cognitive science has the potential to reveal fresh insights about the natural world, which could encourage or discourage particular theological positions. Unlike many of these sciences, cognitive science has the additional potential to reveal to us previously undiscovered insights into human nature itself, particularly how human nature comes to embrace (or reject) and act upon (or ignore) these same theological positions. Other sciences can give us reasons to believe or withhold belief in a god. Cognitive science can also give us reasons *why* we are inclined or not to form such beliefs and act on them.

 Author's Note

As COGNITIVE SCIENCE incorporates some areas of neuroscience and some areas of scientific psychology, many of the themes presented here will abut another book in the Templeton Press's Science and Religion Series, Malcolm Jeeves and Warren S. Brown's *Neuroscience, Psychology, and Religion*. To reduce redundancy, I have not written this book in dialogue with Jeeves and Brown's work. I leave it to readers of both books to find where we agree and where we diverge.

A large number of people gave me constructive suggestions and other help at various stages of this writing project, and deserve credit here. I thank Developing a Christian Mind at Oxford for allowing me to use their program as a vehicle for recruiting discussion-group participants, and thank the participants in those discussions, specifically: Emily Burdett, Michael Burdett, Daniel Darg, Peter Eckley, Linda Fisher-Hoyrem, Donald Hay, Joses Ho, Jo Lewis-Barned, Matthew Lim, and Aku Visala. I also thank Kelly Clark, Michael Murray, Dani Rabinowitz, Jeff Schloss, Roger Trigg, and Aku Visala for trying to educate me on philosophical matters pertaining to sections of the manuscript, and Michael Burdett and Andrew Moore for theological challenges. Sherry Barrett helped reduce the amount of technical and obtuse material. I thank Jean-Luc Jucker for a careful reading of and assistance in manuscript preparation, and Larry Witham and an anonymous reviewer for constructive criticisms. I am grateful to the Centre for Anthropology and Mind and to Regent's Park College (Oxford) and my colleagues there for supporting this project with use of space, good conversation and collegiality, and lots of coffee. Finally, I thank the John Templeton Foundation for supporting research and scholarship drawn upon here, mine and that of others.

 Notes

CHAPTER 1

1. Some theologies that stress the importance of special divine revelation to the exclusion of general, natural revelation might see less application to understanding revelation from cognitive science. Some threads in Muslim thought that emphasize the exclusivity of divine revelation as well as Barthian Reformed Christian theology can be read as approaching such a position. See Alister E. McGrath, *The Open Secret: A New Vision for Natural Theology* (Oxford: Blackwell, 2008). I return to these issues in chapter 5.

2. Rif S. El-Mallakh, Justin L. Barrett, and Richard Jed Wyatt, "The Na, K-ATPase Hypothesis for Bipolar Disorder: Implications of Normal Development," *Journal of Child and Adolescent Psychopharmacology* 3, no. 1 (1993): 37–52.

3. Along with most modern scientists, I am adopting a stance of methodological naturalism when it comes to doing science. That is, science concerns phenomena of the natural world and should proceed to identify natural (as opposed to extra- or supernatural) causes of those phenomena. Such a stance does not imply that natural phenomena cannot be explained in nonnaturalistic ways or that naturalistic science provides complete knowledge by itself. Nevertheless, part of modern science's success in answering questions lies in its broad accessibility to people from varying worldviews. A science that prematurely or unnecessarily imports theological commitments (e.g., god A is the cause of phenomenon X) immediately restricts the range of participants and audiences (e.g., those who reject the existence or efficacy of god A).

4. The claim is that being a Red Sox fan is the default stance into which all babies are born and it is only corrupting influences that lead one to either eschew baseball altogether or become loyal to the Yankees. Though I reject this claim, I must confess that I do so without being acquainted with relevant data.

5. Paul Thagard, *Mind: Introduction to Cognitive Science*, 2nd ed. (Cambridge, MA: MIT, 2005).

6. For a dramatic illustration, see Vilayanur S. Ramachandran, Diane Rogers-Ramachandran, and Steve Cobb, "Touching the Phantom Limb," *Nature* 377 (1995): 489–90.

7. Exactly what one's commitments are on the mind-body problem must be borne in mind, however, when drawing conclusions in relation to some theological questions. If one is committed to human minds being inseparable from human

bodies and that minds are nothing but the functional properties of the body (particularly its nervous system), then the idea that a person's mind can be displaced by a spirit's is nonsense. Note, however, that while this position could be argued to be more or less coherent with the findings of cognitive science, the position that minds are just bodies is a philosophical position and not, strictly, a scientific one. It could not be claimed, then, that cognitive science disproves spirit possession, but more modestly that spirit possession is less coherent with some perspectives on the mind than others. I return to this issue in chapter 5.

CHAPTER 2

1. Vilayanur S. Ramachandran and Edward M. Hubbard, "Hearing Colors, Tasting Shapes," *Scientific American* 288, no. 5 (2003): 52–59; Jamie Ward, *The Frog Who Croaked Blue: Synesthesia and the Mixing of the Senses* (London: Routledge, 2008).

2. Such a view can be found in Aristotle, Abu 'Ali al-Husayn ibn Sina (a medieval Islamic philosopher), Thomas Aquinas, and, most famously, in John Locke's epistemological writings. For an argument against such a view, see Steven Pinker, *The Blank Slate: The Modern Denial of Human Nature* (New York: Viking, 2002).

3. John B. Watson, *Behaviorism*, 2nd ed. (London: Kegan Paul & Co., 1931), 82.

4. Some forms of dualism more modestly propose that minds and bodies are different substances but not separable in reality. These dualists have similar problems to solve concerning the interaction of these substances. A spectrum of positions between the two poles I have presented exists, partly because of attempts to solve these sorts of problems.

5. Sara W. Lazar et al., "Meditation Experience Is Associated with Increased Cortical Thickness," *Neuroreport* 16, no. 17 (2005): 1893–97.

6. Maturational naturalness may involve heavy repetition or practice. Practice is not a distinguishing feature between these two types of naturalness unless we regard "practice" as indicating deliberate, consciously motivated rehearsal. With this narrower view of practice, it might be argued that the maturationally natural does not typically require such deliberate efforts to attain.

7. John Ridley Stroop, "Studies of Interference in Serial Verbal Reactions," *Journal of Experimental Psychology* 18 (1935): 643–62.

8. This rationale motivates the common use of reaction time experiments in the cognitive sciences. The assumption is that if two stimuli are processed at different speeds, they are represented in different ways by the mind, with faster speeds suggesting greater familiarity or ease and slower speeds suggesting greater complexity or unfamiliarity. For instance, reading a word we have never seen before of 5 syllables will be slower than reading a familiar word of the same number of letters and syllables; multiplying 5 times 5 is faster (for most of us) than multiplying 17 times 38.

9. Some thought and behavior related to reproduction appear later but would still qualify as maturationally natural. I add to McCauley's characteristic features of maturational versus practiced naturalness another type of early development. If a trait or capacity has been part of human prehistory for a long time, it is more

likely to be maturationally natural. Practiced natural capacities are relative late-comers: mostly in the last ten thousand years. Robert N. McCauley, *Why Religion Is Natural and Science Is Not* (New York: Oxford University Press, 2011).

10. In this discussion of natural cognition I do not specify just how the brain limits the mind. To do so would be premature in most cases and be beside the point. We do not need to specify exactly how my body limits my ability to be a world-class sprinter (does it have something to do with leg length, fast-twitch muscle fibers, or what?) to know that a physical limitation is in play.

11. George A. Miller, "The Magical Number Seven, Plus or Minus Two: Some Limits on Our Capacity for Processing Information," *Psychological Review* 63, no. 2 (1956): 343–55.

12. Daniel T. Levin and Daniel S. Simons, "Failure to Detect Changes to Attended Objects in Motion Pictures," *Psychonomic Bulletin and Review* 4, no. 4 (1997): 4; Daniel J. Simons and Daniel T. Levin, "Failure to Detect Changes to People During a Real-World Interaction," *Psychonomic Bulletin and Review* 5 (1998): 644–49.

13. Daniel J. Simons and Daniel T. Levin, "Change Blindness," *Trends in Cognitive Science* 1, no. 1 (1997): 7.

14. Daniel J. Simons, "In Sight, Out of Mind: When Object Representations Fail," *Psychological Science* 7, no. 5 (1996): 301–5; Christopher Chabris and Daniel J. Simons, *The Invisible Gorilla: And Other Ways Our Intuitions Deceive Us* (London: HarperCollins, 2010).

15. In fact, if I set off telling you that the manoby has to eat, grows, is made of organic material, and the like, you will think (rightly) that there is something wrong with me. I have violated the normal expectation governing communication that I will only explicitly tell you information that might be novel, important, and meaningful to you—an expectation Dan Sperber and Deirdre Wilson have argued to be a natural part of human cognition pertaining to communication. See Dan Sperber and Deirdre Wilson, *Relevance: Communication and Cognition*, 2nd ed. (Oxford: Blackwell Publishing, 1995).

16. Not all intuitive knowledge is necessarily (maturationally) natural. As suggested in the discussion of practiced versus maturational naturalness, expertise can bring with it deeply ingrained, automatic associations and ideas that become "intuitive." This expertise-based intuitive knowledge, however, will be irregularly acquired by humans and highly variable, whereas the intuitive knowledge that springs from natural cognition will be available to nearly everyone and from an earlier age. For this reason, generally *intuitive* refers to natural cognition as opposed to expertise in the study of cognitive development.

17. For more information on the relevant experiments, see Judy S. DeLoache and Vanessa LoBue, "The Narrow Fellow in the Grass: Human Infants Associate Snakes and Fear," *Developmental Science* 12, no. 1 (2009): 201–7; Arne Öhman and Susan Mineka, "Fears, Phobias, and Preparedness: Toward an Evolved Module of Fear and Fear Learning," *Psychological Review* 108, no. 3 (2001): 483–522; Arne Öhman and Susan Mineka, "The Malicious Serpent," *Current Directions in Psychological Science* 12, no. 1 (2003): 5–9.

18. Andrew N. Meltzoff and N. Keith Moore, "Newborn Infants Imitate Adult Facial Gestures," *Child Development* 54 (1983): 702–9.

19. This seminal study was Marc H. Bornstein, William Kessen, and Sally Weiskopf, "Color Vision and Hue Categorization in Young Human Infants," *Journal of Experimental Psychology: Human Perception and Performance* 2, no. 1 (1976): 115–29. For a more contemporary treatment of the issue, see Anna Franklin, Michael Pilling, and Ian Davies, "The Nature of Infant Color Categorization: Evidence from Eye Movements on a Target Detection Task," *Journal of Experimental Child Psychology* 91, no. 3 (2005): 227–48; Anna Franklin, "Pre-Linguistic Categorical Perception of Colour Cannot Be Explained by Colour Preference: Response to Roberson and Hanley," *Trends in Cognitive Sciences* 13, no. 12 (2009): 501–2. I recognize that there is some conflict in the literature regarding the naturalness of categorical color perception because the infant studies appear to contradict some cross-cultural studies that may show that the color boundaries are weak or absent in adults when their language system does not mark off the color boundary. It may be that in these cases, much like in the case of auditory categorical perception with speech, the (natural) boundaries are lost if not used.

CHAPTER 3

1. Psychologists, particularly cognitive developmentalists, are fairly comfortable with the idea that children and adults have commitments or "beliefs" that they are unable to articulate but nevertheless predictably guide actions. The infant believes that a ball has to be contacted in order for it to move. Some philosophers might regard this psychological use of *belief* to be closer to what they mean by *knowledge*. Knowledge, however, typically carries the connotation of truth: we cannot know something that is false. Here I wish to remain agnostic about the truth of these mental representations I am calling beliefs.

2. Philosophers have had much more to say about the role of testimony in forming justified and unjustified beliefs.

3. A *skill bias* (differentially attending to people who clearly demonstrate superior skill) and a *success bias* (imitating those who achieve good results) might also be used. The boundaries between prestige, skill, and success can be ambiguous at times. For more details on various social biases that impact imitation and trust, see Joseph Henrich and Richard McElreath, "The Evolution of Cultural Evolution," *Evolutionary Anthropology: Issues, News, and Reviews* 12, no. 3 (2003): 123–35; Richard McElreath and Joseph Henrich, "Dual Inheritance Theory: The Evolution of Human Cultural Capacities and Cultural Evolution," in *Oxford Handbook of Evolutionary Psychology*, ed. Robin I. M. Dunbar and Louise Barrett (Oxford: Oxford University Press, 2007), 555–70.

4. One such answer is historical accident. A prestigious individual, who is the first owner of a car on his island nation, might drive on the left (or right) side of the road for no reason in particular or an "accidental" reason such as being right-handed. Subsequently, the majority imitates him and soon an entire empire drives on the left (or right). Context biases plus accident might be sufficient explanations in such cases, but do not do the job for religion.

5. Though a psychologist, Daniel Kahneman won the Nobel Prize in economics. There is no Nobel Prize in psychology.

6. Daniel Kahneman, "A Perspective on Judgment and Choice: Mapping Bounded Rationality," *American Psychologist* 58, no. 9 (2003): 699.

7. Ibid.

8. Even beliefs about facts are dependent upon personal history and cultural context. Unless he has a particular personal history, the average American does not hold a belief about when England last won the World Cup.

9. Justin L. Barrett, *Why Would Anyone Believe in God?* (Walnut Creek, CA: Alta-Mira Press, 2004), chapter 1; Pascal Boyer, *Religion Explained: The Evolutionary Origins of Religious Thought* (New York: Basic Books, 2001), chapter 9; Dan Sperber, "Intuitive and Reflective Beliefs," *Mind and Language* 12 (1997): 67–83.

10. Jonathan Haidt, "The New Synthesis in Moral Psychology," *Science* 316 (2007): 998–1002.

11. Shelly Chaiken and Yaacov Trope, *Dual-Process Theories in Social Psychology* (New York: Guilford Press, 1999); Thomas Gilovich, Dale Griffin, and Daniel Kahneman, *Heuristics and Biases: The Psychology of Intuitive Judgement* (Cambridge: Cambridge University Press, 2002); Alice M. Isen, Thomas E. Nygren, and F. Gregory Ashby, "Influence of Positive Affect on the Subjective Utility of Gains and Losses: It Is Just Not Worth the Risk," *Journal of Personality and Social Psychology* 55, no. 5 (1988): 710–17; David Sloan Wilson, *Darwin's Cathedral: Evolution, Religion, and the Nature of Society* (Chicago: University of Chicago Press, 2002); Timothy D. Wilson, *Strangers to Ourselves: Discovering the Adaptive Unconscious* (Cambridge, MA: Belknap, 2002).

12. This observation does not entail that *all* reflective beliefs can become so automated as to become intuitive.

13. Similarly, I find it more difficult to mount a bicycle from the right side because I have much more practice from the left. Feeling awkward or "wrong" trying to mount from the right and that feeling contributing to reflective ideas about the proper way to mount a bicycle is a nice illustration of how our entire bodies can contribute to belief formation. Even such thoroughly cognitive capacities such as belief formation can be importantly grounded by our embodiment.

14. It may be that testimony plays a role in triggering some content-specific natural cognition, especially early in development. The point here is that once the natural cognition is in place, then there is no point in acquiring nonreflective beliefs that are already in place as part of natural cognition via reflective beliefs.

15. Note too that these forms of cultural scaffolding are among McCauley's indicators of practiced naturalness described in chapter 2.

16. But these nonreflective beliefs might have been formed via reflective beliefs. The point is that we don't consciously, reflectively think our way to beliefs in most occasions.

17. William James, *The Varieties of Religious Experience* (London: Longmans, Green, and Co., 1902). See chapter 1 in particular.

18. William Kingdon Clifford, *Lectures and Essays* (London: Macmillan and Co., 1886), 346.

19. My position is similar to that of philosopher Thomas Reid, *Inquiry into the Human Mind on the Principles of Common Sense*, ed. Derek R Brookes (Edinburgh: Edinburgh University Press, 1997). Reformed epistemologists, inspired

by Reid, argue that beliefs that arise noninferentially from our cognitive faculties (or are first-order derivatives) require no justification. They are warranted beliefs. If we naturally, automatically believe in some kind of God (as John Calvin argued), then that belief too requires no evidence for justification (but evidence to the contrary can unseat it). See Alvin Plantinga, *Warranted Christian Belief* (New York: Oxford University Press, 2000), and also Nicholas P. Wolterstorff, "Can Belief in God Be Rational If It Has No Foundations?" in *Faith and Rationality: Reason and Belief in God,* ed. Alvin Plantinga and Nicholas Wolterstorff (London: University of Notre Dame Press, 1983), 135–86. Such an approach to epistemology taps the work of Thomas Reid, *Inquiry and Essays,* ed. Ronald E Beanblossom and Keith Lehrer (Indianapolis, IN: Hackett Publishing Company, 1983). See Nicholas P. Wolterstorff, *Thomas Reid and the Story of Epistemology* (Cambridge: Cambridge University Press, 2001).

CHAPTER 4

1. Linda Hermer and Elizabeth S. Spelke, "A Geometric Process for Spatial Reorientation in Young Children," *Nature* 370, no. 6484 (1994): 57–59; Linda Hermer-Vazquez, Elizabeth S. Spelke, and Alla S. Katsnelson, "Sources of Flexibility in Human Cognition: Dual-Task Studies of Space and Language," *Cognitive Psychology* 39, no. 1 (1999): 3–36. Verbal shadowing is when someone tries to say what someone else is saying *with* the speaker. It requires listening to another person, anticipating what they are about to say from contextual information, and producing the words immediately after the other person. This task is very difficult and swamps attentional resources.
2. Simons, "In Sight, Out of Mind," 301–5.
3. Much of this section borrows heavily from Justin L. Barrett, "Coding and Quantifying Counterintuitiveness in Religious Concepts: Theoretical and Methodological Reflections," *Method and Theory in the Study of Religion* 20 (2008): 308–38.
4. Frank Keil's treatment of intuitive ontology was inspired by linguistic evidence that how predicates span subjects often has a treelike structure. For instance, if something can be described as "is breathing" (a biological predicate), you can generally assume that "is purple" (a physical predicate) can be applied sensibly (even if inaccurately). See Frank C. Keil, *Semantic and Conceptual Development: An Ontological Perspective* (Cambridge, MA: Harvard University Press, 1979). The converse is not true. Something that can be predicated with "is purple" cannot necessarily be said sensibly to "be breathing." See Fred Sommers, "Structural Ontology," *Philosophia* 1, no. 1 (1971): 21–42.
5. These expectation sets do not capture all properties of things in the world, but appear to provide some conceptual anchoring for those properties that may be particularly foundational or important for further learning about the world. As what is proposed here is a description of how human cognition works, and not how the world is actually carved up ontologically, some things might not fall cleanly into one of the five ontological categories and the boundaries might be fuzzy.

6. Elizabeth S. Spelke and Katherine D. Kinzler, "Core Knowledge," *Developmental Science* 10, no. 1 (2007): 89–96.

7. Hence, it has been dubbed part of "core knowledge" (ibid.).

8. Renee Baillargeon, Laura Kotovsky, and Amy Needham, "The Acquisition of Physical Knowledge in Infancy," in *Causal Cognition: A Multidisciplinary Debate*, ed. Dan Sperber, David Premack, and Ann James Premack (Oxford: Oxford University Press, 1995), 79–116.

9. Giyoo Hatano and Kayoko Inagaki, "Young Children's Naive Theory of Biology," *Cognition* 50, no. 1–3 (1994): 171–88; Karl S. Rosengren et al., "As Time Goes By: Children's Early Understanding of Growth in Animals," *Child Development* 62, no. 6 (1991): 1302–20.

10. Virginia Slaughter, "Young Children's Understanding of Death," *Australian Psychologist* 40 (2005): 1–8; Virginia Slaughter and Michelle Lyons, "Learning about Life and Death in Early Childhood," *Cognitive Psychology* 46, no. 1 (2003): 1–30.

11. Hatano and Inagaki, "Young Children's Naive Theory," 171–88; Ken Springer and Frank C. Keil, "On the Development of Biologically Specific Beliefs: The Case of Inheritance," *Child Development* 60, no. 3 (1989): 637–48.

12. Daniel J. Simons and Frank C. Keill, "An Abstract to Concrete Shift in the Development of Biological Thought: The Insides Story," *Cognition* 56 (1995): 1299–63.

13. Kayoko Inagaki and Giyoo Hatano, *Young Children's Naive Thinking about the Biological World* (New York: Psychology Press, 2002); Kayoko Inagaki and Giyoo Hatano, "Young Children's Conception of the Biological World," *Current Directions in Psychological Science* 15, no. 4 (2006): 177–81; Frank C. Keil, "The Origins of an Autonomous Biology," in *Modularity and Constraints in Language and Cognition: 25th Minnesota Symposium on Child Psychology*, ed. Megan R. Gunnar and Michael Maratsos (Hilldale, NJ: Lawrence Erlbaum Associates, 1992): 103–37.

14. Inagaki and Hatano, *Young Children's Naive Thinking*; Frank C. Keil, *Concepts, Kinds, and Cognitive Development* (Cambridge, MA: MIT Press, 1989).

15. Also known as self-propelledness, see David Premack, "The Infant's Theory of Self-Propelled Objects," *Cognition* 36 (1990): 1–36, or as "force," see Alan M. Leslie, "A Theory of Agency," in *Causal Cognition: A Multidisciplinary Debate*, ed. Dan Sperber, David Premack, and Ann James Premack (New York: Oxford University Press, 1995), 121–41.

16. See Philippe Rochat, Rachel Morgan, and Malinda Carpenter, "Young Infants' Sensitivity to Movement Information Specifying Social Causality," *Cognitive Development* 12 (1997): 537–61, and György Gergely and Gergely Csibra, "Teleological Reasoning in Infancy: The Naive Theory of Rational Action," *Trends in Cognitive Sciences* 7, no. 7 (2003): 287–92; Spelke and Kinzler, "Core Knowledge." Note that children do not automatically extend these Animacy expectations to all living things or natural nonliving objects. A Victorian anthropological argument that many people of the world are naturally and intuitively animists is not supported by this cognitive developmental research. It may be that living things are readily imbued with kind-specific essences or even some kind of life force. Such attributions to living things do appear to be

part of natural cognition. Elaboration of such unseen properties into active, animated "spirits" that also characterize rocks, mountains, and rivers is not wholly natural or intuitive, but might be a slightly counterintuitive cultural elaboration.

17. I justify this decision more thoroughly elsewhere. Barrett, "Coding and Quantifying Counterintuitiveness," 308–38.

18. For an overview of *intuitive dualism* see Paul Bloom, *Descartes' Baby: How Child Development Explains What Makes Us Human* (London: William Heinemann, 2004). Emma Cohen's (2007) ethnographic treatment of Afro-Brazilian spirit possession illustrates the point. She reports that when a person's body is occupied by a possessing spirit, the host's spirit is often reported to be left in a particular location or to travel, both spatial attributions; but no one attributes the spirit with the massive, physical properties subsumed under what I am terming Physicality (personal communication). See Emma Cohen, *The Mind Possessed: The Cognition of Spirit Possession in an Afro-Brazilian Religious Tradition* (New York: Oxford University Press, 2007).

19. As with Physicality, evidence for Animacy expectations appears in early infancy and might be considered core knowledge (Spelke and Kinzler, "Core Knowledge," 89–96). Animacy is readily applied years before a folk biology clearly emerges, before clear evidence of mentalistic reasoning, and has a ready proper domain of application in simple, nonsocial animals (e.g., snails, worms, etc.). These facts motivate me to leave Animacy independent of both Mentality and Biology. This decision does not entail that animals and humans do not normally activate Biology expectations, but only that Animacy and Mentality might be activated without Biology. Hence, some "Animates" could be represented without Biology. It might be that by the time a robust theory of mind or Mentality develops, all animate objects are intuitively expected to be mentalistic agents (Persons), but as this is not clear (do we automatically attribute mental states to earthworms?), I leave Mentality independent of Animacy.

20. The expectation sets are not a class-inclusion hierarchy, but neither are they wholly independent of each other. Some expectation sets automatically activate others. If a concept activates Biology, it likewise activates Physicality, Spatiality, and Universals. Without Physicality, Biology is not activated. To illustrate, the Biology assumption that like-begets-like (e.g., dogs have puppies and not kittens) is wholly deactivated if Physicality is not assumed.

21. Note that contrary to how I understand Boyer's use of the term *person*, here "Person" is not synonymous with "human." Pascal Boyer, *The Naturalness of Religious Ideas: A Cognitive Theory of Religion* (Berkeley: University of California Press, 1994); Boyer, *Religion Explained*.

22. For example, Boyer, *Naturalness of Religious Ideas*.

23. Paul Bloom, *Descartes' Baby*; Gergely and Csibra, "Teleological Reasoning in Infancy," 287–92.

24. György Gergely et al., "Taking the Intentional Stance at 12 Months of Age," *Cognition* 56 (1995): 165–93; Gergely and Csibra, "Teleological Reasoning in Infancy," 287–92; Leslie, "A Theory of Agency"; Premack, "The Infant's Theory of Self-Propelled Objects," 1–36.

25. Rochat, Morgan, and Carpenter, "Young Infants' Sensitivity to Movement,"

537–61; Brian J. Scholl and Patrice D. Tremoulet, "Perceptual Causality and Animacy," *Trends in Cognitive Sciences* 4 (2000): 299–308.

26. Marjorie Taylor, *Imaginary Companions and the Children Who Create Them* (New York: Oxford University Press, 1999); J. Bradley Wigger, "Imaginary Companions, Theory of Mind, and God," in "Cognition, Religion, and Theology" (conference, University of Oxford, June 29, 2010); J. Bradley Wigger, "See-through Knowing: Learning from Children and Their Invisible Friends," *Journal of Childhood and Religion* 2, no. 3 (2011): 1–34.

27. This claim is consistent with Paul Bloom's claim that people are *intuitive dualists*. I find the available data suggestive, but concede that these informed speculations need further, direct empirical support. See Bloom, *Descartes' Baby*.

28. Daniel C. Dennett, *The Intentional Stance* (Cambridge, MA: MIT Press, 1987); Deborah Kelemen, "Functions, Goals, and Intentions: Children's Teleological Reasoning about Objects," *Trends in Cognitive Sciences* 12 (1999): 461–68; Deborah Kelemen and Evelyn Rosset, "The Human Function Compunction: Teleological Explanation in Adults," *Cognition* 111 (2009): 138–43.

29. Krista Casler and Deborah Kelemen, "Reasoning about Artifacts at 24 Months: The Developing Teleo-Functional Stance," *Cognition* 103, no. 1 (2007): 120–30; Krista Casler and Deborah Keleman, "Developmental Continuity in Teleo-Functional Explanation: Reasoning about Nature among Romanian Romani Adults," *Journal of Cognition and Development* 9 (2008): 340–62; Frank C. Keil, "The Growth of Causal Understandings of Natural Kinds: Modes of Construal and the Emergence of Biological Thought," in *Causal Cognition: A Multidisciplinary Debate*, ed. Dan Sperber, David Premack, and Ann James Premack (New York: Oxford University Press, 1995), 234–62.

30. This acquisition advantage is not necessarily because of differences in intrinsic plausibility between intuitive and counterintuitive ideas but because massively counterintuitive ideas are just less likely to be accessible.

31. We might wonder why such a cognitive propensity exists. Is it adaptive to overuse design? Perhaps being carefully cued in to the possible function or purpose of things helps in making good use of the environment and developing artifacts (e.g., that rhino's horn looks good for stabbing; I'll make something similar and it will be good for stabbing). Living in an artifact-rich world could also encourage us to pay particular attention to what things are for. Furthermore, we might wonder if seeing the world as full of intentional purpose—function that was deliberately designed by someone(s)—would be adaptive or maladaptive. Perhaps regarding aspects of the natural world as intentionally designed by someone (such as a god) could provide even greater aid for making use of the natural world. If that rhino's horn doesn't just happen to be useful but was *made* with a purpose in mind, it is a small step to seeing that I could make something comparable with a comparable purpose in mind. On a larger scale, regarding the natural world as designed by someone for some reasons could encourage positive ecological attitudes that prove adaptive for local populations. "If someone made things such as they are, perhaps we should not interfere with that arrangement or we will damage the utility and, possibly, frustrate the purposes of a powerful being." Behaviors in response to such reasoning might prove adaptive. These speculations are all in need of empirical investigation.

32. Deborah Kelemen, "Why Are Rocks Pointy? Children's Preference for Teleo-logical Explanations of the Natural World," *Developmental Psychology* 35 (1999): 1443.

33. Cara DiYanni and Deborah Kelemen, "Time to Get a New Mountain? The Role of Function in Children's Conceptions of Natural Kinds," *Cognition* 97 (2005): 31.

34. Kelemen and Rosset, "The Human Function Compunction."

35. Casler and Kelemen, "Developmental Continuity."

36. Intelligent design theory is the idea that an intelligent being such as a god is needed to account for certain aspects of biological structures. That is, at points during evolution an intelligent being intervened supernaturally to help evolu-tion along. William A. Dembski, *Intelligent Design: The Bridge between Science and Theology* (Downers Grove, IL: InterVarsity Press, 1999).

37. Francis Crick, *What Mad Pursuits* (New York: Basic Books, 1988), 138.

38. This observation that arguments supporting the existence of a divine creator gain plausibility because of their roots in natural cognition does not necessarily undermine such arguments. Arguing that ideas with an intuitive ring should be suspect on that basis runs counter to common sense as well as traditional phil-osophical practice.

   Note that design intuitions are only directly supportive (psychologically) of the idea that someone accounts for perceived natural order. Exactly who or how many someones and what they account for (e.g., why that mountain is over there, why the termites act as they do, or why the cosmos exists) are subject to variable culturally elaborated answers. The point here is that natural cogni-tion gives all of these reflective, theological treatments an intuitive grounding at their cores.

CHAPTER 5

1. Emma Cohen and Justin L. Barrett, "In Search of 'Folk Anthropology': The Cognitive Anthropology of the Person," in *In Search of Self: Interdisciplinary Perspectives on Personhood*, ed. Wentzel van Huyssteen and Erik Wiebe (Grand Rapids: Eerdmans, 2011): 104–23.

2. More specifically, the social brain hypothesis tries to account for human's excep-tionally large neo-cortex (the part of the brain associated with higher cognitive functions including theory of mind) relative to the rest of our brain and body size. Robin I. M. Dunbar, "The Social Brain Hypothesis," *Evolutionary Anthro-pology: Issues, News, and Reviews* 6, no. 5 (1998): 178–90; Robin I. M. Dunbar, *The Human Story* (London: Faber and Faber, 2004).

3. Meltzoff and Moore, "Newborn Infants Imitate."

4. Using eye-gaze to infer mental states and future actions is aided among humans by our unusually large white sclera—the whites of our eyes. Other primates do not have white sclera and are far inferior at detecting eye-gaze direction. Look-ing at eyes is so important in human social interaction that failure to do so is now regarded as a potential early indicator of autism, a developmental disorder char-acterized by theory of mind weakness and related social deficits (among other common symptoms). Simon Baron-Cohen's book title *Mindblindness* plays on

his conviction that failure to use information from the eyes can obscure understanding other's minds. See Simon Baron-Cohen, *Mindblindness: An Essay on Autism and Theory of Mind* (Cambridge, MA: MIT Press, 1995). Likewise, placing eye-spots on an object is sufficient for babies to treat an object as an intentional being with a focus of attention. For a helpful, brief review of research, see Susan C. Johnson, "The Recognition of Mentalistic Agents in Infancy," *Trends in Cognitive Sciences* 4, no. 1 (2000): 22–28.

5. *Folk psychology* is sometimes used to refer to the culturally variable understandings of human psychology by laypeople, whereas *theory of mind* typically refers to the cross-culturally recurrent and early developing conceptual core used to reason about human minds by all normally developing humans. As my focus is on natural cognition, I prefer the term *theory of mind* for this discussion.

6. I use the term *theory of mind* as psychologists do, to refer to how people ordinarily think about other's minds and mental states. I do not mean *philosophy of mind*, the intellectual activity concerning what minds, consciousness, perception, and the like are and how they function. Theory of mind is to philosophy of mind as naïve physics is to the scientific study of physics.

7. For instance, sometimes we cannot say what we are feeling from direct introspection but piece it together through theory-based reasoning: What am I feeling right now? Well, my grandmother just died so I must be sad, but she was suffering, so I am a little relieved for her as well. . . . Occasionally, I forget why I have entered a room and have to look around me and figure it out as if I were considering the behavior of someone else: he is in the kitchen with a tea cup in his hand, maybe he wants tea.

8. Joseph Call and Michael Tomasello, "Does the Chimpanzee Have a Theory of Mind? 30 Years Later," *Trends in Cognitive Sciences* 12 (2008): 187–92; Derek C. Penn and Daniel J. Povinelli, "Causal Cognition in Human and Nonhuman Animals: A Comparative, Critical Review," *Annual Review of Psychology* 58, no. 1 (2007): 97–118.

9. Michael Tomasello, *The Cultural Origins of Human Cognition* (Cambridge, MA: Harvard University Press, 1999). A similar point about higher-order theory of mind in relation to collective religious practice was made by Dunbar, *The Human Story*.

10. Such speculations bear on the problem of pain and suffering applied to animals. Perhaps only recently in evolutionary history have animals emerged that consciously experience pain and are thus capable of what we commonly regard as suffering. Many animals may have pain sensations from which they are averse, but they may not suffer in any way comparable to human suffering. A faint analogue may be when humans engage in contact sports and report that the pain they suffer does not detract at all from the enjoyment of the competition. The pain does not bother them because they are attending to something else. For more on such possibilities and their relation to the philosophical problem of whether a good and powerful god would permit animal pain, see Michael J. Murray, *Nature Red in Tooth and Claw: Theism and the Problem of Animal Suffering* (Oxford: Oxford University Press, 2008), and Peter Harrison, "Theodicy and Animal Pain," *Philosophy* 64, no. 247 (1989): 79–92.

11. Perhaps not. Chimpanzees, bonobos, and some other apes are the only animals

I have any degree of confidence could manage such a relationship, and the available data does not make me certain.

12. But when did such a capacity emerge and when did it first begin to produce collective relationships with personal gods? These are questions for a cognitively informed paleoanthropology.

13. A similar presentation of ideas in this section may be found in Cohen and Barrett, "In Search of 'Folk Anthropology.'"

14. For overviews, see David H. Rakison and Diane Poulin-Dubois, "Developmental Origin of the Animate-Inanimate Distinction," *Psychological Bulletin* 127, no. 2 (2001): 209–28; Karen Wynn, "Some Innate Foundations of Social and Moral Cognition," in *The Innate Mind: Foundations and the Future,* ed. Peter Carruthers, Stephen Laurence, and Stephen P. Stich (Oxford: Oxford University Press, 2008), 330–47.

15. Bloom, *Descartes' Baby*; Henry Wellman and Carl Johnson, "Developing Dualism: From Intuitive Understanding to Transcendental Ideas," in *Psycho-Physical Dualism Today: An Interdisciplinary Approach,* ed. Alessandro Antonietti, Antonella Corradini, and E. Jonathan Lowe (Lanham, MD: Lexington Books, 2008), 3–36.

16. Kayoko Inagaki and Giyoo Hatano, "Vitalistic Causality in Young Children's Naive Biology," *Trends in Cognitive Sciences* 8, no. 8 (2004): 356–62.

17. Inagaki and Hatano, *Young Children's Naive Thinking;* Carolyn A. Schult and Henry M. Wellman, "Explaining Human Movements and Actions: Children's Understanding of the Limits of Psychological Explanation," *Cognition* 62, no. 3 (1997): 291–324.

18. Marc J. Miresco and Laurence J. Kirmayer, "The Persistence of Mind-Brain Dualism in Psychiatric Reasoning about Clinical Scenarios," *American Journal of Psychiatry* 163, no. 5 (2006): 913–18.

19. Paul Bloom develops an argument along these lines in his article, "Seduced by the Flickering Lights of the Brain: fMRI Images Have Captivated Headline Writers, Grant Committees and the Public beyond Their Actual Scientific Worth," Seed Magazine.com, accessed February 16, 2011, http://seedmagazine.com/content/article/seduced_by_the_flickering_lights_of_the_brain/.

20. For a more complete discussion of how ordinary cognitions might structure religious and cultural ideas pertaining to personhood, see Cohen and Barrett, "In Search of 'Folk Anthropology.'"

21. Elizabeth Spelke et al., "Spatiotemporal Continuity, Smoothness of Motion and Object Identity in Infancy," *British Journal of Developmental Psychology* 13, no. 2 (1995): 113–42; Fei Xu and Susan Carey, "Infants' Metaphysics: The Case of Numerical Identity," *Cognitive Psychology* 30, no. 2 (1996): 111–53.

22. Rebekah A. Richert and Paul L. Harris, "Dualism Revisited: Body Vs. Mind Vs. Soul," *Journal of Cognition and Culture* 8, no. 1–2 (2008): 99–115.

23. Ibid., 115.

24. Indeed, if we did not have the intuition that people have some kind of individuating essence, it might be far more difficult (and rare) to attribute to people a personal history for which they are responsible. If every several years our bodies' matter is completely replaced, and our physical appearance, attitudes, and

preferences can change radically over time, why would we regard someone we know now as the same person that he or she was twenty years ago? Why not treat that person as an entirely new individual? Because our intuitions tell us that across these changes, something remains the same. This intuition very well could be part of natural cognition.

25. For instance, see Robert A. Hinde, *Why Good Is Good: The Sources of Morality* (London: Routledge, 2002); Leonard D. Katz, ed., *Evolutionary Origins of Morality: Cross-Disciplinary Perspectives* (Thoverton, UK: Imprint Academic, 2000).

26. Katz, *Evolutionary Origins of Morality*. Cognitive scientist Marc Hauser has developed his naturalness of morality thesis by drawing parallels with Chomskian linguistics. See Marc D. Hauser, *Moral Minds: How Nature Designed Our Universal Sense of Right and Wrong* (New York: Ecco/Harper Collins, 2006). As Chomsky and his intellectual descendants have argued that humans naturally and nearly inevitably possess a *universal grammar* that structures and guides language acquisition and use, likewise Hauser argues for a universal *moral grammar* that structures and guides norm acquisition and normative judgment making. Hauser marshals evidence from experimental philosophy, psychology, and other sources to argue that this moral grammar is an evolved capacity that conferred fitness advantages through facilitating human sociality. That is, as with naïve physics and language, humans may possess something akin to a *morality faculty*, which delivers nonreflective, noninferential moral intuitions and judgments regarding human actions. Hauser's approach is controversial but nicely illustrates the way in which themes from the study of one area of content-specific cognition often inform other areas of study.

27. For instance, in Romans 2:15 St. Paul refers to Gentiles (non-Jews) as having God's "law written on their hearts." Similar themes pertaining to *a priori* moral intuitions common in humans can be found in Plato and (much later) in Immanuel Kant too. Of course, it is not an accident C. S. Lewis referred to this "law written in their hearts" as the *Tao*: it has resonance with ideas in ancient Eastern traditions of thought as well.

28. C. S. Lewis, *The Abolition of Man* (London: Oxford University Press, 1943). A potential fruitful scholarly project would be to compare the list of laws or virtues Lewis points to in this book (especially the appendix "Illustrations of the *Tao*") to evidence being produced by cognitive and evolutionary scientists regarding moral intuitions. Lewis and others' point about such natural moral intuitions is that they characterize people generally but not that any given individual (e.g., suffering from brain damage or developmental malady) or any given group (e.g., systematically conditioned to adopt counternatural values) will manifest the alleged suite of moral intuitions.

29. Elsewhere Lewis agued that this convergence was one "clue to the meaning of the universe" and evidence in support of theism of some sort. C. S. Lewis, *Mere Christianity* (New York: Macmillan, 1960), 13–21.

30. I have listed these roughly in order of how confident I am in the evidence in support of these features' naturalness, but as these constitute active areas of research, evaluating the strength of evidence is difficult.

31. Reid, *Inquiry into the Human Mind*. This "commonsense realism" has been elaborated by Nicholas Woltersdorff among others (Wolterstorff, "Can Belief in God Be Rational?," 135–86; Wolterstorff, *Thomas Reid*).

32. The need for such a link is problematic with abstract entities such as those underlying mathematics. It does not seem to be the case that we require mathematical concepts to *cause* our beliefs in them, and yet we are surely justified in affirming them (but this too is somewhat contentious). Premise (2), then, might be qualified to be only applicable to nonabstractions, but it is not clear what the ontological status of free will, souls, or minds is and whether such a premise would apply to them. For these and other reasons presented here, I reject (2) as applied to beliefs about these things. I am under the impression that most epistemologists would heartily agree and regard such considerations as rather rudimentary, but that many students of the sciences would find this easy rejection of (2) surprising.

33. Wolterstorff, "Can Belief in God Be Rational?" 163–64.

34. Daniel M. Wegner, "The Mind's Best Trick: How We Experience Conscious Will," *Trends in Cognitive Sciences* 7, no. 2 (2003): 65–69.

35. For a recent brief review of evidence see Daniel M. Wegner's "The Mind's Best Trick," and for a more thorough study see Daniel M. Wegner, *The Illusion of Conscious Will* (Cambridge, MA: MIT Press, 2002). For a different theological and neuroscientific treatment, see Malcolm Jeeves and Warren S. Brown, *Neuroscience, Psychology, and Religion: Illusions, Delusions, and Realities about Human Nature* (West Conshohocken, PA: Templeton Press, 2009).

36. Alvin Plantinga has argued that under the strict criteria of requiring evidence to justify beliefs (that many scientists and students of science hold), we cannot arrive at a justified belief in human minds, but that our belief in minds is rational nonetheless. He goes on to argue that as our belief in human minds is justified without the burden of evidence, belief in other minds, such as God's, can be justified without such evidence. See Alvin Plantinga, *God and Other Minds: A Study of the Rational Justification of Belief in God* (Ithaca: Cornell University Press, 1990).

CHAPTER 6

1. Paul Tillich, *The Shaking of the Foundations* (New York: Charles Scribner's Sons, 1940).

2. Deborah Kelemen, "Are Children 'Intuitive Theists'? Reasoning about Purpose and Design in Nature," *Psychological Science* 15 (2004): 295–301.

3. A recent review and discussion appears in Ryan T. McKay and Daniel C. Dennett, "The Evolution of Misbelief," *Behavioral and Brain Sciences* 32 (2009): 493–510.

4. Stewart E. Guthrie, *Faces in the Clouds: A New Theory of Religion* (New York: Oxford University Press, 1993).

5. Justin L. Barrett, "Exploring the Natural Foundations of Religion." *Trends in Cognitive Sciences* 4, no. 1 (2000): 31. See also Barrett, *Why Would Anyone Believe in God?* 32–34.

6. Scholl and Tremoulet, "Perceptual Causality and Animacy," 299–308.

7. Fritz Heider and Marianne Simmel, "An Experimental Study of Apparent Behavior," *American Journal of Psychology* 57 (1944): 243–49.

8. For a brief review of experiments on the topic, see Scholl and Tremoulet, "Perceptual Causality and Animacy,", 299–308.

9. Guthrie's argument raises an interesting epistemological problem. How do we know that these are "false positives"? The agency detection cognitive system (or HADD) would have to be checked against a different, reliable system for identifying when agency has been accurately detected. Do we have such a system, or do we just have the one agency detection system? Maybe when we decide that we did not in fact detect intentional agency, it is at this point that the mistake is sometimes made. See Guthrie, *Faces in the Clouds*. Though evidence for some HADD-like system is strong, that it contributes to belief in gods requires more empirical attention.

   Guthrie uses different language in presenting his argument. He favors the term *anthropomorphism* to capture the tendency to attribute events and states to intentional agents. I avoid this term for three reasons. First, it carries the connotation that all intentional agency is humanlike and this is an open question. In many cases it is not human agency that is being postulated but something different. Second, anthropomorphism is often associated with importantly different approaches such as Freudian or Piagetian, and can carry the assumption that the agency in question is thought to have a humanlike bodily form. My third concern is that the term *anthropomorphism* dodges an important theological matter: to what extent is human agency a reflection of divine agency—theomorphism—rather than the other way around?

10. More evidence for such a claim is needed, but the idea has been entertained by several cognitive scientists of religion; see Barrett, *Why Would Anyone Believe in God?*; Jesse M. Bering and Dominic D. P. Johnson, "'O Lord . . . You Perceive My Thoughts from Afar': Recursiveness and the Evolution of Supernatural Agency," *Journal of Cognition and Culture* 5 (2005): 118–42; Boyer, *Religion Explained*; D. Jason Slone, *Theological Incorrectness: Why Religious People Believe What They Shouldn't* (New York: Oxford University Press, 2004). Note that from a psychological perspective at least, when an improbable event happens, such as winning the lottery, pointing out that given enough time or enough people playing the lottery someone is bound to win does not necessarily remove the desire for an explanation of why. Sure, someone had to win, but why me? Sure, people get struck by lightning, but why me and why now?

11. Adrian Furnham, "Belief in a Just World: Research Progress over the Past Decade," *Personality and Individual Differences* 34, no. 5 (2003): 795–817; Melvin J. Lerner, *The Belief in a Just World: A Fundamental Delusion* (New York: Plenum Press, 1980).

12. Boyer, *Religion Explained*.

13. Jesse M. Bering, "Intuitive Conceptions of Dead Agents' Minds: The Natural Foundations of Afterlife Beliefs as Phenomenological Boundary," *Journal of Cognition and Culture* 2 (2002): 263–308; Jesse M. Bering, "The Folk Psychology of Souls," *Behavioral and Brain Sciences* 29 (2006): 453–62.

14. In one case in which a close friend died, I can remember hearing sounds—actual sounds, not hallucinations—that I automatically assumed were from

him approaching, and had to consciously remind myself that he was dead and the sounds must have a different cause. Similarly, I had chilling dreams of him returning and trying to participate in regular life. It is easy to see how such experiences could set one to wondering whether the deceased really are still active and trying to interact, especially if people have convergent experiences that they share with each other.

15. Justin L. Barrett and Melanie Nyhof, "Spreading Non-natural Concepts: The Role of Intuitive Conceptual Structures in Memory and Transmission of Cultural Materials," *Journal of Cognition and Culture* 1, no. 1 (2001): 69–100; Pascal Boyer and Charles Ramble, "Cognitive Templates for Religious Concepts: Cross-Cultural Evidence for Recall of Counter-Intuitive Representations," *Cognitive Science* 25 (2001): 535–64. See also Justin Gregory and Justin L. Barrett, "Epistemology and Counterintuitiveness: Role and Relationship in Epidemiology of Cultural Representations," *Journal of Cognition and Culture* 9 (2009): 289–314.

16. The metaphor *scaffolding* suggests that extra structures are needed to build up some ideas or practices that are not particularly natural (close to the ground). Further, scaffolding is not permanent and can be removed. Analogously, the cultural conditions or devices that help build up relatively unnatural beliefs and practices can be removed. Previously common knowledge (such as how to start a fire from natural materials) can vanish when the cultural scaffolding is removed.

17. Boyer, *Religion Explained.*

18. An exception to the "usually" in this statement is in cases where there is strong cultural scaffolding, such as institutionalized schools of thought that attempt to keep inferentially poor ideas alive. For more complete treatments of the role of inferential potential on the spread of religious ideas, see Boyer, *Religion Explained*; Pascal Boyer, "Religious Thought and Behavior as By-products of Brain Function," *Trends in Cognitive Sciences* 7 (2003): 119–24.

19. And reasons often do arise. Suppose someone believes his god is fully visible under normal conditions and lives on the top of Mt. Olympus. Repeatedly, he climbs Mt. Olympus and fails to see the god. Either the belief that the god lives on Mt. Olympus or that the god is fully visible or that the specified god exists becomes suspect.

20. David Leech and Aku Visala, "The Cognitive Science of Religion: Implications for Theism?" *Zygon* 46, no. 1 (2011): 47–64; Jeffrey P. Schloss and Michael J. Murray, eds., *The Believing Primate: Scientific, Philosophical, and Theological Reflections on the Origin of Religion* (Oxford: Oxford University Press, 2009); Kelly J. Clark and Dani Rabinowitz, "Knowledge and the Objection to Religious Belief from Cognitive Science," *European Journal of Philosophy of Religion* 3 (2011): 67–81.

21. For a brief, accessible treatment of these issues, see Michael J. Murray, "Four Arguments That the Cognitive Psychology of Religion Undermines the Justification of Religious Beliefs," in *The Evolution of Religion: Studies, Theories, and Critiques*, ed. Joseph Bulbulia et al. (Santa Margarita, CA: Collins Foundation Press, 2008), 365–70.

22. "Seeing, Hearing and Smelling the World: A Report from the Howard Hughes

Medical Institute," Howard Hughes Medical Institute, accessed November 24, 2010, http://www.hhmi.org/senses/b130.html.

CHAPTER 7

1. Stanley Schachter and Jerome Singer's two-factor theory of emotion captures this dynamic. Interestingly, the fact that at least sometimes our physiological states have to be conceptually interpreted to form the experience of an emotion leaves open the possibility that the same physiological arousal can be interpreted or reinterpreted in multiple ways. See Rainer Reisenzein, "The Schachter Theory of Emotion: Two Decades Later," *Psychological Bulletin* 94, no. 2 (1983): 239–64; Stanley Schachter and Jerome Singer, "Cognitive, Social, and Physiological Determinants of Emotional State," *Psychological Review* 69, no. 5 (1962): 379–99.

2. Colin J. Humphreys, *The Miracles of Exodus: A Scientist's Discovery of the Extraordinary Natural Causes of the Biblical Stories* (London: Continuum, 2004). Humphreys does not just make the psychological point that such dramatic, important, and unlikely events would be regarded as miraculous even when mediated by natural causes, but that these events truly are miraculous and reasonably regarded as acts of God via natural causes.

3. Michael B. Lupfer, Karla F. Brock, and Stephen J. DePaola, "The Use of Secular and Religious Attributions to Explain Everyday Behavior," *Journal for the Scientific Study of Religion* 31, no. 4 (1992): 486–503.

4. Michael B. Lupfer, Donna Tolliver, and Mark Jackson, "Explaining Life-Altering Occurrences: A Test of the 'God-of-the-Gaps' Hypothesis," *Journal for the Scientific Study of Religion* 35, no. 4 (1996): 379–91; Bernard Spilka and Greg Schmidt, "General Attribution Theory for the Psychology of Religion: The Influence of Event-Character on Attributions to God," *Journal for the Scientific Study of Religion* 22, no. 4 (1983): 326–39.

5. Kurt Gray and Daniel M. Wegner, "Blaming God for Our Pain: Human Suffering and the Divine Mind," *Personality and Social Psychology Review* 14, no. 1 (2009): 7–16.

6. Originally published in their 1990 book *Rethinking Religion*, the ideas were developed much earlier but were so revolutionary that journal editors were reluctant to publish them. See E. Thomas Lawson and Robert N. McCauley, *Rethinking Religion: Connecting Cognition and Culture* (Cambridge: Cambridge University Press, 1990). Their 2002 book, *Bringing Ritual to Mind,* is a more accessible treatment with developed applications to a particular case study—Harvey Whitehouse's ethnographic observations with a religious splinter group in Melanesia. See Robert N. McCauley and E. Thomas Lawson, *Bringing Ritual to Mind: Psychological Foundations of Cultural Forms* (Cambridge: Cambridge University Press, 2002); Harvey Whitehouse, *Inside the Cult: Religious Innovation and Transmission in Papua New Guinea* (Oxford: Clarendon Press, 1995).

Empirical research supporting or challenging Lawson and McCauley's account remains thin, but see Justin L. Barrett and E. Thomas Lawson, "Ritual Intuitions: Cognitive Contributions to Judgments of Ritual Efficacy," *Journal of Cognition and Culture* 1, no. 2 (2001): 183–201; Justin L. Barrett, "Smart

Gods, Dumb Gods, and the Role of Social Cognition in Structuring Ritual Intuitions," *Journal of Cognition and Culture* 2, no. 4 (2002): 183–94; Justin L. Barrett, "Bringing Data to Mind: Empirical Claims of Lawson and McCauley's Theory of Religious Ritual," in *Religion as a Human Capacity: A Festschrift in Honor of E. Thomas Lawson*, ed. Brian C. Wilson and Timothy Light (Leiden: Brill, 2004), 265–88; Brian Malley and Justin L. Barrett, "Does Myth Inform Ritual? A Test of the Lawson-McCauley Hypothesis," *Journal of Ritual Studies* 17, no. 2 (2003): 1–14; Jesper Sørensen, Pierre Liénard, and Chelsea Finney, "Agent and Instrument in Judgment of Ritual Efficacy," *Journal of Cognition and Culture* 6, no. 3–4 (2006): 463–82.

7. Thus circumscribed, many religious activities such as prayer, spirit possession, or participation in worship services are not counted as "religious rituals" for this theory.

8. I emphasize the most direct or immediate connection because a ritual could connect to a god in more than one way as when a priest uses holy water to perform a blessing. In such cases, determining which is the most direct connection to the god is determined by the relative number of previous rituals required to make the person, substance, or objects special. In the case of a priest using holy water, the priest is "closer" to the god because the water required at least one more ritual—the priest blessing the water to make it holy.

9. In my empirical research with Brian Malley, we found that many of our informants found it difficult to articulate just where the most immediate connection to the divine was. Nevertheless, across individuals enough convergence emerged to give us confidence that people do, at some level and with some error, detect these connections. The case may be comparable to some kinds of arithmetic. A particular sum might not be immediately apparent, but the same underlying intuitions of various individuals, when properly primed, will converge upon the same solution. See Malley and Barrett, "Does Myth Inform Ritual?"

10. Barrett, "Smart Gods, Dumb Gods." See also Theodore Vial's application of Lawson and McCauley's work to historical cases: Theodore M. Vial, *Liturgy Wars: Ritual Theory and Protestant Reform in Nineteenth Century Zurich*, Religion in History, Society, and Culture (New York: Routledge, 2004). See also Barrett and Lawson, "Ritual Intuitions"; Malley and Barrett, "Does Myth Inform Ritual?"

11. Pascal Boyer and Pierre Liénard, "Why Ritualized Behavior? Precaution Systems and Action-Parsing in Developmental, Pathological, and Cultural Rituals," *Behavioral and Brain Sciences* 29, no. 6 (2006): 595–613; Pierre Liénard and Pascal Boyer, "Whence Collective Ritual? A Cultural Selection Model of Ritualized Behavior," *American Anthropologist* 108 (2006): 814–27.

12. Such an account is potentially complementary to Lawson and McCauley's. Boyer and Liénard propose that their approach bears upon a broad range of ritualized behaviors, individual or collective, secular or religious. Lawson and McCauley's theory, however, only applies to a narrow range of actions that meet their conditions for a religious ritual. Some of these will be Boyer and Liénard's ritualized behaviors such as purification or cleansing rituals.

13. Jesus' dispute with religious leaders in the Gospel according to Mark (chapter

7) over the spiritually contaminating effect of Jesus' followers eating with ceremonially unclean hands shows similar threads. Jesus could be interpreted as trying to supplant natural religious impulses in favor of less natural ones.

14. Brian Malley, *How the Bible Works: An Anthropological Study of Evangelical Biblicism* (Walnut Creek, CA: AltaMira Press, 2004).

15. Sperber and Wilson, *Relevance.*

16. Justin L. Barrett, "How Ordinary Cognition Informs Petitionary Prayer," *Journal of Cognition and Culture* 1, no. 3 (2001): 259–69. My emphasis here is on spontaneous acts because they, as compared with carefully crafted liturgical acts, would be more tightly anchored by natural cognition.

17. Justin L. Barrett, "Theological Correctness: Cognitive Constraint and the Study of Religion," *Method and Theory in the Study of Religion* 11 (1999): 325–39.

18. Barrett, "How Ordinary Cognition Informs."

19. Cohen, *The Mind Possessed.*

20. Emma Cohen and Justin L. Barrett, "Conceptualising Possession Trance: Ethnographic and Experimental Evidence," *Ethos* 36, no. 2 (2008): 246–67; Emma Cohen and Justin L. Barrett, "When Minds Migrate: Conceptualising Spirit Possession," *Journal of Cognition and Culture* 8, no. 1–2 (2008): 23–48.

21. Wegner, "The Mind's Best Trick."

22. I leave aside whether or not a possessing spirit really is doing the acting. If it is, then because the spiritualists' conceptual frames are open to the idea that another is acting through their bodies, they understand the possession accurately.

CHAPTER 8

1. For an accessible introduction to cognitive linguistics, see Steven Pinker, *The Language Instinct: How the Mind Creates Language* (New York: Harper-Perennial, 1995). For an early pioneering work in this area, see Noam Chomsky, *Aspects of the Theory of Syntax* (Cambridge, MA: MIT Press, 1965). I remind readers that "natural" does not necessarily mean "hard-wired" or "innate," and so is not subject to some of the criticisms lodged against Chomsky and Pinker.

2. Two points of contrast between language and religion are worth noting. First, arguably language is an adaptation, an evolved faculty (Pinker, *The Language Instinct*). Though we can talk about the collection of content-specific cognitive systems relevant to religious thought as a "religion faculty," or those important for encouraging belief in gods as a "god faculty," the evidence that these "faculties" are united by selective reinforcement is not yet very strong. Attempts to argue for religion as an adaptation have not captured the range of content-specific dimensions discussed here—for example, see Wilson, *Darwin's Cathedral*. Second, but perhaps for similar reasons, religious expression appears to be much less constrained by natural cognition than language is.

3. Kelemen, "Are Children 'Intuitive Theists'?"

4. Guthrie, *Faces in the Clouds.*

5. Bloom, *Descartes' Baby*; Paul Bloom, "Religion Is Natural," *Developmental Science* 10 (2007): 147–51; Paul Bloom, "Religious Belief as an Evolutionary Accident," in *The Believing Primate: Scientific, Philosophical, and Theological*

Reflections on the Origin of Religion, ed. Michael Murray and Jeffrey Schloss (New York: Oxford University Press, 2009), 118–27.

6. Hauser, *Moral Minds*; Katz, ed., *Evolutionary Origins of Morality*.

7. Furnham, "Belief in a Just World"; Lerner, *The Belief in a Just World*.

8. Boyer and Liénard, "Why Ritualized Behavior?"; Liénard and Boyer, "Whence Collective Ritual?"

9. Bloom, *Descartes' Baby*; Cohen and Barrett, "In Search of 'Folk Anthropology.'"

10. These traits are automatic deliverances of the theory of mind system. Guthrie, *Faces in the Clouds*. See also Barrett, *Why Would Anyone Believe in God?*; Justin L. Barrett, *Born Believers: The Science of Childhood Religion* (New York: Free Press, forthcoming).

11. Barrett, "Theological Correctness"; Barrett, *Born Believers*; Justin L. Barrett and Frank C. Keil, "Conceptualizing a Nonnatural Entity Anthropomorphism in God Concepts," *Cognitive Psychology* 31 (1996): 219–47.

12. See Justin L. Barrett, "Why Santa Claus Is Not a God," *Journal of Cognition and Culture* 8, no. 1–2 (2008): 149–61; Bering, "Intuitive Conceptions"; Bering, "The Folk Psychology of Souls"; Boyer, *Religion Explained*.

13. Justin L. Barrett and Rebekah A. Richert, "Anthropomorphism or Preparedness? Exploring Children's God Concepts," *Review of Religious Research* 44 (2003): 300–312; Boyer, *Religion Explained*, chapter 4.

14. Jesse M. Bering and Becky D. Parker, "Children's Attributions of Intentions to an Invisible Agent," *Developmental Psychology* 42 (2006): 253–62. On divine punishment, see also Barrett, *Why Would Anyone Believe in God?* chapter 4; Bering and Johnson, "'O Lord . . . You Perceive My Thoughts from Afar'"; Boyer, *Religion Explained*; Dominic D. P. Johnson, "God's Punishment and Public Goods: A Test of the Supernatural Punishment Hypothesis in 186 World Cultures," *Human Nature* 16 (2005): 410–46.

15. McCauley and Lawson, *Bringing Ritual to Mind*.

16. Mohammad Zia Ullah, *Islamic Concept of God* (London: Kegan Paul, 1984), 19.

17. Gordon Spykman, *Reformational Theology: A New Paradigm for Doing Dogmatics* (Grand Rapids: Eerdmans, 1992), 64–65.

18. For details of these experiments and more thorough discussion of the rationale and implications, see Barrett, "Theological Correctness"; Barrett and Keil, "Conceptualizing a Nonnatural Entity"; Justin L. Barrett and Brant VanOrman, "The Effects of Image-Use in Worship on God Concepts," *Journal of Psychology and Christianity* 15, no. 1 (1996): 38–45; Justin L. Barrett, "Cognitive Constraints on Hindu Concepts of the Divine," *Journal for the Scientific Study of Religion* 37 (1998): 608–19. When querying Hindus in India, various gods' names were used: Brahma, Krishna, Shiva, and Vishnu.

19. Marcia K. Johnson, John D. Bransford, and Susan K. Solomon, "Memory for Tacit Implications of Sentences," *Journal of Experimental Psychology* 98 (1973): 203–5. For explanation and elaboration, see Daniel Reisberg, *Cognition: Exploring the Science of the Mind* (New York: W. W. Norton & Company, 1997).

20. Barrett and Keil, "Conceptualizing a Nonnatural Entity"; Barrett and VanOrman, "The Effects of Image-Use."

21. Barrett and Keil, "Conceptualizing a Nonnatural Entity," 224.

22. Concerned that listening to the stories and the accompanying comprehension questions somehow unfairly pushed a more anthropomorphic God concept than people might otherwise use, we tried a version of the task in which adults read the stories themselves and then answered the questions. Same results. We also tried a task in which adults read some stories and then wrote out their own paraphrased versions. Sure enough, the anthropomorphic intrusion errors cropped up again. Various other comparison conditions were used to show that these results could not be attributable to the seductiveness of the stories. Even if the stories helped lead participants to use a humanlike God concept, it is revealing how susceptible they were to such leading.

23. Michael McCloskey, Alfonso Caramazza, and Bert Green, "Curvilinear Motion in the Absence of External Forces: Naive Beliefs about the Motion of Objects," *Science* 210, no. 4474 (1980): 1139–41; Michael McCloskey and Deborah Kohl, "Naive Physics: The Curvilinear Impetus Principle and Its Role in Interactions with Moving Objects," *Journal of Experimental Psychology: Learning, Memory, and Cognition* 9, no. 1 (1983): 146–56. For a brief review of this type of phenomenon, see Michael McCloskey, "Intuitive Physics," *Scientific American* 248, no. 4 (1983): 122–30; McCloskey, Caramazza, and Green, "Curviliear Motion."

24. See McCauley, *Why Religion Is Natural*; Paul Bloom and Deena Skolnick Weisberg, "Childhood Origins of Adult Resistance to Science," *Science* 316 (2007): 996–97.

25. Boyer, *Religion Explained*, 324; Slone, *Theological Incorrectness*.

26. Slone, *Theological Incorrectness*.

27. The American television series *My Name Is Earl* amusingly illustrates this tendency as the title character struggles with pleasing karma.

28. Indeed, I am deliberately not taking care here to spell out the theologically correct positions because they are somewhat beside the point and any distortion I introduce underlines the point that counterintuitive theology is bound to be distorted.

29. For a more thorough discussion of these issues and an enlightening comparison among religion, theology, and modern science, see McCauley, *Why Religion Is Natural*.

30. Alison Gopnik, Andrew N. Meltzoff, and Patricia K. Kuhl, *The Scientist in the Crib: Minds, Brains, and How Children Learn* (New York: William Morrow & Co., 1999).

31. Incidentally, for the reason of these differences between science versus folk knowledge and theology versus religion, philosopher of science Robert McCauley observes that much of the discussion regarding the nature and relationship between science and religion is oftentime making the wrong comparisons. Science is to theology as folk knowledge is to religion. See McCauley, *Why Religion Is Natural*, forthcoming.

32. For a book-length treatment of how modern-day nautical navigation problems have been solved with cultural scaffolding via distribution of tasks and use of specialized artifacts, see Edwin Hutchins, *Cognition in the Wild* (Cambridge, MA: MIT Press, 1996). Doing theology in the first place likewise is aided by cultural scaffolding. Systems of formal theological education, writing systems,

special mnemonic schemes, specialized terminology and symbols, artifacts for illustrating or recording narratives and ideas are all examples of cultural scaffolding that can assist theology to develop with counterintuitive and other complex concepts.

33. Less than fully natural ideas could originate in any number of ways: careful reflection, dreams, mystical experiences, divine revelation, and so forth. The point of Whitehouse's work, and much work within CSR, is that regardless, the source of the nonnatural or counterintuitive ideas, for them to survive and spread, they either need a good fit with natural cognitive systems *or* require some form of cultural scaffolding. Observing where an idea originated does not explain why it persists and spreads.

34. Harvey Whitehouse, *Arguments and Icons: Divergent Modes of Religiosity* (Oxford: Oxford University Press, 2000); Harvey Whitehouse, *Modes of Religiosity: A Cognitive Theory of Religious Transmission* (Walnut Creek, CA: Alta-Mira Press, 2004).

35. See Frederik Barth, *Ritual and Knowledge among the Baktaman of New Guinea* (New Haven, CT: Yale University Press, 1975). Not all sun dances include piercings, but the practice was made famous by such depictions as a sketch by artist George Catlin of a Sioux man attached to a pole by hooks in his chest.

36. Given recent histories of what appears to be religiously motivated conflict between groups, we may think that religions naturally play a critical role in group identification. Whitehouse has provided two means for such identification: through common shared experiences participating in what seem to be profoundly meaningful life-events, and through shared doctrinal beliefs. Note, however, for religious beliefs to serve as group identifiers, they cannot be beliefs that everyone shares, or no one would be set off. It is tempting to think that by virtue of being somewhat counterintuitive, religious concepts can play this role. Any given counterintuitive concept is not universally held. Nevertheless, it does not appear that being counterintuitive is necessary or sufficient for an idea or commitment to serve as a group marker. Real Madrid fans are unified (in part) by a belief in the superiority of their team, a belief that successfully separates them from Manchester United or AC Milan supporters. Regarding Real Madrid as Europe's greatest football club is not, however, counterintuitive, and all parties in question "believe in" football. Similarly, a particular Tribe A and neighboring Tribe B may have a religious difference that divides them, such as Tribe A having different ancestor spirits that they regard as stronger than Tribe B's ancestors. The difference between the two is not, however, anything counterintuitive. Both tribes believe in ancestors.

37. If religions traffic in ideas close to natural religion, neither mode of religiosity needs to be used to scaffold the religious ideas and practices.

38. For an overview, see Damien Keown, *Buddhism: A Very Short Introduction* (Oxford: Oxford University Press, 1996).

CHAPTER 9

1. Michael Heller, *Creative Tension: Essays on Science and Religion* (Radnor, PA: Templeton Press, 2003), 28.

2. For an introduction to contemporary issues in what I am calling universal natural theology, see William Lane Craig and James Porter Moreland, eds., *The Blackwell Companion to Natural Theology* (Oxford: Wiley-Blackwell, 2009).

3. McGrath, *Open Secret*, 4. Arguably some kind of "theology of nature" is required to get any scientifically informed natural theology off the ground, because the scientific exploration of the natural world builds upon certain metaphysical, ontological, and epistemological assumptions that are not consonant with just any and every worldview. For instance, one has to regard the natural world as orderly, have a rudimentary commitment to causal relations characterizing the way the world works, and regard this causal order as knowable to human minds, but recognize that such knowledge cannot be obtained by introspection or nonempirical means. Westerners often take these premises for granted, but such commitments are not common to all peoples or theologies. For a historical treatment of how Christian theology informed the birth of modern science, see Peter Harrison, *The Fall of Man and the Foundations of Science* (Cambridge: Cambridge University Press, 2008).

4. Richard Dawkins, *The God Delusion* (London: Bantam Press, 2006), 184.

5. Jesse M. Bering, *The Belief Instinct: The Psychology of Souls, Destiny, and the Meaning of Life* (New York: W. W. Norton & Company, 2011), 37.

6. For instance, see Justin L. Barrett, David Leech, and Aku Visala, "Can Religious Belief Be Explained Away? Reasons and Causes of Religious Belief," in *Evolution and Religion*, ed. Ulrich Frey (Marburg: Tectum, 2010), 75–92; Kelly James Clark and Justin L. Barrett, "Reidian Religious Epistemology and the Cognitive Science of Religion," *Journal of the American Academy of Religion* (2011): 1–37; Leech and Visala, "The Cognitive Science of Religion"; Murray, "Four Arguments"; Schloss and Murray, eds., *The Believing Primate*.

7. Bats are not normally blind.

8. For a helpful distinction between "core" and "ancillary" beliefs and their differing relationships with cognitive and evolutionary explanations, see Leech and Visala, "The Cognitive Science of Religion."

9. Roy F. Baumeister and Brad J. Bushman, *Social Psychology and Human Nature* (Belmont, CA: Thomson Wadsworth, 2008); Thomas Gilovich, *How We Know What Isn't So: The Fallibility of Human Reason in Everyday Life* (New York: Free Press, 1991); Schachter and Singer, "Cognitive, Social, and Physiological Determinants"; Wegner, *The Illusion of Conscious Will*.

10. If such a theology exists. Some theological schools (e.g., Barthian Christianity and some within Islam) might acknowledge that we have natural religious ideas but regard them as untrustworthy without correction from special revelation. I do not have in mind such traditions here.

11. Like any science, the current state of the art may prove importantly deficient or flat-out wrong in the future. It is unfair to expect theologies to uncritically and prematurely capitulate to the latest scientific finding or fashion.

12. John D. Barrow, Frank J. Tipler, and John A. Wheeler, *The Anthropic Cosmological Principle* (Oxford: Oxford University Press, 1988); Simon Conway Morris, *Life's Solution: Inevitable Humans in a Lonely Universe* (Cambridge: Cambridge University Press, 2003).

13. Plantinga, *Warranted Christian Belief*, chapter 7.

14. Ibid., 232, emphasis in original. Plantinga is quoting T. H. Huxley here.

15. This is not *entirely* a straightforward empirical matter. Presumably all living animals act in ways that have proven adaptive, but would we regard all living animals as having beliefs of any kind, let alone true beliefs, let alone true beliefs when it comes to contemplating metaphysical claims such as whether or not there exists a god? Consider the garden snail. It acts, but does it act based on beliefs? If not, then it isn't obvious that beliefs need be connected to adaptive action. At best, they might only *happen* to be connected to adaptive action in humans (and perhaps some other animals). If so, why so?

16. Wegner, *The Illusion of Conscious Will.*

17. Plantinga takes up some of these issues without direct consideration of Wegner or others' empirical research on the connection between perceived will and action (Plantinga, *Warranted Christian Belief*). Depending upon the particulars of the theist's view of god, the idea that the god would engineer things thus might nevertheless prove problematic. Would God really arrange things so that we falsely believe, in many situations, that we have free will when in fact we do not? Why would God mislead us so? For a discussion along these lines, see Peter Van Inwagen, "Explaining Belief in the Supernatural: Some Thoughts on Paul Bloom's 'Religious Belief as an Evolutionary Accident,'" in *The Believing Primate: Scientific, Philosophical, and Theological Reflections on the Origin of Religion,* ed. Michael Murray and Jeffrey Schloss (New York: Oxford University Press, 2009): 128–38.

18. McKay and Dennett, "The Evolution of Misbelief," 493–510.

19. Categorical perception of rainbows (see chapter 2) is another example of systematic distortion of reality. Presumably, even if not an adaptation per se, this perceptual strategy is not maladaptive enough to have been selected against. When we look at a rainbow, we naturally form false beliefs about its features. So even in fairly low-level perception, natural selection cannot guarantee accuracy. Suppose I wanted to argue that beliefs are built on percepts, and that percepts (at least) must be reliable for us to survive; hence, our beliefs too must be largely reliable. I must reconcile the fact that adaptive percepts (or at least, not maladaptive percepts) can be systematically in error.

A commonsensible rebuttal of Plantinga's argument is to simply point out that if we had false beliefs about being able to walk through walls, we would knock ourselves out and that wouldn't be adaptive, and so would be weeded out by natural selection, and so natural selection grants us generally reliable minds without a god behind it all. As obvious as this seems, it presumes a number of controversial points such as there being a strong causal connection between beliefs and action (such that if natural selection weeds out maladaptive behaviors, it *must* weed out corresponding false beliefs), and all relevant beliefs (such as those concerning the existence of god or the fact of evolution by natural selection) can be built up from basic behavior-related beliefs. Such an argument also presumes that problems such as navigating in space require corroborating *reflective* beliefs, when, perhaps, nonreflective beliefs are sufficient. When I walk down an irregular path, I don't need to form reflective beliefs about where to place each step; I just step and my motor system takes care of the rest.

20. Wolterstorff, *Thomas Reid.*

21. Johan De Smedt and Helen De Cruz, "The Cognitive Appeal of the Cosmological Argument," *Method and Theory in the Study of Religion* 23 (2011): 103–22.

22. George E. Newman et al., "Early Understanding of the Link between Agents and Order," *Proceedings of the National Academy of Sciences for the United States of America* 107 (2010): 17140–45.

23. Of course, critics often attempt to do just this. Nevertheless, a common strategy used is also to come up with a rational alternative explanation for the existence of the universe, and thereby conclude that the cosmological argument in question fails. For instance, one might argue that the universe has always existed and weave in some clever observations about the nature of time before the moment of the big bang. See J. Brian Pitts, "Why the Big Bang Singularity Does Not Help the Kalām Cosmological Argument for Theism," *British Journal for the Philosophy of Science* 59, no. 675–708 (2008): 675–708. Though perhaps formally providing an adequate *possible* alternative to the idea that the universe was caused, it probably fails to override the natural intuition that the universe still requires a cause. As it represents merely a *possible* alternative, but one that may *seem* unlikely, the proponent of the cosmological argument, therefore, is entitled to his or her intuition that the theistic explanation has *higher probability* of being true than the more radically counterintuitive alternative.

24. See Swinburne's argument from design for a contemporary example that focuses not on the apparent design of objects (such as eyes) but on processes and relationships (such as the laws of gravity). Richard Swinburne, "The Argument from Design," in *Readings in the Philosophy of Religion: An Analytic Approach*, ed. Baruch A. Brody (Englewood Cliffs, NJ: Prentice-Hall, 1992), 189–201; Richard Swinburne, *Is There a God?* (Oxford: Oxford University Press, 1996); Richard Swinburne, *Was Jesus God?* (Oxford: Oxford University Press, 2008).

25. Jennifer Faust, "Can Religious Arguments *Persuade?*" *International Journal for Philosophy of Religion* 63, no. 1 (2008): 71–86.

26. I regard these as empirical claims that could be tested and I could be shown to be wrong.

27. McGrath, *Open Secret.*

28. Barrett, *Born Believers.*

29. Kelly James Clark and Justin L. Barrett, "Reformed Epistemology and the Cognitive Science of Religion," *Faith and Philosophy* 27, no. 2 (2010): 174–89.

30. John Calvin, *Commentaries on the Epistle of St. Paul to the Romans*, ed. Henry Beveridge, trans. John Owen (Grand Rapids, MI: Baker Book House, 1979).

31. See Plantinga, *Warranted Christian Belief;* Alvin Plantinga and Nicholas Wolterstorff, eds., *Faith and Rationality: Reason and Belief in God* (London: University of Notre Dame Press, 1983).

32. Sperber and Wilson, *Relevance*, 48.

33. Malley, *How the Bible Works.* As Sperber has argued in an unpublished paper, this authorship-authority effect might also have a "negative" effect—for example, leading us to assume that the complexity of a text from a renowned philosopher is a sign of relevance, whereas the text actually represents addled thinking. Sperber calls this the "Guru Effect"; see http://www.dan.sperber.fr/?p=113. I thank Jean-Luc Jucker for drawing this to my attention.

34. Leon Festinger, *A Theory of Cognitive Dissonance* (Evanston, IL: Row, Peterson, 1957).
35. Ernst-August Gutt, *Translation and Relevance: Cognition and Context*, 2nd ed. (Oxford: Blackwell, 2000).
36. Barrett, *Born Believers*.
37. http://articles.cnn.com/2009-07-23/health/swine.flu.church.wine_1_swine-flu-chalice-holy-communion?_s=PM:HEALTH. Accessed February 26, 2011.
38. See McCauley and Lawson's work on religious ritual and Theodore Vial's application to concerns in nineteenth-century Zurich: McCauley and Lawson, *Bringing Ritual to Mind*; Vial, *Liturgy Wars*.
39. McCauley and Lawson, *Bringing Ritual to Mind*.
40. Heller, *Creative Tension*, 28.

 Glossary

Accessibility heuristic the bias to regard ideas that come to mind easily as likely to be normative or true.

Anthropomorphism the tendency to attribute humanlike features to non-human things.

Attention the process of focusing on one task, idea, or target while ignoring others.

Belief a mental representation of something being the case in the generation of further thought and action. *Contrast* nonreflective belief *with* reflective belief.

Blank slate *see tabula rasa.*

Bounded rationality the tendency to form a judgment or reach a decision using processes that are suboptimal due to time, information, or cognitive limitations.

Categorical perception perception of a continuous range of sensory information (such as a color spectrum) as consisting of discrete categories.

Change blindness failure to notice changes in a scene across a momentary perceptual interruption.

Cognitive dissonance an effect caused by entertaining two conflicting ideas at the same time. Different intuitive strategies are used to reduce cognitive dissonance.

Cognitive science the interdisciplinary study of the mind and thought.

Cognitive science of religion (CSR) the application of cognitive science to the study of religious thought and practice.

Communication   the process of sharing information, such as through language or gesture. *See also* relevance theory (of communication).

Conceptualization   forming concepts, categories, ideas, and knowledge structures.

Confessional natural theology   the use of science and reason to augment, amplify, or disambiguate theological commitments. *Contrast with* universal natural theology.

Conformity bias   a context bias; the tendency to adopt beliefs and behaviors that characterize most people around us.

Content biases   conceptual tendencies that make some ideas more likely to be acquired. *Contrast with* context biases.

Content-specific cognition   features of cognition that apply to particular domains of content such as information pertaining to physical objects or living things, in contrast with general cognitive dynamics that apply across domains.

Context biases   factors that impact who we are likely to imitate or accept testimony from, including conformity bias, prestige bias, and similarity bias.

Counterintuitive   an idea that runs counter to natural cognition; more specifically, concepts that have a breach or a transfer of expectation sets activated by their ontological category membership.

Credulity principle   the justified tendency for humans to trust the testimony of others unless we have reason to doubt it; giving others the benefit of the doubt.

Cultural scaffolding   peculiar (nonuniversal) features of a cultural environment that help sustain ideas and practices that deviate from natural cognition, sometimes leading to expertise. Examples of cultural scaffolding include artifacts, instructional institutions, and literacy. *Contrast with* natural religion.

Decision-making   the process of forming judgments and choosing between options.

Declarative pointing   gesturing to direct another's attention, usually to a third object.

Episodic memory   long-term memory for particular episodes or events from one's life.

Epistemology any theory of knowledge. *For example, see* reformed epistemology.

Error management the tendency to avoid some kinds of costly errors at the expense of making less costly errors; for example, failing to detect potential food to protect against eating something potentially fatal.

Essentialism the idea that an unseen internal part or substance (essence) accounts for the observable features and behaviors of a living thing that either identify it as a member of a species (species-essentialism) or as a particular individual (person-essentialism).

Expectation set *see* intuitive ontology.

Expertise thought characterized by ease, automaticity, and fluency that arises from explicit instruction, requires artifacts that are not universally part of the human environment, and/or heavy deliberate repetition and practice; typically characterized by relatively late development in life (after the first five years), and considerable variability within and across cultures. Also called practiced naturalness. *Contrast with* naturalness.

Folk anthropology the natural cognitive abilities used in conceptualizing other humans.

Folk psychology *see* theory of mind (ToM).

Free will the nonreflective belief that humans are essentially free in their choices and decisions.

God in cognitive science of religion, a counterintuitive intentional agent that a group of people reflectively believes exists, and that has a type of existence or action that can, in principle, be detected. This use of the term includes not only gods, but also ancestors, demons, ghosts, and other similar agents. *See also* counterintuitive.

HADD experience the detection of an unknown agent or agency that is not easily attributed to humans or known animals and, hence, may be attributable to a god. *See* hypersensitive agency detection device (HADD).

Hard-wired fixed parts of an electrical system, used metaphorically to refer to fixed aspects of human cognition. *Compare with* innate. *Contrast with* naturalness.

Hazard precaution system an evolved ability functioning to keep people away from unseen potential harms such as predators, pathogens, and contaminants. *See also* obsessive-compulsive disorder; ritualized behaviors.

Hypersensitive agency detection device (HADD)   the cognitive system for detecting agency, characterized by a tendency to make detections given ambiguous or inconclusive stimuli perhaps because of a "better-safe-than-sorry" strategy. *See* error management *and* HADD experience.

Imagination   the process of thinking about things that are not necessarily so; how we form mental images (*akin to* percept).

Inferential potential   the ability for a concept to generate a broad range of ideas, inferences, explanations, and predictions about issues that matter to people.

Innate   qualifies the cognitive abilities that are supposedly present at birth or biologically determined. Also called hard-wired. *See also* nature-nurture debate.

Intentional agent   a person; a being that has mental states and the ability to act.

Intrusion error   having remembered something as part of a story or episode that was not in fact present due to prior conceptual expectations.

Intuitive dualism   the natural tendency to nonreflectively regard one's body and one's mind as causally separable. *Not to be confused with* mind-body problem.

Intuitive knowledge   things we know early in development by virtue of being human living in typical human environments, that we are not even conscious of knowing. Also called tacit knowledge. *See also* naturalness.

Intuitive ontology   a collection of ontological categories; intuitive or natural categories of being that include Spatial Entities, Solid Objects, Living Things, Animates, and Persons, and generated by the selective activation of *expectation sets*, including Spatiality, Physicality, Biology, Animacy, and Mentality.

Joint attention   being aware of attending to the same thing as another person.

Just world reasoning   the belief in a reciprocity principle; for example, that immoral actions will be punished. *See also* moral intuitions.

Learning   the process of acquiring new ideas, information, and behaviors.

Maturational naturalness   *see* naturalness.

Memory the process of storing and retrieving information.

Metarepresentation a representation of a representation; for example, a thought about another thought. *See also* representation; theory of mind (ToM).

Mind-body problem the question of how the mind and the body are related; for example, whether biology deterministically causes our thoughts. *Not to be confused with* intuitive dualism.

Modes of religiosity an account of why religious traditions that include relatively unnatural ideas gravitate toward one of two different clusters of psychological, social, and political features known as the doctrinal mode and the imagistic mode. *See also* ritual form theory; sensory pageantry.

Moral intuitions natural intuitions or nonreflective beliefs that pertain to moral behavior such as regarding it as bad to harm members of one's own group. *See also* just world reasoning.

Naturalness thought characterized by ease, automaticity, and fluency. Specifically, the natural cognition that arises in the course of normal human development, typically marked by development in the first five years of life and little variability in aptitude across individuals or cultures, and not dependent upon special artifacts or explicit instruction for acquisition. Also called maturational naturalness. *Contrast with* expertise.

Natural religion the religious thoughts and actions that are generated by natural cognitive systems, and do not necessitate cultural scaffolding to be entertained and transmitted. Natural religion has to be distinguished from theology. *See also* counterintuitive; cultural scaffolding; nonreflective belief; religion; theological correctness; theological incorrectness,

Nature-nurture debate the theoretical problem of whether human thought and behavior are products of our biology or of our environment. *See also* innate.

Nonreflective belief belief or intuition that is nonconscious and automatically produced. Nonreflective beliefs can be products of expertise or natural cognition. *See* belief; *contrast with* reflective belief.

Obsessive-compulsive disorder a condition that features obsessive thoughts, compulsion to perform repeated precautionary acts, and heightened emotional concern to perform these correctly. *See also* hazard precaution system; ritualized behavior.

Ontological category *see* intuitive ontology.

Percept a representation from a perceptual system (e.g., from seeing or hearing).

Perception the process of using our senses to identify patterns and objects.

Person-essentialism *see* essentialism.

Petitionary prayer a prayer in which someone makes a request to a god.

Practiced naturalness *see* expertise.

Preparedness a natural tendency or disposition: for example, to be afraid of snakes independently of learning that snakes are dangerous.

Prestige bias a context bias; the tendency to imitate beliefs and behaviors of prestigious individuals and to weigh their testimony more heavily that others'.

Procedural memory long-term memory for how to perform a task or action.

Promiscuous teleology the tendency to make sense of things in terms of purpose or function, even when such purpose or function is dubious. Also called teleological reasoning.

Proximate cause a cause that is immediately responsible for an effect.

Question begging a fallacy that consists of assuming what has been set out to be concluded as a premise in the argument for the conclusion.

Reasoning conscious reflection on ideas or images to evaluate or draw nonautomatic inferences.

Reflective belief belief that is consciously entertained. *See* belief; *contrast with* nonreflective belief.

Reformed epistemology epistemological position inspired by Thomas Reid and John Calvin under which religious beliefs that are automatic deliverances of cognitive faculties do not require evidence for them to be justifiably held.

Relevance theory (of communication) a cognitive theory of communication centered on the principle that humans attempt to extract as much meaning as possible for as little cognitive investment as possible from a communicative exchange.

Religion   collection of beliefs related to the existence of one or more gods, and the activities that are motivated by these beliefs.

Religious experiencing   any experience that has been represented as meaningfully connected to one or more gods; may occur in religious rituals and ceremonies, petitionary prayer, scripture reading, spirit possession, and similar religious activities or in mundane activities as well.

Religious ritual   according to ritual form theory, an observable action with an agent and patient (object) that brings about some change in states of affairs by appeal to the power of a god, who is usually represented in the ritual structure by a proxy such as a priest or sacred object. *Compare with* ritualized behavior.

Representation (or mental representation)   any thought, idea, or belief that stands for something else; a mental object with meaning or semantic content. For example, when thinking about an apple, one forms a representation of the apple. *See also* metarepresentation.

Ritual form theory   a theory according to which religious rituals come in three forms (special agent ritual or SAR, special instrument ritual or SIR, and special patient ritual or SPR), and according to which people's intuitive expectations about a ritual's centrality, repeatability, reversibility, sensory pageantry, and ability to accommodate substitutions will depend on the form to which it belongs. *See also* modes of religiosity; religious ritual; sensory pageantry.

Ritualized behavior   a personal or cultural action sequence characterized by emotional preoccupation with right sequence and precision of performance, as well as unnecessary repetition, usually pertaining to unseen potential threats that concern the hazard precaution system such as contamination or unseen intruders. *See* hazard precaution system.

Semantic memory   long-term memory for the meaning of ideas, words, or concepts.

Sensory pageantry   a high amount of arousal and emotionality triggered in a particular ritual. *See also* modes of religiosity; ritual form theory.

Sensus divinitatis   in Calvinist theology, the rudimentary or natural sense of the divine.

Similarity bias   a context bias; the tendency to imitate beliefs and behaviors of people we regard as relevantly similar to ourselves.

Simulation a strategy used to reason about other people's mental states; for example, putting ourselves in someone's situation to predict what this person would think or feel. *See also* theory of mind.

Stigmata a condition in which thoughts or feelings appear to trigger remarkable bodily changes such as tissue damage on limbs, and which is commonly regarded as a supernatural sign.

Stroop test a task in which a list of color words are presented in differing colors of print and the reader is instructed to name the color of each word instead of reading the word itself; when the color of the word and the word itself conflict, reading time slows.

Soul a nonbodily, individuating person-essence thought to be a cultural elaboration of nonreflective person-essentialism. *See also* essentialism.

Synesthesia a condition in which sensory qualities typically associated with one domain are perceived in another, as in tasting words or seeing color in numbers.

Tabula rasa view of the mind according to which it is a passive receptor just waiting to be written upon by the environment. Also called blank slate.

Teleological reasoning *see* promiscuous teleology.

Theism a religious system that includes beliefs in some god or gods. *See also* counterintuitive; god; religion.

Theological anthropology the theological study of human nature.

Theological correctness the difference between carefully considered theological beliefs (e.g., about a god) and the theological ideas used in real-time, off-the-cuff situations or conditions of cognitive load.

Theological incorrectness the tendency of theological ideas that are too counterintuititve or cognitively unnatural to be distorted, often unknowingly, by nonexperts into more intuitive and natural versions.

Theory of mind (ToM) the capacity to attribute mental states such as beliefs, desires, emotions, memories, and percepts to other humans, and the understanding of how these mental states are formed and motivate action. Also called folk psychology.

Universal natural theology the attempt to use reason, self-evident truths, and evidence from the natural world to say something about gods or the transcendent, such as to demonstrate that God exists, and to demonstrate what properties God has. *Contrast with* confessional natural theology.

Vitalism   the idea that living things have some internal substance or force or spirit that energizes them and makes them alive.

Working memory   the amount of information that can be consciously attended to or "held in mind" at once.

 Bibliography

Baillargeon, Renee, Laura Kotovsky, and Amy Needham. "The Acquisition of Physical Knowledge in Infancy." In *Causal Cognition: A Multidisciplinary Debate*, edited by Dan Sperber, David Premack, and Ann James Premack, 79–116. Oxford: Oxford University Press, 1995.

Baron-Cohen, Simon. *Mindblindness: An Essay on Autism and Theory of Mind*. Cambridge, MA: MIT Press, 1995.

Barrett, Justin L. *Born Believers: The Science of Childhood Religion*. New York: Free Press, forthcoming.

———. "Bringing Data to Mind: Empirical Claims of Lawson and McCauley's Theory of Religious Ritual." In *Religion as a Human Capacity: A Festschrift in Honor of E. Thomas Lawson*, edited by Brian C. Wilson and Timothy Light, 265–88. Leiden: Brill, 2004.

———. "Coding and Quantifying Counterintuitiveness in Religious Concepts: Theoretical and Methodological Reflections." *Method and Theory in the Study of Religion* 20 (2008): 308–38.

———. "Cognitive Constraints on Hindu Concepts of the Divine." *Journal for the Scientific Study of Religion* 37 (1998): 608–19.

———. "Exploring the Natural Foundations of Religion." *Trends in Cognitive Sciences* 4, no. 1 (2000): 29–34.

———. "How Ordinary Cognition Informs Petitionary Prayer." *Journal of Cognition and Culture* 1, no. 3 (2001): 259–69.

———. "Smart Gods, Dumb Gods, and the Role of Social Cognition in Structuring Ritual Intuitions." *Journal of Cognition and Culture* 2, no. 4 (2002): 183–94.

———. "Theological Correctness: Cognitive Constraint and the Study of Religion." *Method and Theory in the Study of Religion* 11 (1999): 325–39.

———. "Why Santa Claus Is Not a God." *Journal of Cognition and Culture* 8, no. 1–2 (2008): 149–61.

———. *Why Would Anyone Believe in God?* Walnut Creek, CA: AltaMira Press, 2004.

Barrett, Justin L., and Frank C. Keil. "Conceptualizing a Nonnatural Entity: Anthropomorphism in God Concepts." *Cognitive Psychology* 31 (1996): 219–47.

Barrett, Justin L., and E. Thomas Lawson. "Ritual Intuitions: Cognitive Contributions to Judgments of Ritual Efficacy." *Journal of Cognition and Culture* 1, no. 2 (2001): 183–201.

Barrett, Justin L., David Leech, and Aku Visala. "Can Religious Belief Be Explained Away? Reasons and Causes of Religious Belief." In *Evolution and Religion*, edited by Ulrich Frey, 75–92. Marburg: Tectum, 2010.

Barrett, Justin L., and Melanie Nyhof. "Spreading Non-natural Concepts: The Role of Intuitive Conceptual Structures in Memory and Transmission of Cultural Materials." *Journal of Cognition and Culture* 1, no. 1 (2001): 69–100.

Barrett, Justin L., and Rebekah A. Richert. "Anthropomorphism or Preparedness? Exploring Children's God Concepts." *Review of Religious Research* 44 (2003): 300–312.

Barrett, Justin L., and Brant VanOrman. "The Effects of Image-Use in Worship on God Concepts." *Journal of Psychology and Christianity* 15, no. 1 (1996): 38–45.

Barrow, John D., Frank J. Tipler, and John A. Wheeler. *The Anthropic Cosmological Principle.* Oxford: Oxford University Press, 1988.

Barth, Frederik. *Ritual and Knowledge among the Baktaman of New Guinea.* New Haven, CT: Yale University Press, 1975.

Baumeister, Roy F., and Brad J. Bushman. *Social Psychology and Human Nature.* Belmont, CA: Thomson Wadsworth, 2008.

Bering, Jesse M. *The Belief Instinct: The Psychology of Souls, Destiny, and the Meaning of Life.* New York: W. W. Norton & Company, 2011.

———. "The Folk Psychology of Souls." *Behavioral and Brain Sciences* 29 (2006): 453–62.

———. "Intuitive Conceptions of Dead Agents' Minds: The Natural Foundations of Afterlife Beliefs as Phenomenological Boundary." *Journal of Cognition and Culture* 2 (2002): 263–308.

Bering, Jesse M., and Dominic D. P. Johnson. "'O Lord . . . You Perceive My Thoughts from Afar': Recursiveness and the Evolution of Supernatural Agency." *Journal of Cognition and Culture* 5 (2005): 118–42.

Bering, Jesse M., and Becky D. Parker. "Children's Attributions of Intentions to an Invisible Agent." *Developmental Psychology* 42 (2006): 253–62.

Bloom, Paul. *Descartes' Baby: How Child Development Explains What Makes Us Human.* London: William Heinemann, 2004.

———. "Religion Is Natural." *Developmental Science* 10 (2007): 147–51.

————. "Religious Belief as an Evolutionary Accident." In *The Believing Primate: Scientific, Philosophical, and Theological Reflections on the Origin of Religion*, edited by Michael Murray and Jeffrey Schloss, 118–27. New York: Oxford University Press, 2009.

Bloom, Paul, and Deena Skolnick Weisberg. "Childhood Origins of Adult Resistance to Science." *Science* 316 (2007): 996–97.

Bornstein, Marc H., William Kessen, and Sally Weiskopf. "Color Vision and Hue Categorization in Young Human Infants." *Journal of Experimental Psychology: Human Perception and Performance* 2, no. 1 (1976): 115–29.

Boyer, Pascal. *The Naturalness of Religious Ideas: A Cognitive Theory of Religion*. Berkeley: University of California Press, 1994.

————. *Religion Explained: The Evolutionary Origins of Religious Thought*. New York: Basic Books, 2001.

————. "Religious Thought and Behavior as By-products of Brain Function." *Trends in Cognitive Sciences* 7 (2003): 119–24.

Boyer, Pascal, and Pierre Liénard. "Why Ritualized Behavior? Precaution Systems and Action-Parsing in Developmental, Pathological, and Cultural Rituals." *Behavioral and Brain Sciences* 29, no. 6 (2006): 595–613.

Boyer, Pascal, and Charles Ramble. "Cognitive Templates for Religious Concepts: Cross-Cultural Evidence for Recall of Counter-Intuitive Representations." *Cognitive Science* 25 (2001): 535–64.

Call, Joseph, and Michael Tomasello. "Does the Chimpanzee Have a Theory of Mind? 30 Years Later." *Trends in Cognitive Sciences* 12 (2008): 187–92.

Calvin, John. *Commentaries on the Epistle of St. Paul to the Romans*. Translated by John Owen. Edited by Henry Beveridge. Grand Rapids, MI: Baker Book House, 1979.

Casler, Krista, and Deborah Kelemen. "Developmental Continuity in Teleo-Functional Explanation: Reasoning about Nature among Romanian Romani Adults." *Journal of Cognition and Development* 9 (2008): 340–62.

————. "Reasoning about Artifacts at 24 Months: The Developing Teleo-Functional Stance." *Cognition* 103, no. 1 (2007): 120–30.

Chabris, Christopher, and Daniel J. Simons. *The Invisible Gorilla: And Other Ways Our Intuitions Deceive Us*. London: HarperCollins, 2010.

Chaiken, Shelly, and Yaacov Trope. *Dual-Process Theories in Social Psychology*. New York: Guilford Press, 1999.

Chomsky, Noam. *Aspects of the Theory of Syntax*. Cambridge, MA: MIT Press, 1965.

Clark, Kelly James, and Justin L. Barrett. "Reformed Epistemology and the Cognitive Science of Religion." *Faith and Philosophy* 27, no. 2 (2010): 174–89.

———. "Reidian Religious Epistemology and the Cognitive Science of Religion." *Journal of the American Academy of Religion*, forthcoming.

Clark, Kelly J., and Dani Rabinowitz. "Knowledge and the Objection to Religious Belief from Cognitive Science." *European Journal of Philosophy of Religion* 3 (2011): 67–81.

Clifford, William Kingdon. *Lectures and Essays*. London: Macmillan and Co., 1886.

Cohen, Emma. *The Mind Possessed: The Cognition of Spirit Possession in an Afro-Brazilian Religious Tradition*. New York: Oxford University Press, 2007.

Cohen, Emma, and Justin L. Barrett. "Conceptualising Possession Trance: Ethnographic and Experimental Evidence." *Ethos* 36, no. 2 (2008): 246–67.

———. "In Search of 'Folk Anthropology': The Cognitive Anthropology of the Person." In *In Search of Self: Interdisciplinary Perspectives on Personhood*, edited by Wentzel van Huyssteen and Erik Wiebe, 104–23. Grand Rapids: Eerdmans, 2011.

———. "When Minds Migrate: Conceptualising Spirit Possession." *Journal of Cognition and Culture* 8, no. 1–2 (2008): 23–48.

Conway Morris, Simon. *Life's Solution: Inevitable Humans in a Lonely Universe*. Cambridge: Cambridge University Press, 2003.

Craig, William Lane, and James Porter Moreland, eds. *The Blackwell Companion to Natural Theology*. Oxford: Wiley-Blackwell, 2009.

Crick, Francis. *What Mad Pursuits*. New York: Basic Books, 1988.

Dawkins, Richard *The God Delusion*. London: Bantam Press, 2006.

DeLoache, Judy S., and Vanessa LoBue. "The Narrow Fellow in the Grass: Human Infants Associate Snakes and Fear." *Developmental Science* 12, no. 1 (2009): 201–7.

Dembski, William A. *Intelligent Design: The Bridge between Science and Theology*. Downers Grove, IL: InterVarsity Press, 1999.

Dennett, Daniel C. *The Intentional Stance*. Cambridge, MA: MIT Press, 1987.

De Smedt, Johan, and Helen De Cruz. "The Cognitive Appeal of the Cosmological Argument." *Method and Theory in the Study of Religion* 23 (2001): 103–22.

DiYanni, Cara, and Deborah Kelemen. "Time to Get a New Mountain? The Role of Function in Children's Conceptions of Natural Kinds." *Cognition* 97 (2005): 327–35.

Dunbar, Robin I. M. *The Human Story*. London: Faber and Faber, 2004.

———. "The Social Brain Hypothesis." *Evolutionary Anthropology: Issues, News, and Reviews* 6, no. 5 (1998): 178–90.

El-Mallakh, Rif S., Justin L. Barrett, and Richard Jed Wyatt. "The Na, K-Atpase Hypothesis for Bipolar Disorder: Implications of Normal Development." *Journal of Child and Adolescent Psychopharmacology* 3, no. 1 (1993): 37–52.

Faust, Jennifer. "Can Religious Arguments *Persuade?*" *International Journal for Philosophy of Religion* 63, no. 1 (2008): 71–86.

Festinger, Leon. *A Theory of Cognitive Dissonance.* Evanston, IL: Row, Peterson, 1957.

Flavell, John H., Patricia H. Miller, and Scott A. Miller. *Cognitive Development.* Englewood Cliffs, NJ: Prentice-Hall, 1993.

Franklin, Anna. "Pre-Linguistic Categorical Perception of Colour Cannot Be Explained by Colour Preference: Response to Roberson and Hanley." *Trends in Cognitive Sciences* 13, no. 12 (2009): 501–2.

Franklin, Anna, Michael Pilling, and Ian Davies. "The Nature of Infant Color Categorization: Evidence from Eye Movements on a Target Detection Task." *Journal of Experimental Child Psychology* 91, no. 3 (2005): 227–48.

Furnham, Adrian. "Belief in a Just World: Research Progress over the Past Decade." *Personality and Individual Differences* 34, no. 5 (2003): 795–817.

Gergely, György, and Gergely Csibra. "Teleological Reasoning in Infancy: The Naive Theory of Rational Action." *Trends in Cognitive Sciences* 7, no. 7 (2003): 287–92.

Gergely, György, Zoltán Nádasdy, Gergely Csibra, and Szilvia Bíró. "Taking the Intentional Stance at 12 Months of Age." *Cognition* 56 (1995): 165–93.

Gilovich, Thomas. *How We Know What Isn't So: The Fallibility of Human Reason in Everyday Life.* New York: Free Press, 1991.

Gilovich, Thomas, Dale Griffin, and Daniel Kahneman. *Heuristics and Biases: The Psychology of Intuitive Judgement.* Cambridge: Cambridge University Press, 2002.

Gopnik, Alison, Andrew N. Meltzoff, and Patricia K. Kuhl. *The Scientist in the Crib: Minds, Brains, and How Children Learn.* New York: William Morrow & Co., 1999.

Gray, Kurt, and Daniel M. Wegner. "Blaming God for Our Pain: Human Suffering and the Divine Mind." *Personality and Social Psychology Review* 14, no. 1 (2009): 7–16.

Gregory, Justin, and Justin L. Barrett. "Epistemology and Counterintuitiveness: Role and Relationship in Epidemiology of Cultural Representations." *Journal of Cognition and Culture* 9 (2009): 289–314.

Guthrie, Stewart E. *Faces in the Clouds: A New Theory of Religion.* New York: Oxford University Press, 1993.

Gutt, Ernst-August. *Translation and Relevance: Cognition and Context.* 2nd ed. Oxford: Blackwell, 2000.

Haidt, Jonathan. "The New Synthesis in Moral Psychology." *Science* 316 (2007): 998–1002.

Harrison, Peter. *The Fall of Man and the Foundations of Science.* Cambridge: Cambridge University Press, 2008.

———. "Theodicy and Animal Pain." *Philosophy* 64, no. 247 (1989): 79–92.

Hatano, Giyoo, and Kayoko Inagaki. "Young Children's Naive Theory of Biology." *Cognition* 50, no. 1–3 (1994): 171–88.

Hauser, Marc D. *Moral Minds: How Nature Designed Our Universal Sense of Right and Wrong.* New York: Ecco/Harper Collins, 2006.

Heider, Fritz, and Marianne Simmel. "An Experimental Study of Apparent Behavior." *American Journal of Psychology* 57 (1944): 243–49.

Heller, Michael. *Creative Tension: Essays on Science and Religion.* Radnor, PA: Templeton Press, 2003.

Henrich, Joseph, and Richard McElreath. "The Evolution of Cultural Evolution." *Evolutionary Anthropology: Issues, News, and Reviews* 12, no. 3 (2003): 123–35.

Hermer, Linda, and Elizabeth S. Spelke. "A Geometric Process for Spatial Reorientation in Young Children." *Nature* 370, no. 6484 (1994): 57–59.

Hermer-Vazquez, Linda, Elizabeth S. Spelke, and Alla S. Katsnelson. "Sources of Flexibility in Human Cognition: Dual-Task Studies of Space and Language." *Cognitive Psychology* 39, no. 1 (1999): 3–36.

Hinde, Robert A. *Why Good Is Good: The Sources of Morality.* London: Routledge, 2002.

Humphreys, Colin J. *The Miracles of Exodus: A Scientist's Discovery of the Extraordinary Natural Causes of the Biblical Stories.* London: Continuum, 2004.

Hutchins, Edwin. *Cognition in the Wild.* Cambridge, MA: MIT Press, 1996.

Inagaki, Kayoko, and Giyoo Hatano. "Vitalistic Causality in Young Children's Naive Biology." *Trends in Cognitive Sciences* 8, no. 8 (2004): 356–62.

———. "Young Children's Conception of the Biological World." *Current Directions in Psychological Science* 15, no. 4 (2006): 177–81.

———. *Young Children's Naive Thinking about the Biological World.* New York: Psychology Press, 2002.

Isen, Alice M., Thomas E. Nygren, and F. Gregory Ashby. "Influence of Positive Affect on the Subjective Utility of Gains and Losses: It Is Just Not Worth the Risk." *Journal of Personality and Social Psychology* 55, no. 5 (1988): 710–17.

James, William. *The Varieties of Religious Experience*. London: Longmans, Green, and Co., 1902.

Jeeves, Malcolm, and Warren S. Brown. *Neuroscience, Psychology, and Religion: Illusions, Delusions, and Realities about Human Nature*. West Conshohocken, PA: Templeton Press, 2009.

Johnson, Dominic D. P. "God's Punishment and Public Goods: A Test of the Supernatural Punishment Hypothesis in 186 World Cultures." *Human Nature* 16 (2005): 410–46.

Johnson, Marcia K., John D. Bransford, and Susan K. Solomon. "Memory for Tacit Implications of Sentences." *Journal of Experimental Psychology* 98 (1973): 203–5.

Johnson, Susan C. "The Recognition of Mentalistic Agents in Infancy." *Trends in Cognitive Sciences* 4, no. 1 (2000): 22–28.

Kahneman, Daniel. "A Perspective on Judgment and Choice: Mapping Bounded Rationality." *American Psychologist* 58, no. 9 (2003): 697–720.

Katz, Leonard D., ed. *Evolutionary Origins of Morality: Cross-Disciplinary Perspectives*. Thoverton, UK: Imprint Academic, 2000.

Keil, Frank C. *Concepts, Kinds, and Cognitive Development*. Cambridge, MA: MIT Press, 1989.

———. "The Growth of Causal Understandings of Natural Kinds: Modes of Construal and the Emergence of Biological Thought." In *Causal Cognition: A Multidisciplinary Debate*, edited by Dan Sperber, David Premack, and Ann James Premack, 234–62. New York: Oxford University Press, 1995.

———. "The Origins of an Autonomous Biology." In *Modularity and Constraints in Language and Cognition: 25th Minnesota Symposium on Child Psychology*, edited by Megan R. Gunnar and Michael Maratsos, 103–37. Hilldale, NJ: Lawrence Erlbaum Associates, 1992.

———. *Semantic and Conceptual Development: An Ontological Perspective*. Cambridge, MA: Harvard University Press, 1979.

Kelemen, Deborah. "Are Children 'Intuitive Theists'? Reasoning about Purpose and Design in Nature." *Psychological Science* 15 (2004): 295–301.

———. "Functions, Goals, and Intentions: Children's Teleological Reasoning about Objects." *Trends in Cognitive Sciences* 12 (1999): 461–68.

———. "Why Are Rocks Pointy? Children's Preference for Teleological Explanations of the Natural World." *Developmental Psychology* 35 (1999): 1440–53.

Kelemen, Deborah, and Evelyn Rosset. "The Human Function Compunction: Teleological Explanation in Adults." *Cognition* 111 (2009): 138–43.

Keown, Damien. *Buddhism: A Very Short Introduction*. Oxford: Oxford University Press, 1996.

Kosslyn, Stephen M., Giorgio Ganis, and William L. Thompson. "Neural Foundations of Imagery." *National Review of Neuroscience* 2, no. 9 (2001): 635–42.

Lawson, E. Thomas, and Robert N. McCauley. *Rethinking Religion: Connecting Cognition and Culture*. Cambridge: Cambridge University Press, 1990.

Lazar, Sara W., Catherine E. Kerr, Rachel H. Wasserman, Jeremy R. Gray, Douglas N. Greve, Michael T. Treadway, Metta McGarvey, Brian T. Quinn, Jeffery A. Dusek, Herbert Benson, Scott L. Rauch, Christopher I. Moore, and Bruce Fischl. "Meditation Experience Is Associated with Increased Cortical Thickness." *Neuroreport* 16, no. 17 (2005): 1893–97.

Leech, David, and Aku Visala. "The Cognitive Science of Religion: Implications for Theism?" *Zygon* 46, no. 1 (2011): 47–64.

Lerner, Melvin J. *The Belief in a Just World: A Fundamental Delusion*. New York: Plenum Press, 1980.

Leslie, Alan M. "A Theory of Agency." In *Causal Cognition: A Multidisciplinary Debate*, edited by Dan Sperber, David Premack, and Ann James Premack, 121–41. New York: Oxford University Press, 1995.

Levin, Daniel T., and Daniel S. Simons. "Failure to Detect Changes to Attended Objects in Motion Pictures." *Psychonomic Bulletin and Review* 4, no. 4 (1997):501–6.

Lewis, C. S. *The Abolition of Man*. London: Oxford University Press, 1943.

———. *Mere Christianity*. New York: Macmillan, 1960.

Liénard, Pierre, and Pascal Boyer. "Whence Collective Ritual? A Cultural Selection Model of Ritualized Behavior." *American Anthropologist* 108 (2006): 814–27.

Lupfer, Michael B., Karla F. Brock, and Stephen J. DePaola. "The Use of Secular and Religious Attributions to Explain Everyday Behavior." *Journal for the Scientific Study of Religion* 31, no. 4 (1992): 486–503.

Lupfer, Michael B., Donna Tolliver, and Mark Jackson. "Explaining Life-Altering Occurrences: A Test of the 'God-of-the-Gaps' Hypothesis." *Journal for the Scientific Study of Religion* 35, no. 4 (1996): 379–91.

Malley, Brian. *How the Bible Works: An Anthropological Study of Evangelical Biblicism*. Walnut Creek, CA: AltaMira Press, 2004.

Malley, Brian, and Justin L. Barrett. "Does Myth Inform Ritual? A Test of the Lawson-McCauley Hypothesis." *Journal of Ritual Studies* 17, no. 2 (2003): 1–14.

McCauley, Robert N. *Why Religion Is Natural and Science Is Not*. New York: Oxford University Press, 2011.

McCauley, Robert N., and E. Thomas Lawson. *Bringing Ritual to Mind: Psychological Foundations of Cultural Forms*. Cambridge: Cambridge University Press, 2002.

McCloskey, Michael. "Intuitive Physics." *Scientific American* 248, no. 4 (1983): 122–30.

McCloskey, Michael, Alfonso Caramazza, and Bert Green. "Curvilinear Motion in the Absence of External Forces: Naive Beliefs about the Motion of Objects." *Science* 210, no. 4474 (1980): 1139–41.

McCloskey, Michael, and Deborah Kohl. "Naive Physics: The Curvilinear Impetus Principle and Its Role in Interactions with Moving Objects." *Journal of Experimental Psychology: Learning, Memory, and Cognition* 9, no. 1 (1983): 146–56.

McElreath, Richard, and Joseph Henrich. "Dual Inheritance Theory: The Evolution of Human Cultural Capacities and Cultural Evolution." In *Oxford Handbook of Evolutionary Psychology*, edited by Robin I. M. Dunbar and Louise Barrett, 555–70. Oxford: Oxford University Press, 2007.

McGrath, Alister E. *The Open Secret: A New Vision for Natural Theology*. Oxford: Blackwell, 2008.

McKay, Ryan T., and Daniel C. Dennett. "The Evolution of Misbelief." *Behavioral and Brain Sciences* 32 (2009): 493–510.

Meltzoff, Andrew N., and N. Keith Moore. "Newborn Infants Imitate Adult Facial Gestures." *Child Development* 54 (1983): 702–9.

Miller, George A. "The Magical Number Seven, Plus or Minus Two: Some Limits on Our Capacity for Processing Information." *Psychological Review* 63, no. 2 (1956): 343–55.

Miresco, Marc J., and Laurence J. Kirmayer. "The Persistence of Mind-Brain Dualism in Psychiatric Reasoning about Clinical Scenarios." *American Journal of Psychiatry* 163, no. 5 (2006): 913–18.

Murray, Michael J. "Four Arguments That the Cognitive Psychology of Religion Undermines the Justification of Religious Beliefs." In *The Evolution of Religion: Studies, Theories, and Critiques*, edited by Joseph Bulbulia, Richard Sosis, Erica Harris, Russell Genet, Cheryl Genet, and Karen Wyman, 365–70. Santa Margarita, CA: Collins Foundation Press, 2008.

———. *Nature Red in Tooth and Claw: Theism and the Problem of Animal Suffering*. Oxford: Oxford University Press, 2008.

Newman, George E., Frank C. Keil, Valerie Kuhlmeier, and Karen Wynn. "Early Understanding of the Link between Agents and Order." *Proceedings of the National Academy of Sciences for the United States of America* 107 (2010): 17140–4.

Öhman, Arne, and Susan Mineka. "Fears, Phobias, and Preparedness: Toward an Evolved Module of Fear and Fear Learning." *Psychological Review* 108, no. 3 (2001): 483–522.

———. "The Malicious Serpent." *Current Directions in Psychological Science* 12, no. 1 (2003): 5–9.

Penn, Derek C., and Daniel J. Povinelli. "Causal Cognition in Human and Nonhuman Animals: A Comparative, Critical Review." *Annual Review of Psychology* 58, no. 1 (2007): 97–118.

Pinker, Steven. *The Blank Slate: The Modern Denial of Human Nature.* New York: Viking, 2002.

———. *The Language Instinct: How the Mind Creates Language.* New York: HarperPerennial, 1995.

Pitts, J. Brian. "Why the Big Bang Singularity Does Not Help the Kalām Cosmological Argument for Theism." *British Journal for the Philosophy of Science* 59 (2008): 675–708.

Plantinga, Alvin. *God and Other Minds: A Study of the Rational Justification of Belief in God.* Ithaca: Cornell University Press, 1990.

———. *Warranted Christian Belief.* New York: Oxford University Press, 2000.

Plantinga, Alvin, and Nicholas Wolterstorff, eds. *Faith and Rationality: Reason and Belief in God.* London: University of Notre Dame Press, 1983.

Premack, David. "The Infant's Theory of Self-Propelled Objects." *Cognition* 36 (1990): 1–36.

Rakison, David H., and Diane Poulin-Dubois. "Developmental Origin of the Animate-Inanimate Distinction." *Psychological Bulletin* 127, no. 2 (2001): 209–28.

Ramachandran, Vilayanur S., and Edward M. Hubbard. "Hearing Colors, Tasting Shapes." *Scientific American* 288, no. 5 (2003): 52–59.

Ramachandran, Vilayanur S., Diane Rogers-Ramachandran, and Steve Cobb. "Touching the Phantom Limb." *Nature* 377 (1995): 489–90.

Reid, Thomas. *Inquiry and Essays.* Edited by Ronald E Beanblossom and Keith Lehrer. Indianapolis, IN: Hackett Publishing Company, 1983.

———. *Inquiry into the Human Mind on the Principles of Common Sense.* Edited by Derek R. Brookes. Edinburgh: Edinburgh University Press, 1997.

Reisberg, Daniel. *Cognition: Exploring the Science of the Mind.* New York: W. W. Norton & Company, 1997.

Reisenzein, Rainer. "The Schachter Theory of Emotion: Two Decades Later." *Psychological Bulletin* 94, no. 2 (1983): 239–64.

Richert, Rebekah A., and Paul L. Harris. "Dualism Revisited: Body Vs. Mind Vs. Soul." *Journal of Cognition and Culture* 8, no. 1–2 (2008): 99–115.

Rochat, Philippe, Rachel Morgan, and Malinda Carpenter. "Young Infants' Sensitivity to Movement Information Specifying Social Causality." *Cognitive Development* 12 (1997): 537–61.

Rosengren, Karl S., Susan A. Gelman, Charles W. Kalish, and Michael McCormick. "As Time Goes By: Children's Early Understanding of Growth in Animals." *Child Development* 62, no. 6 (1991): 1302–20.

Schachter, Stanley, and Jerome Singer. "Cognitive, Social, and Physiological Determinants of Emotional State." *Psychological Review* 69, no. 5 (1962): 379–99.

Schloss, Jeffrey P., and Michael J. Murray, eds. *The Believing Primate: Scientific, Philosophical, and Theological Reflections on the Origin of Religion.* Oxford: Oxford University Press, 2009.

Scholl, Brian J., and Patrice D. Tremoulet. "Perceptual Causality and Animacy." *Trends in Cognitive Sciences* 4 (2000): 299–308.

Schult, Carolyn A., and Henry M. Wellman. "Explaining Human Movements and Actions: Children's Understanding of the Limits of Psychological Explanation." *Cognition* 62, no. 3 (1997): 291–324.

Simons, Daniel J. "In Sight, Out of Mind: When Object Representations Fail." *Psychological Science* 7, no. 5 (1996): 301–5.

Simons, Daniel J., and Frank C. Keill. "An Abstract to Concrete Shift in the Development of Biological Thought: The Insides Story." *Cognition* 56 (1995): 129–63.

Simons, Daniel J., and Daniel T. Levin. "Change Blindness." *Trends in Cognitive Science* 1, no. 7 (1997): 261–67.

———. "Failure to Detect Changes to People during a Real-World Interaction." *Psychonomic Bulletin and Review* 5 (1998): 644–49.

Slaughter, Virginia. "Young Children's Understanding of Death." *Australian Psychologist* 40 (2005): 1–8.

Slaughter, Virginia, and Michelle Lyons. "Learning about Life and Death in Early Childhood." *Cognitive Psychology* 46, no. 1 (2003): 1–30.

Slone, D. Jason. *Theological Incorrectness: Why Religious People Believe What They Shouldn't.* New York: Oxford University Press, 2004.

Sommers, Fred. "Structural Ontology." *Philosophia* 1, no. 1 (1971): 21–42.

Sørensen, Jesper, Pierre Liénard, and Chelsea Finney. "Agent and Instrument in Judgment of Ritual Efficacy." *Journal of Cognition and Culture* 6, no. 3–4 (2006): 463–82.

Spelke, Elizabeth, Roberta Kestenbaun, Daniel J. Simons, and Debra Wein. "Spatiotemporal Continuity, Smoothness of Motion and Object Identity in Infancy." *British Journal of Developmental Psychology* 13, no. 2 (1995): 113–42.

Spelke, Elizabeth S., and Katherine D. Kinzler. "Core Knowledge." *Developmental Science* 10, no. 1 (2007): 89–96.

Sperber, Dan. "Intuitive and Reflective Beliefs." *Mind and Language* 12 (1997): 67–83.

Sperber, Dan, and Deirdre Wilson. *Relevance: Communication and Cognition.* 2nd ed. Oxford: Blackwell Publishing, 1995.

Spilka, Bernard, and Greg Schmidt. "General Attribution Theory for the Psychology of Religion: The Influence of Event-Character on Attributions to God." *Journal for the Scientific Study of Religion* 22, no. 4 (1983): 326–39.

Springer, Ken, and Frank C. Keil. "On the Development of Biologically Specific Beliefs: The Case of Inheritance." *Child Development* 60, no. 3 (1989): 637–48.

Spykman, Gordon. *Reformational Theology: A New Paradigm for Doing Dogmatics.* Grand Rapids: Eerdmans, 1992.

Stroop, John Ridley. "Studies of Interference in Serial Verbal Reactions." *Journal of Experimental Psychology* 18 (1935): 643–62.

Swinburne, Richard. "The Argument from Design." In *Readings in the Philosophy of Religion: An Analytic Approach*, edited by Baruch A. Brody, 189–201. Englewood Cliffs, NJ: Prentice-Hall, 1992.

———. *Is There a God?* Oxford: Oxford University Press, 1996.

———. *Was Jesus God?* Oxford: Oxford University Press, 2008.

Taylor, Marjorie. *Imaginary Companions and the Children Who Create Them.* New York: Oxford University Press, 1999.

Thagard, Paul. *Mind: Introduction to Cognitive Science.* 2nd ed. Cambridge, MA: MIT, 2005.

Tillich, Paul. *The Shaking of the Foundations.* New York: Charles Scribner's Sons, 1940.

Tomasello, Michael. *The Cultural Origins of Human Cognition.* Cambridge, MA: Harvard University Press, 1999.

Van Inwagen, Peter. "Explaining Belief in the Supernatural: Some Thoughts on Paul Bloom's 'Religious Belief as an Evolutionary Accident.'" In *The Believing Primate: Scientific, Philosophical, and Theological Reflections on the Origin of Religion*, edited by Jeffrey P. Schloss and Michael J. Murray, 128–38. New York: Oxford University, 2009.

Vial, Theodore M. *Liturgy Wars: Ritual Theory and Protestant Reform in Nineteenth Century Zurich.* Religion in History, Society, and Culture. New York: Routledge, 2004.

Ward, Jamie. *The Frog Who Croaked Blue: Synesthesia and the Mixing of the Senses.* London: Routledge, 2008.

Watson, John B. *Behaviorism.* 2nd ed. London: Kegan Paul & Co., 1931.

Wegner, Daniel M. *The Illusion of Conscious Will*. Cambridge, MA: MIT Press, 2002.

———. "The Mind's Best Trick: How We Experience Conscious Will." *Trends in Cognitive Sciences* 7, no. 2 (2003): 65–69.

Wellman, Henry, and Carl Johnson. "Developing Dualism: From Intuitive Understanding to Transcendental Ideas." In *Psycho-Physical Dualism Today: An Interdisciplinary Approach*, edited by Alessandro Antonietti, Antonella Corradini, and E. Jonathan Lowe, 3–36. Lanham, MD: Lexington Books, 2008.

Whitehouse, Harvey. *Arguments and Icons: Divergent Modes of Religiosity*. Oxford: Oxford University Press, 2000.

———. *Inside the Cult: Religious Innovation and Transmission in Papua New Guinea*. Oxford: Clarendon Press, 1995.

———. *Modes of Religiosity: A Cognitive Theory of Religious Transmission*. Walnut Creek, CA: AltaMira Press, 2004.

Wigger, J. Bradley. "Imaginary Companions, Theory of Mind, and God." Presented at the Cognition, Religion, and Theology Conference, Merton College, University of Oxford, June 29, 2010.

———. "See-through Knowing: Learning from Children and Their Invisible Friends." *Journal of Childhood and Religion* 2, no. 3 (2011): 1–34.

Wilson, David Sloan. *Darwin's Cathedral: Evolution, Religion, and the Nature of Society*. Chicago: University of Chicago Press, 2002.

Wilson, Timothy D. *Strangers to Ourselves: Discovering the Adaptive Unconscious*. Cambridge, MA: Belknap, 2002.

Wolterstorff, Nicholas P. "Can Belief in God Be Rational If It Has No Foundations?" In *Faith and Rationality: Reason and Belief in God*, edited by Alvin Plantinga and Nicholas Wolterstorff, 135–86. London: University of Notre Dame Press, 1983.

———. *Thomas Reid and the Story of Epistemology*. Cambridge: Cambridge University Press, 2001.

Wynn, Karen. "Some Innate Foundations of Social and Moral Cognition." In *The Innate Mind: Foundations and the Future*, edited by Peter Carruthers, Stephen Laurence, and Stephen P. Stich, 330–47. Oxford: Oxford University Press, 2008.

Xu, Fei, and Susan Carey. "Infants' Metaphysics: The Case of Numerical Identity." *Cognitive Psychology* 30, no. 2 (1996): 111–53.

Zia Ullah, Mohammad. *Islamic Concept of God*. London: Kegan Paul, 1984.

Index